Henry Cha[illegible]

The College Environment

The College Environment

by

Alexander W. Astin
Director, Office of Research
American Council on Education

American Council on Education

1785 MASSACHUSETTS AVENUE N.W.

WASHINGTON, D.C. 20036

LIBRARY OF CONGRESS CARD CATALOG NUMBER 68-19998

Preface

MY INTEREST in studying the college environment began in the summer of 1960, when I joined the research staff of the National Merit Scholarship Corporation to assume responsibility for conducting a two-year study of factors influencing the "Ph.D. productivity" of undergraduate institutions. One of the earliest findings to emerge from this study was that certain types of institutions are more effective than others in encouraging their undergraduate students to go on for the Ph.D. degree. Even before the project was completed, however, it had become abundantly clear that our understanding of differences between college environments—and, hence our ability to account for such differential influences—was very limited.

My principal goals in undertaking the study reported in this book were to identify some of the major differences in undergraduate college environments and to develop a set of objective measurements of these environmental differences. I was especially concerned with employing observational and measurement procedures that were consistent with my own theoretical views of what an environment is and what it is not. Although I do not feel that I have been entirely successful in articulating these views, I think that some progress has been made toward more adequately uniting conceptual and methodological approaches.

In some ways, this has been a kind of "shotgun" study: a large number of students at a large number of institutions have made a great many observations—more than 12 million in all—concerning the characteristics of their undergraduate college environments. The labor involved in planning the study and in collecting, editing, and reducing this massive amount of data to manageable proportions has, of course, been considerable, and a number of people have contributed their energies to the task.

All of the planning and collection of data and much of the processing was carried out between early 1962 and December, 1964, while I was associated with the National Merit Scholarship Corporation. This portion of the work was supported by grants to NMSC from the Ford Foundation, the Carnegie Corporation of New York, and the National Science Foundation. I am indebted to my former colleagues at NMSC, John L. Holland, Robert C. Nichols, and John M. Stalnaker for their encouragement and support, as well as their many helpful suggestions during this phase of the project. Special thanks are also due Mary Salmon, my research assistant at

NMSC, who bore the main burden of editing the data files and setting up and running many dozens of the early factor analyses, rotations, and factor scoring procedures.

The final data analyses and all of the writing were completed at the American Council on Education between January, 1965, and August, 1967. I should like to thank Robert J. Panos, John A. Creager, John L. Holland, and C. Robert Pace for their critical readings of the manuscript. I should also like to express my appreciation to Janet D. Griffith for her assistance in editing and data processing, to Laura Kent for her skillful editing of the entire manuscript, and especially to Barbara A. Blandford, who typed and proofread every draft.

September, 1967 ALEXANDER W. ASTIN

Contents

List of Figures

List of Tables

Appendix Tables

1

Design of the Study

THE HETEROGENEITY of American higher education has become a popular topic of discussion and study in recent years. That institutional diversity is more than just a cliché is attested to by the very uneven distribution of student talent, research funds, and other resources among the nation's 2,200 colleges and universities,[1] and by the weight that today's high school student attaches to the problem of choosing a college.

While these facts suggest that college environments differ greatly in their quality and character, administrators, faculty, students, and others concerned with such institutional differences are handicapped by the dearth of accurate comparative data. Much of the available descriptive information about the college environment—as presented in college catalogues, for example—tends to be vague and highly subjective. The information contained in the several commercially published "guides," although more systematic and comparable across colleges than is the information in college catalogues, consists largely of superficial data about costs, admission requirements, course offerings, and the like. For the most part, meaningful information about the intellectual and social climate of the institution is missing from these sources. This lack of comparative information has been in part responsible for the current interest among educational researchers in studying the college environment.

The study reported here is concerned with describing and measuring some of the important differences among the environments of undergraduate institutions. It is hoped that both the findings and the measurement techniques developed in this research will be useful to teachers, to administrators, to prospective college students, and to researchers who may be interested in measuring institutional differences and assessing their impact on student development.

THE FUNCTION OF ENVIRONMENTAL MEASURES

The American system of higher education, with its diverse educational policies and practices, offers an ideal setting for natural "experiments" con-

[1] For example, see Holland (1959a; 1966), McConnell and Heist (1962), Astin (1965d), and Astin and Holland (1962).

cerning the differential impact of various college environments on the student's development. Purely experimental studies must, of course, be ruled out because students are not assigned to colleges at random. But the considerable overlap in student characteristics from institution to institution makes it possible to estimate comparative institutional impact by means of longitudinal studies in which statistical adjustments are made to compensate for inequalities in the student inputs of different institutions. The major function of environmental measures in such studies is to provide a basis for interpreting any differential institutional effects that may be observed. It is not sufficient to know simply that one college differs from another in its impact on a particular kind of student. On the contrary, unless the effects can be accounted for by identifiable institutional characteristics, we cannot arrive at the generalizations needed for improving educational theory and for formulating sound educational policy.

In brief, the task of defining the college environment is one of identifying and measuring those institutional characteristics that are likely to have some impact on the student's development.

The importance of an adequate environmental interpretation of differential college influence can be made clearer with an illustration. To simplify, let us assume that we are interested in comparing the differential impact of a state university and a private liberal arts college on the development of students. Suppose that we find that students attending the private liberal arts college are more likely to go on to graduate school after completing the baccalaureate degree than are comparable students attending the state university. (For purposes of discussion, we shall assume that this is indeed a differential effect of the two colleges, and not an artifact arising from our failure to control adequately some extraneous variable.[2]) How can we explain this observed difference in the relative impact of the two institutions? Is it because the two faculties differ in the extent to which they encourage students to go on to seek a degree beyond the baccalaureate, or is it because of some difference in the motivational stimulation provided by the other students? Can the result be caused by more subtle institutional differences in living conditions, type of town, or administrative practices? Perhaps a relative neglect of undergraduate instruction at the state univer-

[2] For example, the typical student entering the private liberal arts college may be brighter and more highly motivated to begin with than the typical student entering the state university. Unless such initial differences have been adequately controlled in our analysis, the observed differences in subsequent rates of graduate school attendance may be attributable simply to differences in the student inputs of the two institutions, rather than to their differential effects on the student's motivation. For a fuller discussion of this problem, see Astin (1962b, 1963a).

sity makes the students cynical about the importance of graduate education. Clearly, the observed differential effect of the two institutions is subject to a variety of rival interpretations.

There are two important stages in the interpretation of differential college influence. The first, the purely descriptive task of defining and assessing differences between the two institutions, is both a conceptual and a technical problem: The investigator seeks to measure adequately all relevant differences between the environments of the two institutions. The second stage in the interpretative process is primarily methodological and statistical: The investigator attempts to identify the particular environmental differences that account for the observed effect. This book is primarily concerned with the first stage of this process, that of measuring relevant differences between institutional environments. If appropriate measurement techniques are developed, then they can in turn be used in studies of differential impact.

It must be emphasized again that information concerning differential college impact is of little value unless we have meaningful interpretations of these effects. Studies that produce only this information may be of interest to the particular institutions that are involved in the research, but they contribute little to scientific knowledge and are of small benefit either to other institutions or to the educational community at large. However, if we can account for observed differences in terms of measurable characteristics of institutions, the resulting findings will be generally useful in educational theory, policy formulation, research, and guidance.

THE COLLEGE ENVIRONMENT AS A STIMULUS

Webster's *New Collegiate Dictionary* defines *environment* as "the aggregate of all the external conditions and influences affecting the life and development of an organism." In the broadest sense, we can define the "college environment" as including any characteristic of the college that constitutes a potential stimulus for the student, i.e., that is capable of changing the student's sensory input.[3] These changes in sensory input may have one (or a combination) of four consequences:

1. A change in the student's immediate subjective experience.
2. A temporary or situational change in the student's overt behavior.
3. A lasting or relatively permanent change in the student's experience.
4. A lasting or relatively permanent change in the student's behavior.

[3] Although our discussion will, for the sake of simplicity, concentrate on the student's environment, the stimulus model is equally applicable to the environments of faculty and staff.

To illustrate these four types of environmental effect, let us assume that a new student enrolls at an institution which has very high academic standards and where the following types of environmental stimuli occur relatively frequently: classroom examinations, discussions among students about grades, studying, intellectual arguments among students, and debates between faculty and students. The new student would be exposed to these and any related stimuli both in the classroom and in his social interactions with fellow students. As an example of the first type of effect—a change in the student's immediate subjective experience—the student feels anxiety about possible academic failure. Other possible subjective effects are fear of or hostility toward fellow students, increased feelings of competitiveness, pride in the institution, and feelings of inferiority. It is important to note here that these hypothetical environmental effects are in fact *differential* effects (that is, the student would be affected differently if he attended a less competitive college).

The second type of environmental effect—a temporary or situational change in the student's overt behavior—can be illustrated by an increase in the time he devotes to study, a reduction in the time he devotes to social activities, and perhaps increased intellectual aggression (argumentativeness, for example) toward faculty and fellow students. Obviously, changes in a person's overt behavior are often caused by changes in his subjective experience, and practically any change in behavior creates "response-produced" stimuli which can, in turn, produce changes in subjective experience. The student who spends more time studying, for example, and less in social or interpersonal contacts, may consequently experience feelings of loneliness and isolation.

The last two types of environmental effects involve changes in the student which persist when he is away from the college environment and sometimes after he has completed college. Changes of the third type would include any lasting alteration in the student's self-concept. For example, as a result of four years in a highly competitive college, the student's self-esteem may be considerably greater (or less, for that matter). He may generalize his increased competitiveness, anxiety, or other feelings to persons outside of the college community.

Effects of the fourth type, relatively permanent changes in behavior, include any learned behavioral patterns that persist beyond college and any changes in behavior that result from the experiential changes (for example, devoting a great deal of time to the job or competing constantly with others).

Most educational practices are probably designed to produce changes of the latter two types, changes of a relatively lasting nature in experience or behavior. The goals expressed in college catalogues, for example, have to do with the student's intellectual and character development. The college, it would seem, tries to assist the student in making the fullest possible use of his talents and in becoming an effective, responsible member of society. Presumably, such effects on vocational and social behavior will, in turn, result in a more satisfying and rewarding life experience.

Many prospective college students find the last two types of goals remote and difficult to conceive. They are probably more interested in goals of the first type: that is, in their actual experiences during the undergraduate years. This attitude is exemplified by the college student who says that he is interested in "enjoying college life" or "having a good time in college." Such experiences include not only the social and extracurricular activities of the student, but also the personal stimulation resulting from his academic and other intellectual pursuits.

Ordinarily, interest in the college environment is generated by a concern with one or several of these four types of consequences. In the research described in this report, it is assumed that by focusing on the observable stimulus properties of the environment, we can identify some of the specific environmental variables that affect the student's development.

One possible problem in using the "stimulus" definition of the environment in studies of environmental influence is the circularity suggested by "external conditions . . . affecting the life and development of an organism." (This is somewhat like the circularity involved in defining the psychological term "reinforcement.") We have attempted to avoid this problem by defining the environment in terms of *potential* stimuli. A more basic definitional problem, however, concerns the methods used to identify or measure potential stimuli. Since, in the final analysis, it is necessary to use human observers to collect environmental data, we shall further qualify our definition of an environmental stimulus as follows: *any behavior, event, or other observable characteristic of the institution capable of changing the student's sensory input, the existence or occurrence of which can be confirmed by independent observation.*

PREVIOUS APPROACHES TO ENVIRONMENTAL ASSESSMENT

Our "stimulus" view of the college environment can be better illustrated by comparing it to previous approaches to assessing the college environment.

The "Image" Approach

The first systematic empirical approach to measuring the college environment was the College Characteristics Index (CCI) of Pace and Stern (1958) (See also Stern, 1963). The CCI, which was developed in part from Murray's (1938) need-press theory and from the later work of Stern, Stein, and Bloom (1956) on personality assessment, is based on the notion that the college environment or "press" can be characterized in terms of its potential for reinforcing certain personality needs. The CCI is thus designed to measure 30 different environmental presses, each of which corresponds to a parallel personality need. A college's "press for achievement," for example, indicates that college's capacity for satisfying the student's "need for achievement." An environment characterized by a relatively high achievement press would be more likely to satisfy the student's need for achievement than one with a relatively low achievement press.

Briefly, the CCI consists of 300 items describing different impressions of the college environment (e.g., "There is not much to do except go to class and study"). Observers (usually students) are requested to indicate whether or not each item accurately describes their college. Responses are scored on 30 ten-item scales, and scale scores are averaged across observers to yield the 30 environmental press scores for the institution.

Since most of the CCI items are concerned with the observer's impressions of the total institutional climate (e.g., "There is a lot of group spirit"), the resulting scales are more an indication of the student's "image" of the college environment than they are a direct measure of potential environmental stimuli. In Murray's (1938) terminology, CCI items represent an attempt to measure the "beta press," whereas the stimulus approach used in the present study represents an attempt to measure the "alpha press."

This essential difference between the college image and the college environment can be made clearer by examining an item from the "Harmavoidance" scale of the CCI: "Many students drive sports cars" (keyed "false"). Here the observer is being asked to make a quantitative judgment ("many") about the habits of the entire student body. Even if the student has access to the relevant information (i.e., if he were able regularly to observe what kinds of cars the majority of students drive), he must still resort to a subjective judgment concerning what constitutes "many." It is obvious that, to a large degree, the item reflects no more than the impression of the observer; the Harmavoidance scale, in turn, reflects the aggregate of the observer's perceptions.

The "sports car" item as phrased does not satisfy the definition of an environmental stimulus, since the observer's judgment can neither be validated by independent observation or, in itself, change the sensory input to other students. If we take the "stimulus" approach, and if we assume that driving a sports car is a potentially important stimulus in the college environment, we would ask a sample of students, "Did you drive a sports car at college during the past year?" The environmental measure consists of the percentage of students at the college who respond positively. Or, alternatively, we might ask the students to indicate how many times they have driven sports cars; the environmental measure in this instance could be the mean or median number of times, based on all student observers. Differences among institutions with respect to this particular stimulus (driving a sports car) are thus defined in terms of its relative frequency of occurrence.

Revisions of the CCI have been developed, although the college "image" aspect of the instrument has been retained. Thistlethwaite (1960), for example, has separated the CCI items into "faculty press" and "student press" scales. More recently, Pace (1960, 1963) has shortened and simplified the CCI by means of a factor analysis and an item analysis that resulted in the development of five College and University Environmental Scales (CUES). One of the major purposes of this revision was to identify the CCI items which actually differentiate among college environments. Scoring of the CUES scales is accomplished not by averaging the scale scores for individual observers, but simply by counting the number of keyed items about which at least two-thirds of the observers at a particular college agree. Although this modification eliminates much of the redundancy in the original 30 CCI scales, most of the 150 CCI items retained in CUES can still be classified as impressionistic items concerned with the college "image."

The Student Characteristics Approach

A somewhat different approach to assessing the college environment is represented by the Environmental Assessment Technique (EAT) developed by Astin and Holland (1961). EAT is based on the assumption that environments are transmitted by people and that the college environment depends on the personal characteristics of the students, faculty, administration, and staff of the institution. Since the undergraduate's personal contacts are chiefly with fellow students, it is further assumed that a major portion of the student's environment is determined by the characteristics of his fellow students. Accordingly, the environment was defined in terms of eight characteristics of the student body: average intelligence, size, and six personal orientations based on the proportions of the students in six broad areas of study: Realistic, Scientific, Social, Conventional, Enterprising, and Artistic. Since the classification of major field choices is based on Holland's (1959b, 1966) theory of personality types, the student's choice of a major field of study is regarded as a miniature personality "test."

An early test of the validity of the EAT (Astin and Holland, 1961) indicated that a large portion of the reliable variances in the 30 CCI scales could be accounted for by the eight EAT scores. Correlations between individual EAT and CCI scales (e.g., the EAT Realistic Orientation and the CCI Press for Humanism) ran as high as −.81 in a sample of 33 institutions. In another test of the validity of the EAT (Astin, 1963b), several specific hypotheses concerning the meanings of the various EAT measures were confirmed.

DEFINING THE ENVIRONMENTAL STIMULI: THE INVENTORY OF COLLEGE ACTIVITIES (ICA)

The preceding discussion suggests that the data used in the "image" and "student characteristics" approaches to assessing the college environment do not satisfy our criterion of a potential stimulus. Although the student's perception of his college environment ("There is a lot of group spirit") may influence his behavior toward his fellow students, his perception alone cannot function as a stimulus for others.[4] Nor do his intelligence, attitudes, values, and other personal characteristics constitute stimuli by our definition, although such traits may be manifested in certain behaviors which can in turn serve as stimuli for fellow students.

Stimulus data for the study described in the following chapters were obtained using a specially designed instrument called the Inventory of College Activities (ICA). To clarify further the essential differences between the "image," the "personal characteristics," and the "stimulus" approaches, Figure 1 shows examples of the kinds of data derived from each. The upper box gives examples of student behaviors, or "stimulus" data of the kind used in the ICA. The lower left box shows samples of student perceptions of the kind used in the CCI and CUES. The lower right box shows examples of student traits and personal characteristics of the type used in the EAT.

[4] Even though one person's perceptions cannot be directly observed by another person, perceptions can, of course, serve as internal stimuli for the perceiver. The point is that, unlike his overt behavior, the individual's perceptions cannot operate directly as stimuli for others with whom he comes in contact.

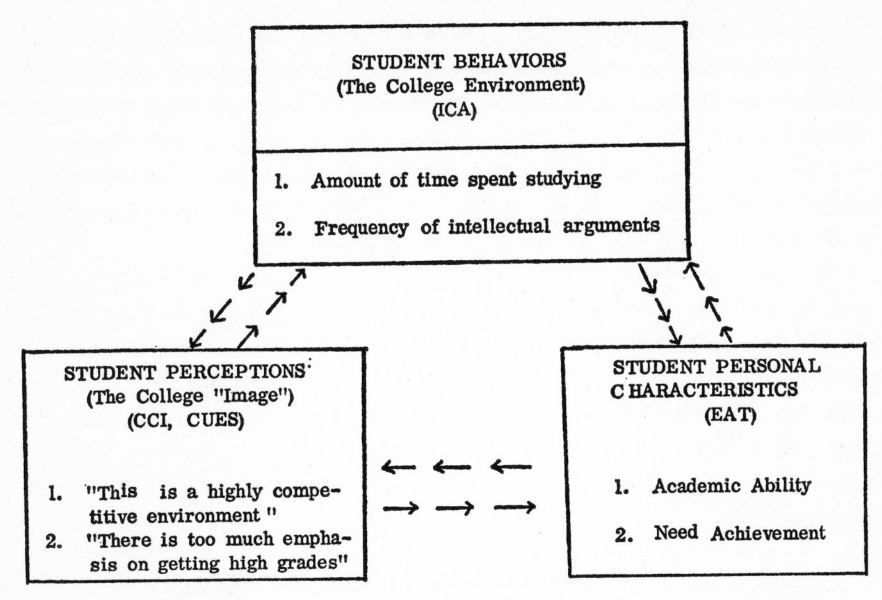

Fig. 1. Examples of the three types of information obtained by different approaches to assessing the college environment.

Our goal in designing the ICA was to identify as many environmental stimuli as possible that could be observed by undergraduate students and reported in a questionnaire. We tried to cover four broad categories of stimuli: the peer environment, the classroom environment, the administrative environment, and the physical environment. A series of staff discussions and a review of existing tests and inventories resulted in the formulation of 275 items covering these four categories. In addition, 77 items concerning the college image and 48 items concerning the students' personal characteristics were included in order to explore the relationships among these three types of data.

Examples of the types of items used to obtain information about the college environment, the college image, and the students' personal characteristics are given in Table 1. (The complete 400-item questionnaire is shown in Appendix A.)

SAMPLES OF INSTITUTIONS AND STUDENTS

In an earlier study of 1961 entering freshman classes (Astin, 1965d), 248 institutions were selected to represent the population of accredited four-year colleges and universities. The larger and wealthier institutions were over-represented, however, in order to maximize heterogeneity within the sample; a strictly random sample would comprise mostly very small, poorly

Table 1

Types of Items Used in the Inventory of College Activities (ICA)

- I. The College Environment:
  - A. Peer Environment
    1. Average number of hours per week spent in various activities (bull sessions, studying)
    2. Frequency of dates of different types
    3. Roommate's behavior ("messy," "liked to talk")
    4. Typical mode of dress (for class, for dinner)
    5. Membership in campus organizations
  - B. Classroom Environment
    1. Observations of instructor's behavior (frequency of lectures versus discussion, types of assignments)
    2. Observations of behavior of self and other students in class (asked questions, took notes)
    3. *Modus operandi* of class (seating assigned, smoking permitted, roll taken)
  - C. Administrative Environment
    1. Disciplinary consequences of potential violations (drinking, cheating, demonstrations, etc.)
    2. Frequency of actual violations of regulations
  - D. Physical Environment
    1. Characteristics of living quarters (number of roommates, wall displays)
    2. Distance to classrooms, library
    3. Climate
- II. The College Image:
  - A. Subjective impressions ("There is a lot of school spirit on this campus")
  - B. Ratings of environmental traits ("liberal," "friendly," "practical")
  - C. Evaluations (satisfaction with curriculum, social life)
- III. Personal Characteristics of the Students:
  - A. Educational and vocational plans (highest degree sought)
  - B. Self-ratings (intelligence, drive to achieve)
  - C. Ratings of roommate's traits (same as III, B)

financed institutions. Each of the 127,212 entering freshmen was asked to provide information about his socioeconomic background, academic and extracurricular achievements in high school and his future educational and vocational plans. The sample of 246 institutions used in the present study was drawn from this earlier sample.[5]

The general plan of the current study was to use the students from the earlier study as observers of the college environment by asking them to fill out the ICA after completing their first year in college. Since certain aspects of the college environment undoubtedly change systematically between the

[5] Two institutions with entering classes of fewer than 30 students were dropped from the original sample of 248 institutions because the number of observers was not large enough for us to obtain reliable measures of the college environment.

freshman year and subsequent years in college, we felt that, by restricting this survey to college freshmen, we would reduce the possibility of confounding such changes. Moreover, using only freshmen gives a more accurate picture of the types of stimuli that the prospective new college student can reasonably expect to encounter.

In order to reduce project costs, a subsample of 60,505 students was selected for the follow-up survey conducted in the summer of 1962 (i.e., after completion of the freshman year in college). Approximately 250 students were chosen from each college. For institutions enrolling fewer than 300 freshmen in 1961, all students were selected; for the larger institutions, samples of 250 students were selected at random. The arbitrary figure of 250 was chosen with the expectation that the rate of return would be about 50 percent. The 100-125 returns for a given college would thus enable us to obtain a reasonably stable estimate of that college's relative position on each item. In the hope that it would be possible to study subenvironments within the complex university, approximately 500 students were selected from several of the large universities.

Copies of the ICA were mailed from the National Merit Scholarship Corporation to each of the 60,505 subjects during the last week of August, 1962. (Home addresses had been provided by the students when they first entered college in 1961.) Since fourth-class mail was used, few questionnaires were forwarded beyond the initial address, and undelivered questionnaires were not returned to the Corporation. Although no follow-ups of nonrespondents were conducted, completed questionnaires continued to arrive daily until well into 1963. For purposes of analysis, however, the cut-off date of December 31, 1962, was set, by which time we had received approximately 34,500 returns. Since it is unlikely, because of the year-old addresses, that more than 90 percent of the 60,505 questionnaires actually reached the students, we estimate that between 64 and 70 percent of the students who received the questionnaire eventually returned it.

In order to simplify the task of data processing, subjects who had omitted or only partially completed large sections of the questionnaire were excluded. This procedure reduced the sample used for analysis to 30,570 subjects—slightly more than half of the original 60,505 students.

The percentage of usable questionnaires by institution varied from 23 percent to 81 percent; the absolute number varied from 33 to 322. However, only two of the institutions produced fewer than 50 respondents, and 100 or more usable returns were received from 70 percent of the 246 institutions.

A series of analyses was performed to determine the extent and potential effects of the bias in the sample of respondents (see Appendix B). Although certain biases clearly existed in the mean scores on some items, (e.g., students with relatively high grades in their senior year in high school were more likely to return the questionnaire than were students with relatively low grades), they did not appear to have any appreciable effect on the *relationships* among the items. Since this study is primarily concerned with such relationships (i.e., the *relative* ordering of colleges on various items), it is unlikely that the responding bias had any pronounced effect on the findings.

METHOD OF ANALYSIS

The principal purpose of the analyses of data obtained through the ICA was to identify patterns of environmental stimuli that differentiate among institutions. The initial step was to compute mean scores on each item separately for each of the 246 institutions. Means for the dichotomous ("true—false" or "yes—no") items consisted of percentages of students answering "true" or "yes" to the item. Thus, for each institution we determined the percentage of students who reported that they had flunked a course during their freshman year, the percentage who reported that they had changed their field of study during their freshman year, the percentage who reported that they had got married during their freshman year, and so forth. Percentages were similarly computed for a long list of student behaviors to which the response was trichotomous: "frequently," "occasionally," or "not at all."[6] For the majority of these trichotomous items we collapsed the "frequently" and "occasionally" categories and computed for each college the percentage of students who gave either one of these two responses (i.e., the percentage of students who engaged in the particular behavior at least occasionally during their freshman year). However, on some items (e.g., "Studied in the library," "Went to the movies"), the mean scores of nearly all institutions were near 100 percent. In order to increase interinstitutional variability on such items, we collapsed the "occasionally" and "not at all" categories and computed only the percentage of students who checked "frequently."

A different method of computing averages was used for those items in which students were asked to specify how frequently an event occurred.

[6] Pretests of different item response formats in several earlier questionnaires had suggested that students found this particular trichotomous format easy to use and that the differentiation between "frequently" and "occasionally" was, for most items, not difficult to make.

For instance, the student was asked to indicate the average number of hours per week he spent on each of 19 activities (attending class, watching TV, sleeping, etc.) and to report on the average number of various types of dates he had per month. To minimize the influence of those few students who may have reported impossibly high rates of dating or impossibly large numbers of hours per week spent on various activities, we computed the median instead of the mean score for each institution on these items.

It is important to note here that these mean scores for each of the 246 institutions represent our basic measures of environmental characteristics. Although it would be possible to profile any institution in terms of its scores on all 275 stimulus items, such a large number tends to be unwieldy and undoubtedly includes a substantial amount of redundant information. Accordingly, a second phase in the analysis was designed to examine the relationships among the mean scores on each of the 275 stimulus items and at the same time to reduce this large pool of stimuli to a smaller number of more general environmental dimensions. To accomplish these aims we performed a series of factor analyses in which the institutions were used as the units of sampling. Factor analyses were done separately on items having to do with the student peer environment, the classroom environment, the administrative environment, and the physical environment of the institution. For exploratory purposes we also performed factor analyses of items having to do with the college image and of items concerning personal characteristics of students.[7] (Lists of the items used in each analysis are given in Appendix G.) Scores for each institution on each obtained factor were com-

[7] Several different methods of analysis were attempted with the various matrices. For example, both normalized and non-normalized variables were tried, with no appreciable difference in the outcomes. Since the distributions on many of the variables showed pronounced departures from normality, however, we elected to perform all factor analyses using normalized distributions.

All factor analyses of the correlation matrices were performed using the method of principal components. Communality estimates for matrices of less than 75 variables consisted of squared multiple correlation coefficients between each variable and all others. In order to reduce computing costs (i.e., to avoid inverting the matrix), communality estimates for larger matrices consisted of the highest correlation coefficient. (We repeated two of the analyses of the smaller matrices using this latter method for estimating communalities, with results almost identical to those obtained using the squared multiple correlations method.)

All rotations were performed with the normalized varimax method. In each problem, we rotated different numbers of factors in order to identify the most meaningful solution. The final determination of the number of factors to be retained was primarily a decision of the author.

Two of the early analyses were repeated using revised estimates of communalities based on the number of factors finally retained. Since these iterations proved to have little effect on the final rotated loadings, iterations of the remaining analyses were not done.

puted using stepwise linear multiple regression analyses in which the factor loading of the item was used as the criterion correlation. In most instances, it was possible to obtain a relatively accurate estimate of each factor by using the first three items that entered the equation with their appropriate weights as determined by the regression analysis (see Appendix D).

The final step in the analysis involved correlating each obtained factor score with every available item of information about the institution. These items—approximately 650 in all—included not only the 400 items from the ICA employed in the original factor analysis, but also a variety of other information about the institution, such as its type of control and location. Additional data about administrative policies and practices were obtained from all but six of the institutions through a questionnaire sent to the institutional representative (usually the Registrar) who supervised the collection of data when the students first entered college in 1961. (This questionnaire is reproduced in Appendix E.) For 43 of the institutions, the National Opinion Research Center provided mean item scores from a questionnaire administered to the graduating seniors of 1961.[8] It was our belief that an exploratory correlational analysis of this type, in which all known information about the institution is related to each obtained factor, would help to clarify the meaning of the factors.

In the remaining chapters of the book we shall present the results and the interpretations of these analyses.

[8] The author is indebted to Norman Bradburn and James Davis of NORC for providing these scores.

2

The Peer Environment

FROM THE POINT of view of the prospective college student, the stimuli provided by his peers may represent the most significant aspect of the college environment. The potential impact of the peer environment becomes apparent when one realizes the great variety of roles that the student and his classmates can play with respect to each other: friend, competitor, adviser or confidant, sexual partner, intellectual companion, and so on. Thus, insofar as sheer variety and frequency of personal contacts are concerned, no other source of stimulation is likely to rival the student's peers. The effects of such stimuli will probably be especially pronounced for those students who live away from home in dormitories or in other types of college housing shared by fellow students.

The fact that the student on the campus serves both as a recipient of stimuli and as a source of stimulation for his peers suggests an interesting hypothesis about the dynamics of college environments: To the extent that the stimuli provided by fellow students alter the behavior of the individual student, thus altering in turn the stimuli that he provides for others, college environments are in a process of continual change. Evidence from recent studies (Astin, 1965b; Davis, 1965) lends partial support to the notion that environments (defined in terms of student behaviors) tend to become more homogeneous with time, or—to put it more simply—that students in a particular college tend to become more alike with time. Although it was beyond the scope of this project to make a systematic study of these alterations, one should keep in mind that the student's peer environment may undergo continual change as he progresses through college.

In this chapter, we shall describe and analyze some of the many stimuli provided by students at the 246 institutions. Our major objectives are to identify those student behavioral stimuli that show the greatest differences in frequency of occurrence among the different institutions and to identify some of the interinstitutional patterns created by these peer stimuli.

ICA items concerning student behavioral stimuli presented certain special problems for analysis. To begin with, the pool of 161 items was too large to be accommodated by available factor analytic computer programs, so it was necessary to separate the large pool into two smaller pools. The first contained items describing student interpersonal behavior (e.g., "Participated in informal group singing"), and the second consisted of items describing student behavior of a noninterpersonal sort (e.g., "Studied in the library"). The division of the peer behavior items into these two groups was to some extent arbitrary, since it is possible that many of the behaviors classified as "noninterpersonal" typically involve other students (e.g., "Went to the movies"). Our criterion for including an item in the interpersonal category was that the behavior as described in the item necessarily involved at least one other person (e.g., "Played table tennis").

INTERPERSONAL STUDENT BEHAVIOR

A total of 84 items was used in the analysis of the interpersonal peer environment. Distributions of the mean item scores among the 246 institutions revealed remarkable diversity in the frequency of most student interpersonal behaviors. A sample of these behaviors, selected primarily because they had high loadings in the resulting factor analyses, is shown in Table 2. These data suggest, for example, that at some institutions nearly all of the students arranged a date for another student at least once during their freshman year, and at other institutions fewer than one student in eight did so. The frequency with which students at different colleges vote in student elections is similarly diverse, ranging from fewer than one student in ten to

Table 2

Students' Interpersonal Behavior: Diversity Among 246 Institutions

Behavior	Frequency of Occurrence:*		
	Lowest Inst.	Median Inst.	Highest Inst.
Participated in informal group singing**	35.0	74.5	96.4
Arranged a date for another student	13.8	54.5	95.3
Voted in a student election**	9.0	59.3	91.8
Went to an overnight or week-end party	5.3	25.0	80.9
Participated in a student demonstration against some administrative policy	0.0	11.4	80.6
Was a member of a college athletic team	1.4	15.8	75.5
Argued with other students**	1.8	20.6	61.1
Gambled with cards or dice	0.0	20.0	54.0
Median number of casual (coke or study) dates per month	1.9	2.9	9.2

* Unless indicated otherwise, the data shown are percentages of students who reported engaging in the behavior ("frequently" or "occasionally") during their freshman year.

** Percentages based only on those engaging in the behavior "frequently."

more than nine in ten. That the items shown in Table 2 are not an unrepresentative sample of this diversity is demonstrated by the fact that on fully 26 of the student interpersonal items, the highest institution differed at least 50 percentage points from the lowest institution. (A complete list of all items, together with the scores for the highest, lowest, and median institution, is given in Appendix C.)

The factor analysis of the institutions' mean scores on the 84 items revealed five distinct patterns of student interpersonal interaction: Competitiveness versus Cooperativeness, Organized Dating, Independence, Cohesiveness, and Informal Dating.[1]

Table 3 shows the variables that are correlated with the first interpersonal factor, Competitiveness versus Cooperativeness. This factor is clearly bipolar in character: that is, two groups of items distinctly different in content define the opposite extremes of the factor. Both the content of the items and the correlation of .80 between this factor and percentage of men in the student body indicate that it has a strong masculinity-femininity component. The positive end, competitiveness, reflects a style of interaction that is characterized by risk-taking, adventurousness, and—perhaps most importantly—an aggressive desire to defeat or overcome an opponent (e.g., through gambling, making bets, playing chess). Other behaviors such as becoming intoxicated, picking up dates in bars, attending burlesque shows, and driving cars fast also suggest an impulsive, irresponsible person. In contrast, the negative (cooperative) end of the factor reveals a pattern of interpersonal behaviors characterized by participation in organized student activities, by religious interests, and by sensitivity to and concern for the needs of others.

Students at institutions with highly competitive environments tend to see the college as impersonal and as treating the students like "numbers in a book." Students in cooperative environments, on the other hand, are more likely to see the college as being warm and having high morale, and to see the faculty as going out of their way to help the student. Liberal arts colleges obtain very low (cooperative) scores on this factor, as do women's colleges; indeed, no woman's college obtained a score as high as any one of the men's colleges (see Figure 2), and even the highest scoring woman's college scored below more than three-fourths of the coeducational colleges.

[1] Diagonal values were the highest correlation. A total of eight components, accounting for 90 percent of the total communality, were retained for varimax rotation. Of the three rotated factors not described in this chapter, two are unidentifiable residual factors; the third seemed to be an artifact of the presence or absence of social fraternities or sororities on the campus. See Appendix G for the complete correlation and factor matrices.

Table 3

Competitiveness Versus Cooperativeness

Variable	r with Factor Score
A. Correlated Peer Stimuli	
Gambled with cards or dice	.87*
Made a bet on a game or other event	.82
Played chess	.68
Pushed a stalled car	.67
Became intoxicated	.66
Picked up a hitchhiker	.64
Picked up a date in a bar or restaurant	.63
Attended a burlesque show	.60
Discussed sports with other students	.60
Drank beer	.58
Drove a car over 80 mph	.54
Drinking vs. Religiousness factor	.52
Participated in informal group singing	−.88*
Cried	−.82
Listened to a friend discuss a personal problem	−.72
Discussed religion with other students	−.64
Attended a student stage play	−.62
Artistic & Musical Activity factor	−.62
Voted in a student election	−.58*
Tried on clothes in a store without buying anything	−.57
Said grace before meals	−.57
Number of students called by first name	−.56
Femininity factor	−.56
Time spent on personal care and grooming	−.55
Sang in a choir or glee club	−.54
Read the Bible	−.53
Attended a public recital	−.53
Said "hello" to students you didn't know	−.51
B. Correlated Classroom Stimuli	
Instructor was a woman	−.64
Instructor called students by their first names	−.56
C. Correlated Student Personal Characteristics	
Male	.80
Value money (NORC)	.58
Value leadership (NORC)	.57
Prefer to work with things	.54
Prefer to work with people	−.59
Value being helpful (NORC)	−.53
D. Correlated Aspects of the College Image	
Impersonal	.61
Most of the students are more like "numbers in a book"	.52
Warm	−.61
Faculty go out of their way to help the student	−.54
High morale	−.52
E. Correlated Characteristics of the College	
Masculinity of entering class	.74
Pragmatism of entering class	.63
Social orientation (EAT)	−.63
Women's college	−.54
Liberal arts college	−.51
Artistic orientation (EAT)	−.50

* Used in computing the factor score.

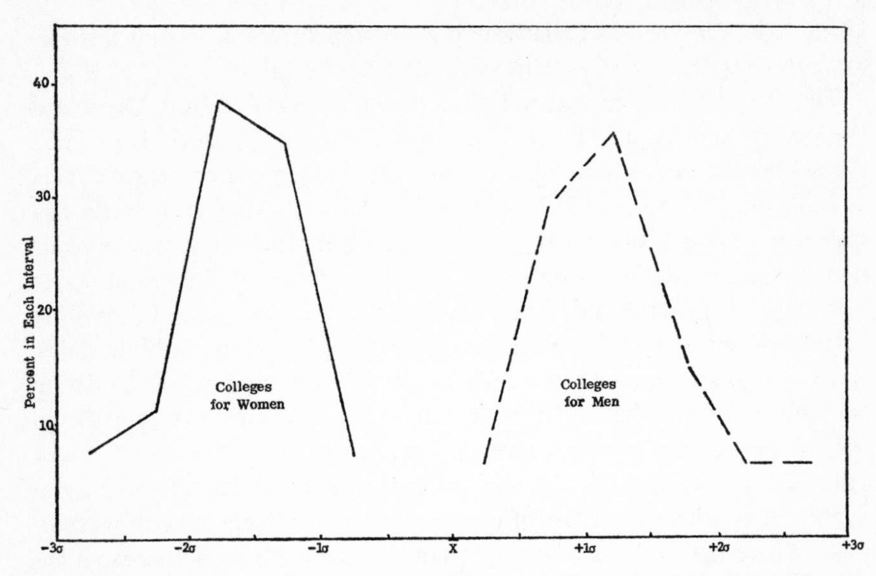

Fig. 2. Scores of Colleges for Men (N = 31) and Colleges for Women (N = 26) on Competitiveness vs. Cooperativeness.

Table 4
Organized Dating

VARIABLE	R WITH FACTOR SCORE
A. Correlated Peer Stimuli	
Arranged a date for another student	.93*
Had a blind date	.87*
Went to an overnight or week-end party	.76*
Danced the twist	.71
Went to a party	.68
Number of formal dates to dances and big parties	.57
Drank whiskey	.54
Do not date at all	−.57
B. Correlated Student Personal Characteristics	
Father's occupation in Enterprising class	.66
Father's occupation in Realistic class	−.58
C. Correlated Aspects of the College Image	
Sophisticated	.51

* Used in computing the factor score.

Universities tend to have relatively high (competitive) scores on this factor, although not as high as those of the men's colleges.

The correlates of the second student interpersonal factor, Organized Dating, are shown in Table 4. Interestingly enough, the analysis revealed the existence of two distinct patterns of dating behavior: organized dating and informal dating (the fifth interpersonal factor). Apparently, sheer frequency of dating is not, by itself, a meaningful measure of student interaction. Organized dating is defined primarily in terms of the frequency of dates that are prearranged. The three items that make up the factor score have to do with arranging dates for other students, going on blind dates, and going to an overnight or week-end party. The rate of organized dating is highly related to the frequency with which the students go to parties, go out on formal dates (to big dances and major parties), and dance the twist (this last item is undoubtedly obsolete for the current crop of college students). A relatively high rate of organized dating is likely to occur on campuses where the students come from families in which the father is an entrepreneur (e.g., salesman, business executive). Organized dating occurs less frequently on campuses where the students' fathers are in Realistic occupations (mainly skilled trades). Students in the colleges where there is much organized dating tend to see their college environment as very sophisticated.

Table 5 shows the variables that are highly correlated with the third behavioral pattern in the interpersonal peer environment, Independence. It is obvious that institutional environments characterized by a high degree of independence have contentious students who are prone to participate in intercollegiate athletics, to argue with their teachers, and to participate in demonstrations against administrative policies. There is also a relatively high rate of drinking in the independent environment; oddly enough, the rate of studying is also high, perhaps because of the relatively superior ability of the students in this environment. The independent environment might also be characterized as highly aggressive.

Faculty in the independent environment tend to prefer essay exams to objective exams and are likely to be men. Their students feel that they emphasize theoretical rather than practical concerns. Students in this environment are highly motivated toward graduate training and are interested in careers either as scientists or as entrepreneurs. They tend to have above-average academic ability, and their fathers are highly educated. Colleges with the more independent environments are apt to be very selective and to put little emphasis on Social (mainly teaching) occupations.

Table 5

Independence

Variable	r with Factor Score
A. Correlated Peer Stimuli	
Argued with other students	.79*
Was a varsity athlete (NORC)	.75
Member of college athletic team	.74*
Participated in a student demonstration against some administrative policy	.65*
Argued with a teacher in class	.64
Drinking vs. Religiousness Factor	.58
Became intoxicated	.57
Drank beer	.57
Argued openly with the instructor	.56
Discussed sex with other students	.56
Verbal Aggressiveness factor	.55
Overslept and missed a class or appointment	.54
Hours per week spent in sports or practice sessions	.54
Took a nap or rest during the day	.53
Argued openly with other students in class	.53
Hours per week spent studying	.52
Drank whiskey	.52
Married (NORC)	−.78
Hours per week spent in personal care	−.62
Prayed	−.57
Cooked a complete meal	−.56
Attended a fashion show	−.56
Got married during freshman year	−.52
Attended Sunday School	−.52
Took a laxative	−.51
B. Correlated Classroom Stimuli	
Examinations were usually of the "objective" rather than the "essay" type	−.60
Instructor was a woman	−.53
C. Correlated Student Personal Characteristics	
Father's educational level (NORC)	.64
Very nonreligious (NORC)	.63
Planning graduate training or study	.62
Home is located in the suburbs (NORC)	.61
Father's educational level	.60
Planning to get a Ph.D. degree	.58
Major in Scientific field	.57
Father a professional or executive	.57
Academic ability (NMSQT composite)	.57
Social science achievement (NMSQT)	.57
Natural science achievement (NMSQT)	.56
Took NMSQT in high school	.55
Vocational choice in Scientific class	.54

* Used in computing the factor score.

Table 5 (Continued)

Variable	r with Factor Score
Word usage (NMSQT)	.53
Father's occupation in Scientific class	.53
Lazy (self rating)	.51
Planning a career in Enterprising class	.51
Religious (self-rating)	−.63
Father's occupation in Realistic class	−.51
D. Correlated Aspects of the College Image	
Positive evaluation of teachers (NORC)	.73
High calibre of students (NORC)	.69
Professional standing of faculty (NORC)	.65
Intellectual atmosphere is definitely on the theoretical, rather than the practical side	.58
Campus paper and humor magazine are carefully censored by the administration	−.57
E. Correlated Characteristics of the College	
Status of the entering class	.59
Intellectualism of entering class	.59
Selectivity	.56
Social orientation (EAT)	−.50

In general, the NORC items that had substantial correlations with the Independence factor were consistent with the ICA items. For instance, Independence correlates .75 with the percentage of NORC graduating seniors who reported being a varsity athlete and .74 with the percentage of students who reported on the ICA that they were a member of a college athletic team during their freshman year. Similarly, the father's educational level of the NORC students correlated .64 with Independence, as compared with a correlation of .60 between Independence and the father's educational level as reported by the students in our sample. Independence correlated —.52 with the percentage of freshmen who reported on the ICA that they got married and −.78 with the percentage of NORC graduates who reported being married, the higher NORC correlation no doubt resulting from the inevitable increase in the proportion of married students as the students get older.

Of the various types of institutions, colleges for men, technological institutions, and private nonsectarian institutions tend to score significantly above average on Independence.

Table 6

Cohesiveness

Variable	r with Factor Score
A. Correlated Peer Stimuli	
Number of close friends among fellow students	.88*
Discussed how to make money with friends	.68*
Freshmen have to take orders from upperclassmen	.64*
Said "hello" to students you didn't know	.59
Time spent watching athletic events	.53
Drank wine	−.59
Bought a paperback book (not for a class)	−.54
Listened to folk music	−.51
B. Correlated Classroom Stimuli	
We sometimes had unannounced or "pop" quizzes	.57
Lectures followed the textbook closely	.52
Instructor was engaged in research	−.56
C. Correlated Student Personal Characteristics	
Home is on a farm (NORC)	.82
Value getting along with people (NORC)	.67
Home is located in the suburbs (NORC)	−.65
Word usage (NMSQT)	−.64
Academic ability (NMSQT composite)	−.62
Social science reading aptitude (NMSQT)	−.62
Unconventional (NORC)	−.62
Value being original (NORC)	−.60
English aptitude (NMSQT)	−.59
Natural science reading aptitude (NMSQT)	−.59
High school grades	−.56
Mathematics aptitude (NMSQT)	−.55
Intellectual factor	−.54
Took NMSQT in high school	−.50
Had poems, short stories, etc., published in high school	−.50
D. Correlated aspects of the College Image	
Practical-minded	.52
Tense	−.52
Intellectual atmosphere is definitely on the theoretical, rather than the practical side	−.50
There is a large group of "avant-garde" students on the campus	−.50
E. Correlated Characteristics of the College	
Selectivity	−.60

* Used in computing factor score.

The fourth pattern of student interpersonal behavior, Cohesiveness, is shown in Table 6. This factor is defined primarily by the median number of fellow students who, according to the student observer, are his close friends. Other student behaviors closely associated with Cohesiveness include discussing with fellow students how to make money, having to take orders from upperclassmen, saying hello to other students who are strangers, and spending a relatively large amount of time watching athletic events. (It should be noted here that whereas Independence is related to the degree of student *participation* in athletics, Cohesiveness is related to the frequency with which students are *spectators* at athletic events.) A comparatively high percentage of students in the cohesive environment come from farm or rural backgrounds and value getting along with people. The students' perception of the cohesive environment is that it is practical-minded rather than theory-oriented.

By contrast, students in the less cohesive environments are more likely to come from the suburbs of the large cities, to have high academic ability, and to see their college environment as tense. They also appear to have achieved more during high school in both academic and extracurricular activities. The less cohesive environment, furthermore, has students who tend to rate themselves as unconventional and who value being original. As one

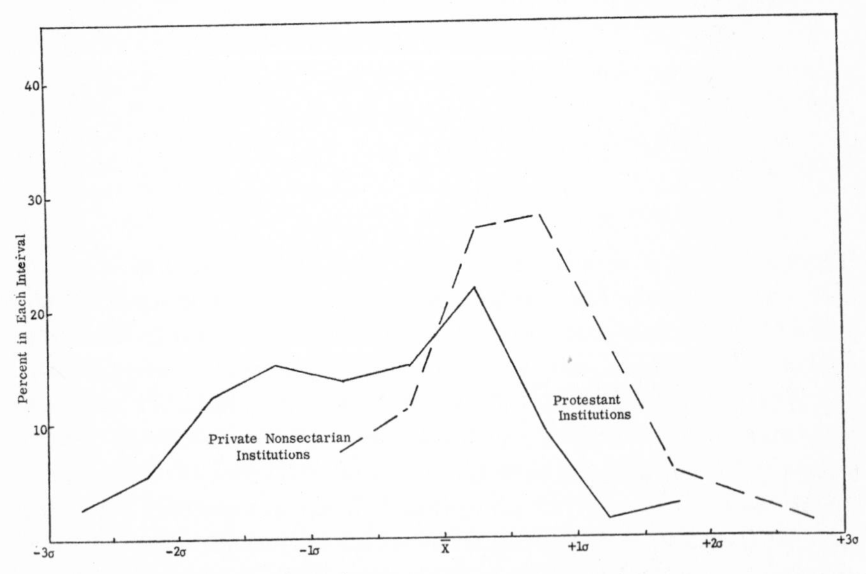

Fig. 3. Scores of Private Nonsectarian Institutions (N = 73) and Protestant Institutions (N = 89) on Cohesiveness.

would expect from these findings, institutions with less cohesive environments are usually more selective than are typical institutions.

Of the various types of institutions, Protestant liberal arts colleges tend to obtain the highest scores on Cohesiveness; nonsectarian liberal arts colleges and universities tend to obtain the lowest scores. Figure 3 compares the scores of the nonsectarian and Protestant colleges. More than 40 percent of the nonsectarian colleges have Cohesiveness scores below the lowest-scoring Protestant colleges. Conversely, 80.9 percent of the Protestant colleges, as compared to only 35.6 percent of the nonsectarian colleges, had above-average scores on Cohesiveness.

The fifth and last student behavioral pattern identified in the analyses of the interpersonal peer environment, Informal Dating, is shown in Table 7.

Table 7

Informal Dating

Variable	r with Factor Score
A. Correlated Peer Stimuli	
Number of casual coke, coffee, or study dates	.92*
Fell in love	.76*
Number of informal dates to movies, student gatherings, etc.	.70
Broke up with girlfriend or boyfriend	.54
Discussed sex with other students	.19*
B. Correlated Aspects of the College Image	
Not enough dates	−.68
C. Correlated Characteristics of the College	
Men's college	−.60

* Used in computing the factor score.

Informal Dating is defined primarily in terms of the frequency of casual coke, coffee, or study dates. The proportion of students who report falling in love and the proportion who break up with a girlfriend or boyfriend during their freshman year are also highly correlated with Informal Dating. Although the frequency with which the students discuss sex with each other entered into the scoring of the Informal Dating factor with a small weight, the correlation between this item and the factor is negligible.

Not surprisingly, the rate of informal dating is negatively correlated with the frequency of complaints about not having enough dates. Naturally enough, too, informal dating is fairly infrequent at women's colleges, though not nearly so much so as at men's colleges (all 31 men's colleges had below-average scores). Perhaps women's colleges are more strategically located as far as accessibility of dates is concerned, or perhaps women are more industrious then are men in overcoming the handicap of a single-sex institution. In any event, the overlap between men's colleges and coeducational colleges in the rate of informal dating is only about 10 percent.

Informal Dating is the only one of the five student interpersonal factors that shows pronounced differences by geographic region: it is relatively frequent at colleges located in the West and Southwest and relatively infrequent at colleges located in the Northeast. Probably this finding is a consequence of the high concentration of noncoeducational colleges in the Northeast and the rarity of such institutions in the West and Southwest.

Table 8 shows intercorrelations of the five student interpersonal behavior factors. Although half of these intercorrelations are statistically

Table 8

Intercorrelations of Five Patterns of Student Interaction

N= 246 Institutions

Student Interaction Factor*	2	3	4	5
1. Competitiveness vs. Cooperativeness	−.04	.26	−.07	−.26
2. Organized Dating		.10	−.13	.06
3. Independence			−.20	−.24
4. Cohesiveness				.10
5. Informal Dating				

* All factor scores have been normalized.

significant, none is as high as .30. Thus, the five patterns can, for most practical purposes, be regarded as independent. However, the correlations in Table 8 do suggest the presence of a second-order factor involving, on the one end, competitiveness and independence, and, on the other, cooperativeness, cohesiveness, and informal dating. The rate of organized dating is not related to the other factors.

NONINTERPERSONAL STUDENT BEHAVIOR

The *noninterpersonal* peer environment includes all student behaviors which do not by definition require the participation of two or more students. The diversity among colleges in frequency of occurrence of this kind of behavior (Table 9) is at least as great as the diversity found for the interpersonal behaviors. This variation is aptly illustrated by two items—"Prayed (not including grace before meals)" and "Drank beer"—both of which span nearly the entire possible range in frequency of occurrence.

Table 9

Students' Noninterpersonal Behavior: Diversity Among 246 Institutions

BEHAVIOR	FREQUENCY OF OCCURRENCE		
	Lowest Inst.	Median Inst.	Highest Inst.
Prayed (not including grace before meals)*	7.1	48.3	100.0
Attended a public recital or concert	33.0	77.2	98.9
Drank beer	1.8	50.6	93.4
Stayed up all night	8.7	57.3	89.9
Checked out a book or journal from the college library	15.4	56.4	88.8
Attended a ballet performance	0.0	6.5	79.9
Listened to folk music	4.5	21.9	74.7
Been interviewed as a client in the college counseling center	0.0	10.2	56.4
Median number of hours per week spent sleeping	39.0	49.0	54.0
Median number of hours per week spent studying	15.8	28.0	38.6

* Percentage based only on those engaging in the behavior "frequently."

That institutions should vary so much in the proportion of their students who use the college library is surprising. In particular, it is difficult to understand why, at some institutions, fewer than one student in six checks out a book from the library during his freshman year. Even more remarkable is the degree of diversity among institutions in the amount of time their students spend studying; it varies from as little as two hours a day to more than five hours a day. In contrast, the variation among student bodies in the average amount of time spent sleeping is somewhat less: the median number of hours ranges from slightly less than six hours to almost eight hours per night. At no institution, apparently, does the typical freshman average as much as eight hours of sleep per night.

The factor analyses of the 77 items of student noninterpersonal behavior produced ten identifiable factors: Femininity, Drinking versus Religiousness, Musical and Artistic Activity, Leisure Time, Career Indecision, Regularity of Sleeping Habits, Use of the Library, Conflict with Regulations, Student Employment, and Use of Automobiles.[2]

[2] The component extraction was performed using the highest r as the diagonal value. Twelve components, accounting for 90 percent of the total communality, were retained for the varimax rotation (these components included all of those accounting for at least 2 percent of the communality). Two of the rotated factors appeared to be uninterpretable residuals. This analysis was actually performed with the five interpersonal peer factors as "marker variables" to test for possible redundancy. However, certain errors in the scoring of these five factors, which were not detected until several months after the analysis was completed, markedly lowered their correlations with the noninterpersonal items. Although it is unlikely that these errors seriously affected the resulting factor structure, the correlations and factor loadings involving these five variables should be disregarded (see Appendix G, Table G-2).

Table 10

Femininity

Variable	r with Factor Score
A. Correlated Peer Stimuli	
Tried on clothes in a store without buying anything	.90*
Took Metrecal or similar dietary formula	.88*
Cried	.73
Listened to a friend discuss a personal problem	.71
Painted (oil, water color, pastel, etc.)	.65
Attended a fashion show	.57
Time spent on personal care (bathing, fixing hair, shaving, putting on make-up, etc.)	.56
Attended a ballet performance	.56*
Took a laxative	.51
Discussed sports with other students	−.63
Played chess	−.60
Competitiveness vs. Cooperativeness factor	−.56
Gambled with cards or dice	−.54
Made bets on games or other events	−.52
Frequency of informal dates to movies, student gatherings, etc.	−.50
Member of intramural athletic team	−.50
B. Correlated Classroom Stimuli	
Instructor was a woman	.64
C. Correlated Student Personal Characteristics	
Major in Artistic field	.57
Prefer to work with people	.53
Wanted to take a course but couldn't because of other requirements	.53
Value being helpful (NORC)	.51
Major in Social field	.51
Vocational choice in Social class	.50
Male	−.77
Masculinity of entering class	−.64
Major in Scientific field	−.53
Vocational choice in Scientific field	−.50
D. Correlated Aspects of the College Image	
Artistic orientation (EAT)	.53
Women's college	.53
Men's college	−.59

* Used in computing the factor score.

Table 10 shows the variables that correlated at least .50 with Femininity, the first noninterpersonal student behavior factor. Although other student behavior factors also contained elements of masculinity-femininity, we decided to label this particular pattern "Femininity" because each one of the highest-loading items appears to reflect stereotyped feminine characteristics and behaviors. Student behaviors with the highest positive loadings include trying on clothes in a store without buying anything, taking dietary formulas, crying, and attending fashion shows and ballet performances. The nonfeminine behaviors include discussing sports, playing chess, gambling, and playing intramural sports.

Students in the more feminine institutions are more likely than are students in other kinds of institutions to major in artistic or social fields of study and to prefer working with people; students at institutions with less feminine environments are more likely to major in scientific fields and to plan careers in these fields. There was virtually no overlap between men's colleges and women's colleges on the Femininity factor, as Figure 4 shows. Nevertheless, that some variability occurs within both the men's colleges and the women's colleges does suggest that the Femininity score, although closely related to the sex of the student body, is not synonymous with it.

Femininity has much in common with the negative (cooperative) end of the Competitiveness versus Cooperativeness factor identified in the analysis of interpersonal behavior. Although Femininity and Cooperativeness both correlate approximately .80 with the percentage of women in the student body, they correlate only about .56 with each other. The major differentiating features are that Femininity is characterized more by a concern with one's appearance, an emphasis on organized dating, and a rela-

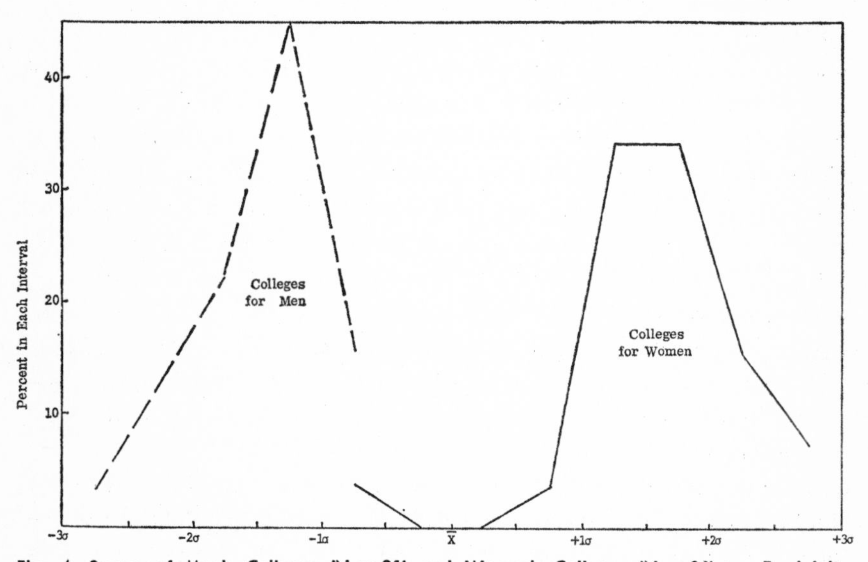

Fig. 4. Scores of Men's Colleges (N = 31) and Women's Colleges (N = 26) on Femininity.

tive lack of interest in science, whereas Cooperativeness is characterized more by interest and participation in group activities (group singing, student stage plays, student elections, etc.). Cooperativeness is also more characteristic of liberal arts colleges than is Femininity.

The second pattern of noninterpersonal student behavior, Drinking versus Religiousness, accounted for a larger proportion of the Common variance among the 77 behavioral items than did any of the other nine factors. The variables correlating most highly with Drinking versus Religiousness are given in Table 11. The many high positive and high negative correlations indicate once again that a bipolar factor is present. The positive end is clearly related to the frequency of student drinking. The negative end, on the other hand, involves, almost exclusively, formal religious behavior: attending church and Sunday school, praying, saying grace before meals, and reading the Bible. That these two types of student behavior, drinking and religiousness, are negatively related is perhaps to be expected. It is surprising, however, that these two clusters form opposite poles of the same factor. This finding indicates that information concerning the frequency of the two types of behavior on a given campus is, for the most part, interchangeable. That is, if one knows the extent of student drinking that occurs on the campus, he can use this information as a fairly accurate inverse measure of the amount of religious behavior among the students; conversely, if he knows the frequency of formal religious behavior, he can make a reasonable estimate of the amount of drinking that goes on.

Some of the other items with high positive loadings on this factor suggest that the students in colleges where the rate of drinking is relatively high are more argumentative, independent, and competitive in their behavior than are typical students. Also, they tend to be considerably brighter academically, to be more highly motivated toward graduate training, and to come from higher socioeconomic backgrounds. In contrast, more of the students in highly religious environments rate themselves as religious and select fields of study and vocations in a Social field (education and social science). Also they seem to be more friendly than do students in "drinking" environments. This pattern of student personal characteristics is further reflected in the college characteristics: the bibulous colleges tend to be more selective, and the pious institutions tend to score higher on the Social orientation.

As would be expected, the private nonsectarian institutions tend to obtain high scores on Drinking versus Religiousness: nearly eight of ten score above average on the factor, as compared to fewer than two in ten of the Protestant institutions. All four of the institutions that are affiliated with

Table 11

Drinking vs. Religiousness

Variable	r with Factor Score
A. Correlated Peer Stimuli	
Drank beer	.94*
Drank whiskey or other hard liquor	.91
Drank wine	.89*
Became intoxicated	.86
Drank in a bar	.75
Argued with other students	.71
Argued with a teacher in class	.69
Bought a paperback book (not for class)	.64
Listened to folk music	.62
Picked up a date in a bar, restaurant, or similar place	.59
Went to a foreign movie	.59
Independence factor	.58
Gambled with cards or dice	.57
Argued openly with other students in class	.57
Argued openly with the instructor	.53
Took No-Doz or other stay-awake pills	.53
Bet on a game or other event	.52
Competitiveness vs. Cooperativeness factor	.52
Overslept and missed a class or appointment	.51
Attended Sunday school	−.72
Prayed (not including grace before meals)	−.68*
Read the Bible	−.67
Said grace before meals	−.64
Time spent on personal care (bathing, fixing hair, shaving, putting on make-up, etc.)	−.62
Said "hello" to students you didn't know	−.61
Attended church	−.61
Attended a fashion show	−.54
B. Correlated Classroom Stimuli	
Students permitted to smoke in class	.61
Instructor engaged in research	.53
Examinations were usually of the "objective" rather than "essay" type	−.54
Involvement in the Class factor	−.53
Instructor was a woman	−.51
C. Correlated Student Personal Characteristics	
Lazy (self-rating)	.63
Intellectualism	.60
Mathematics aptitude (NMSQT)	.60
Social science reading aptitude (NMSQT)	.59
Academic ability (NMSQT composite)	.57
Natural sciences reading aptitude (NMSQT)	.57
Word usage aptitude (NMSQT)	.55

* Used in computing the factor score.

Table 11 (Continued)

Variable	r with Factor Score
Planning to get graduate degree	.53
Argumentative (self-rating)	.52
Vocational choice in Scientific class	.52
Status	.51
Took NMSQT in high school	.51
Planning to get Ph.D. degree	.51
Father's occupation in Scientific class	.50
Masculinity	.50
Religious (self-rating)	−.75
Major in Social field	−.59
Vocational choice in Social class	−.57
D. Correlated Aspects of the College Image	
Liberal	.63
Intellectual atmosphere is definitely on the theoretical, rather than the practical side	.61
There is a large group of "avant-garde" students on campus	.58
A great deal of independence is granted the student	.55
Victorian	−.69
Campus paper and magazine are carefully censored by the administration	−.63
High morale	−.60
Warm	−.54
Practical-minded	−.52
Number of fellow students who are close friends	−.50
E. Correlated Characteristics of the College	
Selectivity	.56
Social orientation (EAT)	−.60

the Seventh-Day Adventist Church score below the sixth percentile. Catholic institutions, despite their strong religious affiliations, obtain average scores.

The students' impressions that correlate highly with Drinking versus Religiousness are generally consistent with the other correlates. Students in the colleges characterized by a high degree of drinking and a low degree of religious behavior feel that they are granted a good deal of independence and perceive the institution as liberal. They also feel that theoretical concerns are emphasized over practical concerns and that avant-garde students are well represented on the campus. Students in religious environments, on the other hand, are more likely to see their college as Victorian, practical-minded, and warm, and as having high morale. They also report that the campus paper and humor magazine are censored by the administration.

The data shown in Table 11 suggest that the highly religious college environment is an interesting combination of formal religious behavior, strict disciplinary control by the administration, and friendliness among the students. In contrast, the college environment characterized by a high rate of drinking combines a permissive administrative policy with a student body that is highly motivated, competitive, independent, and academically able.

What is the explanation for this inverse relationship between drinking and religious behavior in the college environment? There is strong reason to infer from the data in Table 11 that the kinds of students initially recruited by the college are a major factor. However, the close relationship between this particular pattern of environmental stimuli and the administration's disciplinary practices (see Chapter IV) raises the possibility that the degree of administrative permissiveness may also contribute to shaping these patterns of student behavior.

Musical and Artistic Activity, the third pattern of noninterpersonal student behavior, is shown in Table 12. This factor seems to reflect the degree of the students' involvement in musical activities (both as performers and as listeners) and the rate of their attendance at cultural events such as public lectures, stage plays, and art exhibits. Musical and Artistic Activity appears to be relatively frequent at institutions where the students live predominantly in dormitories. Institutions with relatively low rates of musical and artistic activity tend to manifest a high degree of competitiveness and to have relatively severe grading practices; this latter relationship may indicate that professors in courses such as music and art are more permissive in their grading practices than other professors are or that the students who major in such fields have been more thoroughly screened (on the basis of their abilities, motivation, and preparation) than have students who major in other fields.

The data in Table 12 also suggest that the college environment where there is a good deal of musical and artistic activity tends to be more friendly and intimate than the environment where such activity is limited. Correlations with the data provided by NORC are generally consistent with the other correlations. The NORC data indicate that students in the musical-artistic environment more often come from higher socioeconomic levels than do typical students. (Although items involving socioeconomic level in our sample also had relatively high correlations with this factor, they are not shown in Table 12 because the coefficients did not reach .50.) In any

Table 12

Musical and Artistic Activity

Variable	r with Factor Score
A. Correlated Peer Stimuli	
Attended a public recital	.89*
Played a musical instrument	.78*
Attended an orchestral concert	.73
Time spent participating in musical, dramatic, or artistic activities	.66
Listened to classical music	.63
Participated in informal group singing	.62
Attended a public lecture	.58
Percent of friends living in a dormitory	.57
Attended a student stage play	.57
Discussed religion with other students	.55
Listened to a friend discuss a personal problem	.54
Attended an art exhibit	.52
Cried	.50
Lived in a dormitory during freshman year	.50
(Listened to folk music)	(.45*)
Competitiveness vs. Cooperativeness factor	−.62
Severity of Grading factor	−.58
Picked up a hitchhiker	−.55
Made bets on a game or other event	−.54
Gambled with cards or dice	−.52
Pushed a stalled car (other than your own)	−.50
Flunked a course	−.50
B. Correlated Student Personal Characteristics	
Musical and dramatic activities (NORC)	.72
Father's educational level (NORC)	.62
Mother's educational level (NORC)	.62
Father a professional (NORC)	.62
Positive evaluation of faculty (NORC)	.62
Religious preference none (NORC)	.61
Father's occupation in Social class	.59
College should provide basic education and appreciation of ideas (NORC)	.59
High calibre of students (NORC)	.54
Major in Artistic field	.52
Exhibited works of art in high school	.52
Wanted to take a course but couldn't because of other requirements	.52
Parental income (NORC)	.52
Parent's religion none (NORC)	.52
Value being helpful (NORC)	.51
College should provide career training (NORC)	−.64
Male	−.51
Plan to remain at home after college (NORC)	−.51

* Used in computing the factor score.

Table 13

Leisure Time

Variable	r with Factor Score
A. Correlated Peer Stimuli	
Time spent attending movies and plays	.93*
Went to the movies	.85*
Time spent playing games (cards, chess, etc.)	.63*
B. Correlated Student Personal Characteristics	
Value having a good time (NORC)	.60
Value getting along with people (NORC)	.59

* Used in computing the factor score.

event, it appears as though students in the highly musical and artistic environment come from relatively well educated and affluent families.

Nearly eight of every ten universities and all six of the technological institutions obtained below-average scores on Musical and Artistic Activity.

Correlates of Leisure Time, the fourth pattern of student noninterpersonal behavior, are shown in Table 13. Only three items from the ICA—the ones used in computing the factor score—correlated as high as .50 with the factor. Two of them were from the student's time diary—time spent attending movies and plays and time spent playing games—and one was from the behavior inventory and concerned the frequency of attendance at movies. The two correlated NORC items seem to justify labeling this pattern of behavior "Leisure Time." Additional confirmation is provided by correlations with several other ICA items. For example, Leisure Time is significantly and positively related to the amount of time spent watching athletic events (.34), reading for pleasure (.31), and watching TV (.25). It is negatively related to time spent studying (−.32), and positively re-

Table 14

Career Indecision

Variable	r with Factor Score
A. Correlated Peer Stimuli	
Changed your major field	.87*
Changed your long-term career plans	.77*
Been interviewed as a client in the college counseling center	.59*

* Used in computing the factor score.

lated to failing a course (.33). Finally, students tend to rate the environment characterized by a large amount of Leisure Time as carefree (.47).

Career Indecision, the fifth factor derived from the analysis of items concerning student noninterpersonal behavior, is shown in Table 14. Students in college environments characterized by a high rate of career indecision tend to change their major fields and their long-term career plans relatively often. Also, they are relatively likely to be clients of the counseling center during their freshman year. The presence of this last item raises questions as to the possibility of a causal relationship with the first two items. In future research, it would be interesting to determine whether the proportion of students who receive counseling is merely a consequence of the rate of career indecision or whether counseling in fact exacerbates or contributes to that indecision.

The great variability among institutions in the three Career Indecision items is striking. The range among institutions in the percentages of students who change major fields during their freshman year is from four to 43, with a median of 26. The percentage of students who change their long-range career plans is similarly varied: from 7 percent to 39 percent, with a median of 26. The most outstanding variation, however, occurs in the percentage of students who are interviewed as clients in the college counseling center during their freshman year. These percentages range from zero to 56, with a median of 10. That more than half of the freshmen at one institution seek the services of the counseling center is indeed remarkable.

The sixth pattern of student noninterpersonal behavior, Regularity of Sleeping Habits, is shown in Table 15. This factor is one of the most consistent and homogeneous of all those identified, in that virtually all of the highly correlated behaviors have to do with some aspect of sleep. Compared with typical students, students in the college characterized by regular sleeping habits spend more time sleeping, are more likely to attend church, and, most interestingly, are more likely to live at home. They are also more likely to have college friends who live at home, to rate themselves as religious, and to be of the Roman Catholic faith. Only future longitudinal studies can determine whether this last finding is a consequence of a greater proportion of commuter students attending Catholic institutions or of characteristic administrative policies of Catholic institutions (such as more stringent dormitory policies about "lights out").

Students in the colleges characterized by irregular sleeping habits are more likely than are other students to stay up all night, to oversleep and miss a class, to take a nap or rest during the day, and to use stay-awake

Table 15

Regularity of Sleeping Habits

Variable	r with Factor Score
A. Correlated Peer Stimuli	
Time spent sleeping	.75*
Attended church	.51
Stayed up all night	−.86*
Overslept and missed a class or appointment	−.69
Took a nap or rest during the day	−.63
Took No-Doz or other stay-awake pills	−.63*
Member of fraternity or sorority (NORC)	−.62
Discussed sex with other students	−.51
B. Correlated Student Personal Characteristics	
Very religious (self-rating) (NORC)	.64
Religion Roman Catholic (NORC)	.64
Parent's religion Roman Catholic (NORC)	.63
Value getting along with people (NORC)	.51
Parents' income (NORC)	−.62
Father's educational level (NORC)	−.62
Mother's educational level (NORC)	−.61
Parents' religion Protestant (NORC)	−.52
Father a professional (NORC)	−.51
Father's educational level	−.50
C. Correlated Aspects of the College Image	
Not enough sleep	−.53
D. Correlated Physical Stimuli	
Lived at home (NORC)	.55
Friends lived at home during freshman year	.53
Lived at home during freshman year	.51
Distance of college from hometown	−.52

* Used in computing the factor score.

pills. As might be expected, their college tends to be located farther from home than the colleges of the students who have regular sleeping habits, and the students are more apt to complain that they have not had enough sleep during their freshman year. They are also more likely to come from highly educated and well-to-do families and to be of the Protestant faith.

The relationships shown between this factor and the NORC items are highly consistent with the ICA correlates already discussed. Two correlates, living at home and educational level of parents, are especially closely related to regularity of sleeping habits in both sets of data.

Of the various types of institutions, those controlled by the Roman Cath-

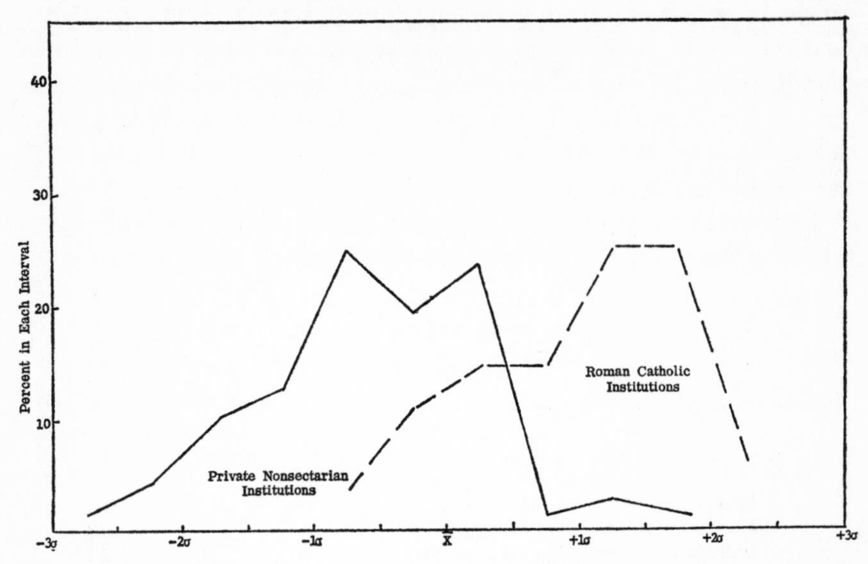

Fig. 5. Scores of Private Nonsectarian Institutions (N = 73) and Roman Catholic Institutions (N = 28) on Regularity of Sleeping Habits.

olic church obtained by far the highest scores on Regularity of Sleeping Habits. (This finding is consistent with the NORC correlates discussed earlier.) The Catholic institutions showed only a slight degree of overlap with private nonsectarian institutions, as Figure 5 shows.

It is of some interest to note that Regularity of Sleeping Habits had a modest positive relationship (.38) to the rated strictness of the head resident or housemother and a negative relationship (−.38) to the resident or housemother's being rated permissive.

Although this particular pattern of student behavior can be adequately explained only after more detailed longitudinal studies, one can formulate a provocative hypothetical picture of how it develops. The relatively well-educated and affluent family is more likely than is the typical family to send its children away from home for their freshman year in college. (This tendency may be simply a matter of finances, but it may also reflect a prevailing attitude among more educated families about the type of college experience that is most valuable.) The freshman year is probably the resident student's first experience with being away from home for an extended period. Either because he is, for the first time, free of direct parental supervision or because he is stimulated by other students in the living quarters, the resident student's normal sleeping habits become disrupted. He tends to stay up late at night and to sleep late in the morning, and so his chances of getting up in time to attend church are reduced. (It should be remembered, however, that his lower rate of church attendance may be a consequence of the differences in religious background and religious interests revealed in some of the other items.) In any case, the pattern of items correlating with this factor suggests strongly that the student's sleeping habits may be altered drastically if he lives away from home while attending college.

The seventh factor identified in the analysis of student noninterpersonal behavior, Use of the Library, is shown in Table 16. It was only moderately

Table 16

Use of the Library

Variable	r with Factor Score
A. Correlated Peer Stimuli	
Checked out a book or journal from the college library	.85*
Studied in the library	.85*
(Time spent reading for pleasure)	(.40*)
B. Correlated Student Personal Characteristics	
Value being helpful (NORC)	.52
College should provide basic education and appreciation of ideas (NORC)	.51
College should provide career training (NORC)	−.51

* Used in computing the factor score.

correlated with several ICA items that are suggestive of studiousness and intellectual interests: time spent reading for pleasure (.40), attending public lectures (.37), participating in class discussion (.35), and typing written assignments (.35). However, the frequency of the use of the library is unrelated to both the academic ability and the academic competitiveness of the students and has only a slight negative relationship (−.20) to the distance of the library from the students' living quarters. Apparently, this factor represents a fairly independent pattern of student behavior at most colleges and universities.

The relevance of the three NORC items that correlate with Use of the Library is not immediately apparent, except for the one concerning the college's emphasis on basic education and appreciation of ideas. (However, it should be recognized that because of the relatively small overlapping sample [33 institutions] and large number of NORC items, some of the correlations above .50 between the factor and the NORC items may be attributable to chance.) One possible explanation for the presence of the other two NORC items is that technical institutions tend to obtain very low scores on Use of the Library (r=.34). Thus, it is likely that students majoring in engineering place a relatively high value on training for a career and a relatively low value on being helpful. Some of the correlates listed above (e.g., typing written assignments) may also be accounted for by the low scores of the technical institutions on Use of the Library.

The eighth factor identified in the analysis of noninterpersonal student behavior, Conflict with Regulations, is shown in Table 17. This factor appears to reflect the frequency with which students are disciplined for committing infractions of college rules and regulations. One peculiarity of the factor score is that it combines, with positive weights, two items—"Attended church" and "Drank in a bar or club"—that are *negatively* correlated (−.32) with each other. But to the extent that a high rate of church attendance among students is associated with greater severity of the rules and regulations, this apparently contradictory combination is compatible with the meaning of the factor. In other words, at institutions that have stringent rules, coupled with a relatively large amount of drinking (potential infraction of those rules), there is likely to be a fairly high rate of lost privileges among those students found drinking. The tendency for students at Roman Catholic institutions to break regulations relatively frequently may indicate that such institutions impose rather severe penalties for such

Table 17

Conflict with Regulations

Variable	r with Factor Score
A. Correlated Peer Stimuli	
Lost privileges for infraction of college rules	.80*
Attended church	.57*
Prayed (not including grace before meals)	.51
(Drank in a bar or club)	(.35*)
B. Correlated Student Personal Characteristics	
Religion Roman Catholic (NORC)	.53
Parents have influenced plans (NORC)	.52
Parents' religion Roman Catholic (NORC)	.50
C. Correlated Characteristics of the College	
Roman Catholic	.54

* Used in computing the factor score.

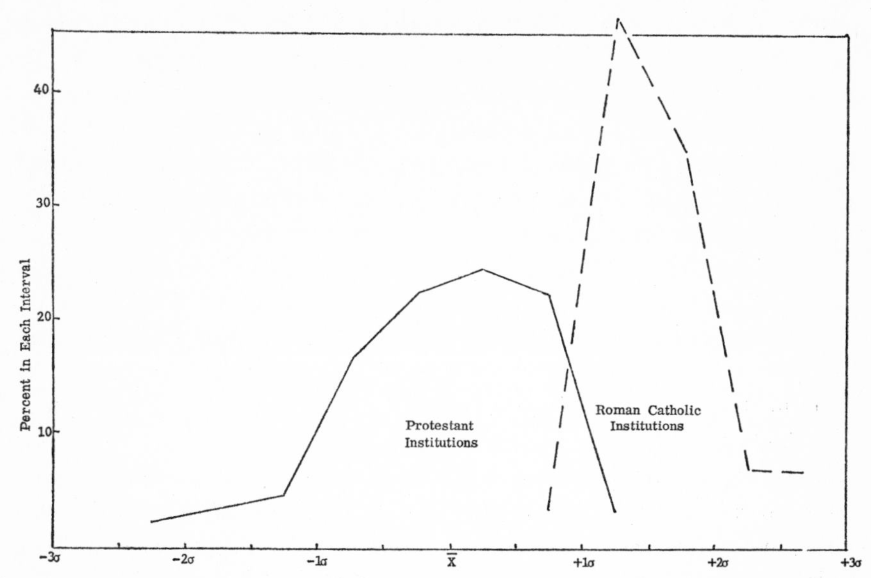

Fig. 6. Scores of Protestant Institutions* (N = 89) and Roman Catholic Institutions (N = 28) on Conflict with Regulations.

* Includes 4 Seventh Day Adventist Colleges.

infractions, although other evidence (see Chapter 4) indicates that such is not the case. Another possible interpretation is that the Catholic institutions enforce rules more diligently than do most institutions. In any case, these findings suggest that the incompatibility between regulations and student behavior tends to be greater at Catholic colleges and universities than at other types of institutions.

It was somewhat surprising to find that while the Catholic institutions show a very high degree of conflict with regulations, institutions affiliated with Protestant denominations show only an average degree of such conflict (see Figure 6). Protestant institutions, furthermore, tend to have even more restrictive policies concerning student conduct than the Catholic institutions (see Chapter 4). In short, these facts indicate that students attending Protestant colleges are more inclined to accept (or at least to conform to) the regulations governing student conduct than are students attending Catholic colleges.

The ninth factor identified in the analysis of the noninterpersonal items, Student Employment, is shown in Table 18. This pattern of behavior is defined primarily in terms of the percentage of students who are employed and the average amount of time that the students spend working for pay. Why the percentage of freshmen who report cheating on examinations ap-

Table 18

Student Employment

Variable	r with Factor Score
A. Correlated Peer Stimuli	
Regularly employed during the school year	.91*
Amount of time spent working for pay	.86
Cheated on examinations	.58*
(Drank in a bar or club)	(.48*)
(Median time spent studying)	(−.45)

* Used in computing the factor score.

pears in this factor is difficult to explain. It may be that the working student finds it easier than does the nonworking student either to justify cheating on examinations or to admit to cheating. Another possible interpretation is that the working student, because he has less time available for study, more often finds it necessary to cheat in order to pass examinations. This second interpretation is partially supported by the moderate negative correlation (−.45) between this factor and the amount of time spent by the students in studying.

The final factor identified in the analysis of student noninterpersonal behavior, Use of Automobiles, is shown in Table 19. The pattern of highly correlated items suggests that an institution's score on this factor will be determined primarily by the proportion of students who have access to a car during their freshman year. The presence of the item "Listened to New Orleans (Dixieland) jazz" is puzzling. A possible clue to this apparent

Table 19

Use of Automobiles

Variable	r with Factor Score
A. Correlated Peer Stimuli	
Drove a car	.76*
Listened to New Orleans (Dixieland) jazz	.66*
Drove a car over 80 mph	.61
Rode in a sports car	.57
Pushed a stalled car (other than your own)	.50
B. Correlated Student Personal Characteristics	
Negro (NORC)	−.50
(Cheated on Examinations)	(−.45*)

* Used in computing the factor score.

mystery is provided by two other pieces of evidence: institutions located in the Southeastern region of the country tend to obtain high scores on the factor (70 percent of the institutions located in this region have above-average scores), but the seven predominantly Negro institutions in the sample (all located in the South) obtain very *low* scores (none scored above the 15th percentile). The Negro institutions' very low scores on Use of Automobiles are reflected in the correlation of −.50 between the factor score and percentage of Negroes as reported by NORC and also in the correlation of −.36 with the dichotomous institutional characteristic "predominantly Negro." In fact, the seven predominantly Negro institutions obtained lower scores than all but one of the 43 non-Negro Southern institutions in the sample. In view of this finding, one should expect that use of automobiles will be related to any other variable that differentiates between these two groups of institutions.

Although these two groups of institutions differ substantially in their use of automobiles, an inspection of the scores on the individual ICA items revealed that they differ even more in their inclination to listen to Dixieland music. It is easy to understand why Dixieland jazz is generally popular among students attending Southern institutions, but it is not clear why this type of music—which was created almost entirely by the Southern Negro—would be so unpopular with students attending the predominantly Negro colleges. One possible answer is provided by the fact that the predominantly Negro colleges were among the *highest* of all 246 institutions in the frequency with which their students listened to progressive jazz. (The non-Negro Southern institutions obtained average scores on this item.) These results suggest that the Southern Negro college student may reject Dixieland, in contrast to modern jazz, because it symbolizes his historically subordinate role in the South. Modern jazz, on the other hand, may be very popular among these students because it is symbolic of the Negro's intellectual advancement and more recent social emancipation.

The correlations among the 10 noninterpersonal factor scores are shown in Table 20. Although several of the 45 coefficients are statistically significant, only seven are as large as ±.20, and none exceeds ±.35. The three largest coefficients indicate that the following student behavioral patterns tend to occur together: femininity and musical and artistic activity; religiousness and regular sleeping habits; and using automobiles and little musical or artistic activity. For the most part, however, these 10 noninterpersonal factors can be regarded as relatively independent patterns of student behavior.

Table 20

Intercorrelations of Ten Patterns of Noninterpersonal Student Behavior
(*N*=246 Institutions)

Noninterpersonal Factor	2	3	4	5	6	7	8	9	10
1. Femininity	−.21	.31	.05	.09	.13	.19	.18	−.09	−.02
2. Drinking vs. Religiousness		−.13	.05	.13	−.34	−.03	−.05	.00	.01
3. Musical & Artistic Activity			−.16	.12	−.22	.17	−.16	−.12	−.35
4. Leisure Time				−.10	−.04	.00	.09	−.14	.19
5. Career Indecision					−.04	.07	.01	.12	.03
6. Regularity of Sleeping Habits						.08	.18	.17	.07
7. Use of the Library							.14	.07	−.21
8. Conflict with Regulations								.23	−.07
9. Student Employment									.16
10. Use of Automobiles									

Table 21 shows the correlations between the ten noninterpersonal and the five interpersonal factors from the peer environment. The last column in Table 21 shows the multiple correlations of the five interpersonal factors with each of the ten noninterpersonal factors; the bottom row of Table 21 shows the multiple correlations of the ten noninterpersonal factors with

Table 21

Correlations Between Patterns of Interpersonal and Noninterpersonal Student Behavior
(*N*=246 Institutions)

Noninterpersonal Factors	Interpersonal Factors					Multiple R from Interpersonal Factors
	Competitiveness vs. Cooperativeness	Organized Dating	Independence	Cohesiveness	Informal Dating	
Femininity	−.56	.38	−.42	−.08	.38	.78
Drinking vs. Religiousness	.52	.33	.58	−.48	−.18	.84
Musical & Artistic Activity	−.62	.07	.11	−.15	.29	.70
Leisure Time	.23	.24	.13	.34	.28	.59
Career Indecision	−.09	.09	.04	−.25	.14	.27
Regularity of Sleeping Habits	−.03	−.30	−.42	.14	−.15	.55
Use of the Library	−.27	.09	.05	.03	.07	.38
Conflict with Regulations	−.08	.12	−.09	.22	−.12	.45
Student Employment	.17	−.39	−.12	−.01	.08	.43
Use of Automobiles	.31	.05	−.25	.17	.06	.52
Multiple R from Interpersonal Factors	.88	.72	.76	.61	.64	—

each of the five interpersonal factors. While these multiple correlations reveal a significant amount of overlap between the two sets of student behavioral factors, the degree is less than 50 percent[3] for ten of the 15 factors. The greatest overlap seems to occur between the noninterpersonal factors and the bipolar interpersonal factor Competitiveness versus Cooperativeness. Highly competitive environments are characterized by relatively high rates of drinking, leisure time, and use of automobiles. Highly cooperative environments, on the other hand, reveal relatively high rates of femininity, religiousness, musical and artistic activity, and use of the library. The multiple regression weights indicate that a relatively good estimate of the competitiveness (or cooperativeness) of a college's peer environment can be derived from a knowledge of the amount of musical and artistic activity, femininity, and drinking (as opposed to religiousness) manifested by the students at the college.

A relatively high degree of overlap was also found between the five interpersonal factors and the noninterpersonal factor Drinking versus Religiousness. College environments characterized by a high rate of drinking and a low rate of religious behavior tend to have a high degree of independence, competitiveness, organized dating, and incohesiveness. The multiple regression solution indicates that these four interpersonal factors receive approximately equal weights in computing an estimate of Drinking versus Religiousness.

These findings lend some support to the concern expressed earlier that dividing stimuli from the peer environment into interpersonal and noninterpersonal behaviors is rather arbitrary. None of the factors identified in either category was independent of patterns identified in the other, and several of the factors showed a moderate to substantial degree of overlap across the two categories. It is likely that many of the noninterpersonal behavioral stimuli—particularly those having to do with drinking, religiousness, musical activity, leisure time, and use of automobiles—typically involve the participation of other students. While the high multiple correlations associated with one or two of the 15 factors indicate that eliminating these factors would result in only a small loss of information, it is important to point out that every one of the 15 contains a significant amount of information not present in the other factors.[4]

[3] Using the conventional R^2 (multiple R square) to estimate the proportion of common variance. These and subsequent R's (Tables 32, 39, 45, and 57) were computed by means of step-wise regression procedures.

[4] In no case did the R^2 for any factor approach the reliability of the factor (see Appendix F).

STUDENT'S MODE OF DRESS

Although the analyses of items dealing with student noninterpersonal behavior indicated that items describing students' typical mode of dress should not be included in that group of factors, the results concerning this subject proved interesting enough to justify their being reported separately. One of the major problems here is that the types of clothes worn by male and female students are, with a few exceptions, qualitatively different. Consequently, our primary objective in analyzing the students' mode of dress was to determine whether comparable patterns of dress for men and women exist on college campuses. If they do, it would then be possible to develop measures of the students' mode of dress that could be used for coeducational and noncoeducational institutions alike.

In the course of preliminary discussions with staff and students from several local campuses, it was suggested that the typical campus attire for attending classes often differs systematically from the attire typically worn to dinner. For this reason, it was decided to perform separate analyses of the kinds of clothes students wear in these two situations.

Items for describing different modes of dress were arranged on a continuum from the most formal to the most informal. The separate continua for men and women are shown below, in order of descending formality:

Men's Dress	Women's Dress
Suit	Suit or dress
Sport jacket & tie	Skirt w/sweater or blouse
Sport jacket (no tie)	Slacks
Sport shirt and slacks	Blue jeans, levis, dungarees
Sweat shirt or T-shirt and slacks	Bermudas
Blue jeans, levis, dungarees	Shorts

Students were asked to report whether they wore each of these styles of dress "usually," "occasionally" or "seldom or never." The several student research assistants who helped to develop these two continua were in agreement about the ordering of the items on the male continuum, but could not agree on the relative degree of informality of four of the items on the female continuum: slacks, blue jeans (levis, dungarees), bermudas, and shorts. Consequently, all four of these items were assigned the same score ("1") in computing a measure of formality of dress for women. The item, "skirt with sweater or blouse," was assigned a score of "2," and "suit or dress" was assigned a score of "3" (the most formal). The measure of formality for male students ranged from a low score of "1" (blue jeans) to a high score of "6" (suit). A measure of variability in dress was obtained by computing the standard deviation of the scores on the formality continuum. Note that "variability" by this definition refers to the variation *among* the students in their typical mode of dress (rather than the day-to-day variations of individual students) and that low variability indicates a high degree of conformity in the students' typical mode of dress.

In an attempt to identify common patterns of dress for men and women, the analysis of students' mode of dress was confined to the 175 coeducational institutions. A total of 32 measures of mode of dress were computed for each institution. These included (separately by sex and separately for clothes worn to class and clothes worn to dinner): (1) a measure of formality, (2) a measure of variability, and (3) the percentages of students who reported wearing each of the six specific items of dress "usually."

The results of the factor analysis were unfruitful: no comparable modes of dress for the two sexes emerged. Four of the six factors identified paralleled the four separate measures of formality: class and dinner, separately for men and women. A fifth factor was concerned with the variability in dress worn to dinner by female students. The sixth factor was concerned with the tendency for male students to wear blue jeans (to class and dinner). (The correlation and factor matrices from this analysis are shown in Appendix G.)

The factor analysis of items concerning the students' mode of dress was next repeated with each item scored as the percentage of students who wore each type of dress "usually" *or* "occasionally." Essentially the same results were obtained.

In order to explore the relationships between styles of dress for men and for women more directly, the individual correlations between each mode of dress for men and each mode of dress for women were inspected. Table 22 shows the between-sex correlations that equaled or exceeded ±.40. These coefficients suggest that the sexes are more consistent in the types of clothes they wear to dinner than in the types of clothes they wear to class. The tendency for girls to wear slacks to dinner, for example, is moderately related to the tendency for boys to wear either T-shirts and slacks or blue jeans to dinner. Similarly, girls at colleges where the boys frequently eat dinner in T-shirts and slacks are more likely to come to dinner dressed in bermudas or blue jeans than are girls at other types of colleges.

Table 23 shows the correlations among the various measures of formality and variability. As might be expected from the previous table, the greatest similarity between male and female dress occurs in the degree of for-

Table 22

Similarity in Types of Clothes Worn to Class and to Dinner by Male and Female Undergraduates
(N=175 Coeducational Institutions)

Type of Clothes (place worn)		r
Men	Women	
T-shirt & slacks (dinner)	Slacks (dinner)	.63
Blue jeans (dinner)	Blue jeans (dinner)	.53
T-shirt & slacks (class)	Bermudas (class)	.51
Blue jeans (dinner)	Slacks (dinner)	.50
T-shirt & slacks (dinner)	Bermudas (dinner)	.50
T-shirt & slacks (dinner)	Blue jeans (dinner)	.49
T-shirt & slacks (class)	Slacks (class)	.49
Suit (dinner)	Suit or dress (dinner)	.47
Blue jeans (class)	Blue jeans (dinner)	.46
Sport jacket & tie (dinner)	Slacks (dinner)	−.44

Table 23

Correlations Between Formality and Variability in the Mode of Dress of Male and Female Undergraduates
(N=175 Coeducational Institutions)

Pattern of Dress, Place, Sex	2	3	4	5	6	7	8
Degree of Formality							
1. At class, men	.29	.18	.24	.02	−.06	−.24	−.09
2. At dinner, men		−.08	.48	−.23	.29	−.09	−.27
3. At class, women			.29	−.07	−.01	−.68	−.12
4. At dinner, women				−.23	.03	−.27	−.70
Degree of Variability							
5. At class, men					−.34	.22	.24
6. At dinner, men						.02	.14
7. At class, women							.35
8. At dinner, women							

mality of clothes usually worn to dinner (r=.48). The formality of clothes worn to class and the two measures of variability reveal very little similarity between the sexes. Two relatively high negative correlations (−.68 and −.70) in Table 23 indicate that formality of dress is related to conformity in dress for coeds, but not for male students (the comparable correlations were .02 and .29).[5]

[5] Since the formality of dress was scored on a six-point scale for males and on only a three-point scale for females, these differential relationships between the means and the standard deviations may be to an extent artifactual.

In brief, these results suggest that common patterns of dress for male and female students do not generally exist in coeducational institutions. While there was some correlation found between the two sexes in the degree of formality of their dinner dress, the magnitude of the relationship is not large enough for us to say that equivalent measures for the two sexes can be used to assess the environments of noncoeducational as well as coeducational institutions.

It is difficult to explain why no comparable patterns exist. Apparently, the factors that determine the predominant styles of dress—climate, administrative policies, and so forth—are not the same for the two sexes. Perhaps the types of clothes preferred by coeds are determined by national and international fads and by other factors extraneous to the college environment.

SUMMARY

In this chapter, we have examined the college environment with respect to the stimuli provided by its students. An analysis of 246 institutional environments in terms of 161 different student behaviors resulted in the identification of 15 relatively independent patterns of student behavior: Competitiveness versus Cooperativeness, Organized Dating, Independence, Cohesiveness, Informal Dating, Femininity, Drinking versus Religiousness, Musical and Artistic Activity, Leisure Time, Career Indecision, Regularity of Sleeping Habits, Use of the Library, Conflict with Regulations, Student Employment, and Use of Automobiles.

In addition to the great variety of stimuli suggested by the above patterns, the analyses revealed a remarkable diversity among the 246 institutions in the frequencies of occurrence of many of the stimuli. Thus, the proportion of students who engage in a particular activity (e.g., dating, going to church, drinking beer, voting in a student election) often varies from virtually no students in some institutions to nearly all students in others. This considerable diversity suggests that the peer environment has great potential for influencing the experience and behavior of the individual student. Several hypotheses concerning the specific nature of these influences were suggested by the data.

3

The Classroom Environment

ALTHOUGH THE UNDERGRADUATE student generally spends less time attending class than he does engaging in other campus activities, the stimuli provided by the classroom experience are probably among the most significant sources of influence during the undergraduate years. The nature of the classroom environment is of special importance to the commuter student, whose exposure to the college is often confined mainly to the time he spends in class.

In developing measures of environmental stimuli in the classroom, we attempted first to sample a reasonably representative cross-section of classes taken by the freshmen at each institution. While it might have been possible to obtain from the student global judgments about all of his freshman-year instructors or all of his introductory classes, we chose instead to obtain explicit observations from each student about a particular class. Consequently, on one page of the questionnaire (see Appendix A), the student was asked to "Name below the course you took this past year which was most closely related to your primary field of interest." He was next asked to record the name of the course, the department, and the time of the day that the class met and to estimate the number of students in the class (lecture portion only) and the age of the instructor. It was our assumption that by having each student rate a specific class in his field, we would obtain a fairly representative sampling of professors and classes and that the different fields of study would be represented roughly in proportion to the number of student majors and faculty members in these fields.

The student was next asked to indicate whether or not each of 32 different statements accurately described the class. In designing these items, we attempted to measure classroom stimuli of three different types:

1. The behavior of the instructor ("The instructor called students by their first names," "The instructor spoke in a monotone," etc.)
2. The behavior of the student ("I took notes regularly in class," "I sometimes argued openly with the instructor," etc.)
3. The *modus operandi* or over-all organization and structure of the

were "The instructor wore a coat and tie to class" and "The instructor was a woman." (The correlation between these two items was −.80.) Accordingly, the analysis was repeated with the "coat-and-tie" item omitted, and six interpretable factors emerged: Involvement in the Class, Verbal Aggressiveness, Extraversion of the Instructor, Familiarity with the Instructor, Organization in the Classroom, and Severity of Grading.[1]

The first factor from the classroom environment, Involvement in the Class, accounted for the greatest amount of item variance (30 percent). Table 25 shows the variables that correlated highly with this factor. The behaviors of instructors and students that define the factor suggest a high degree of personal interest and involvement in the activities of the classroom. Instructors in colleges characterized by a high degree of classroom involvement know their students' names, encourage class discussion, and call students by their first names. The additional effort required to prepare and score pop quizzes and to take attendance every day seems to be a further reflection of the instructor's high degree of involvement in his classroom work. Students in colleges characterized by a high degree of classroom involvement are more likely to engage in religious activities, to rate themselves as religious, to select major fields in education and social science, to like teaching and working with people, and to feel that their vocational plans have been influenced by academic advisers and by their parents. This pattern of personal traits suggests that these students are more social, responsible, and dependent than are the students in colleges where the degree of involvement in the class is relatively low.

Colleges in which there is a relatively low degree of involvement in the class tend to have classes that are somewhat larger than average and their instructors are likely to be engaged in research. Students in these colleges frequently oversleep and miss their classes and often do not speak out in class unless called upon. They tend to prefer vocations in the sciences, to be brighter (particularly in mathematics and natural sciences) than average students, and to value being original. In many ways, the students attending institutions that score at opposite extremes on this factor strongly resemble two of Holland's (1966) model personalities: the Social (high involvement) types and the Scientific or Intellectual (low involvement) type.

Institutions scoring high on Involvement in the Classroom tend to be

[1] Diagonal values consisted of the R^2 between each variable and all others. Each of the first eight components accounted for 3 percent or more of the total common variance. However, the best simple structure was obtained by rotating seven factors, one of which turned out to be difficult to interpret.

Table 25

Involvement in the Class

Variable	r with Factor Score
A. Correlated Classroom Stimuli	
Instructor encouraged a lot of class discussion	.86*
Instructor knew me by name	.79*
Instructor called students by their first names	.57
We sometimes had unannounced or "pop" quizzes	.55
Instructor was a woman	.55
Attendance was usually taken every day	.54
Overslept and missed a class or appointment	−.71*
I almost never spoke in class unless called on	−.59
Size of the class	−.54
Students were permitted to smoke in class	−.54
Instructor was engaged in research	−.51
B. Other Correlated Peer Stimuli	
Prayed (not including grace before meals)	.56
Attended church	.55
Read the Bible	.55
Took No-Doz or other stay-awake pills	−.62
Became intoxicated	−.58
Friends lived in fraternity houses	−.54
Drinking vs. Religiousness factor	−.53
Stayed up all night	−.50
C. Correlated Student Personal Characteristics	
Religious (self-rating)	.59
Adviser influenced plans (NORC)	.59
Vocational choice in Social class	.58
Parents influenced plans (NORC)	.56
Prefer teaching	.51
Prefer to work with people	.50
Vocational choice in Scientific class	−.58
Mathematics aptitude (NMSQT)	−.55
Intellectualism	−.54
Natural science reading aptitude (NMSQT)	−.53
Value being original (NORC)	−.50
D. Correlated Aspects of the College Image	
Warm	.54
Campus paper and humor magazine censored by the administration	.53
Good curricular offerings (NORC)	−.61
Good facilities for research (NORC)	−.60
Student publications often openly ridicule the administration	−.59
Not enough contact with faculty	−.52
Not enough personal direction in studies and in course selection	−.51
Administration is not really very concerned about the individual student	−.51
E. Correlated Characteristics of the College	
Social orientation (EAT)	.58
Size of entering class	−.58
University	−.54
Selectivity	−.53
Per student expenditures for educational and general purposes	−.52

* Used in computing the factor score.

seen by the students as warm. They are likely to exercise a relatively high degree of censorship over student publications and to award a relatively large proportion of their baccalaureate degrees in social fields. In contrast, students in colleges characterized by a low level of classroom involvement feel that the administration is not really very concerned about the individual student and that students do not have enough contact with faculty or enough personal direction in their studies and selection of courses. On the other hand, they are more likely than are students in institutions with great classroom involvement to feel that the curricular offerings and facilities for research are high in quality, perhaps because such institutions tend to be larger, wealthier, and more selective.

Teachers colleges and universities tend to score at opposite extremes on Involvement in the Classroom (see Figure 7): 85 percent of the teachers colleges, as compared to only 4 percent of the universities, obtained above-average scores on this factor.

The correlates of classroom involvement, like the correlates of several factors from the peer environment, suggest certain interesting causal hypotheses about the effects of environmental stimuli on student development. One might predict, for example, that students are more likely to become involved in what goes on in the classroom if their instructors know

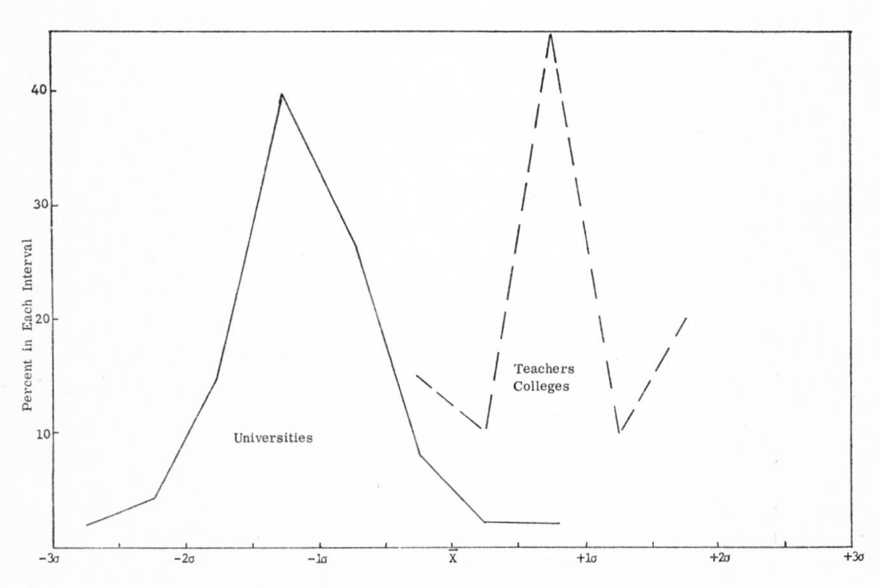

Fig. 7. Scores of Universities (N = 48) and Teachers Colleges (N = 20) on Involvement in the Classroom.

their names, encourage class discussion, give pop quizzes, and take roll. One should keep in mind, however, that in such traits as intelligence, religiousness, and vocational interest, students in colleges that score high on this factor differ markedly from those at colleges that score low. Clearly, the observed relationship in Table 25 could arise from either one of these two types of influences or from both.

The second factor identified in the analysis of stimuli from the classroom environment, Verbal Aggressiveness, is shown in Table 26. The classroom stimuli that correlate highly with this factor are perhaps more homogeneous than are the correlates of any of the other five factors from the classroom environment. Students in colleges characterized by a high degree of verbal aggressiveness in the classroom are likely to argue frequently both with the instructor and with other students, to ask questions frequently, and to make

Table 26

Verbal Aggressiveness

Variable	r with Factor Score
A. Correlated Classroom Stimuli	
I sometimes argued openly with the instructor	.91*
Asked questions in class	.78*
I sometimes argued openly with other students	.76
Argued with a teacher in class	.70
Made wisecracks in class	.61*
Argued with other students	.54
I almost never spoke in class unless I was called on	−.53
Examinations were usually of the "objective" rather than the "essay" type	−.52
B. Other Correlated Peer Stimuli	
Was a varsity athlete (NORC)	.56
Worked on the school paper (NORC)	.54
Independence factor	.54
Bought a paperback book (not for class)	.51
C. Correlated Student Personal Characteristics	
Home is located in the suburbs (NORC)	.63
Planning to pursue graduate training	.52
Married (NORC)	−.72
Value steady progress (NORC)	−.56
D. Correlated Aspects of the College Image	
Intellectual atmosphere is definitely on the theoretical, rather than the practical side	.50

* Used in computing factor score.

wisecracks in class. They tend to speak out without waiting to be called on. Interestingly enough, in colleges where there is a high degree of verbal aggressiveness, the instructors are relatively more inclined to give essay (rather than objective) examinations.

As might be expected, Verbal Aggressiveness is related to the Independence factor from the peer environment. Whereas Verbal Aggressiveness is primarily a reflection of the students' behavior in the classroom, Independence appears to be a more pervasive pattern involving such diverse activities as student demonstrations, athletics, drinking, and similar manifestations of aggressiveness, rebelliousness, and independence.

The third classroom environmental factor, Extraversion of the Instructor, is shown in Table 27. The five items in the table suggest that this factor is concerned exclusively with the extent to which the instructor is judged to be stimulating and enthusiastic. Extraversion of the Instructor is almost identical to a factor identified in an earlier analysis of these items in which the student was used as the unit of sampling (Astin, 1965c), and it is also similar to classroom factors identified earlier by Ryans (1960) and Gibb (1957). The high loading of the item "The instructor was exceptionally well-grounded in the course subject matter" suggests that a halo effect may be present in the factor—that the student's over-all regard for the instructor affects his judgments of traits that are in reality unrelated.

Table 27

Extraversion of the Instructor

Variable	r with Factor Score
A. Correlated Classroom Stimuli	
Instructor was enthusiastic	.87*
Instructor had a good sense of humor	.68*
Instructor was exceptionally well-grounded in the course subject matter	.57
Instructor was often dull and uninteresting	−.94*
Instructor spoke in a monotone	−.61

* Used in computing factor score.

It is of some interest that Extraversion of the Instructor is not highly related to other aspects of the college, to other student behaviors, or even to students' impressions of the college environment. One possible reason for this is that the variation among the 246 institutions on the three items defining this factor was much smaller than was true for the items defining most of the other environmental factors. The median percentage of students rating the instructor as enthusiastic, for example, is 85.5, and the range between the lowest and highest colleges is only from 62 percent to 98 percent. The instructor's rated sense of humor shows an almost identical range of scores and median score. The percentage of students rating the instructor as dull and uninteresting varies between 4 percent and 43 percent among the 246 institutions, with a median of only 19 percent. Thus the factor analysis shows that although the students at any college tend to be consistent in how they rate their instructors on these three items, the absolute extent of the differences is small. In short, most freshmen at most institutions regard their instructors as extraverted, enthusiastic, and knowledgable in the subject matter of their courses.

Table 28 shows the correlates of Familiarity with the Instructor, the fourth factor identified in the analyses of classroom stimuli. The three most highly correlated items (which are the same ones used to compute the factor score), suggest a close personal acquaintance between student and in-

Table 28

Familiarity with the Instructor

Variable	R with Factor Score
A. Correlated Classroom Stimuli	
I knew the instructor's first name	.84*
I was a guest in the instructor's home one or more times	.83*
I was in the instructor's office one or more times	.81*
B. Other Correlated Peer Stimuli	
Lived in a dormitory	.53
Was a varsity athlete (NORC)	.53
C. Correlated Student Personal Characteristics	
Musical and dramatic activity (NORC)	.72
Worked on the school paper (NORC)	.62
Father's educational level (NORC)	.56
Mother's educational level (NORC)	.53
College should provide a basic education and appreciation of ideas (NORC)	.52
Single (NORC)	.51
Father a professional (NORC)	.50
D. Correlated Aspects of the College Image	
Positive evaluation of faculty (NORC)	.62
E. Correlated Characteristic of the College	
Size of freshman class	−.52

* Used in computing factor score.

structor. The content of these items indicates that familiarity with the instructor is not in fact a "classroom" factor, but rather a pattern of interactions between faculty and students occurring outside the classroom. It is important to recognize that the degree of familiarity with the instructor is relatively independent of the verbal interaction that takes place in the classroom and of faculty and student involvement in classroom activity (see Table 31).

The finding that the student's familiarity with the instructor is inversely related to the size of the student body offers support for the common assumption that, at larger institutions, the amount of personal interaction between the teacher and his students is necessarily limited. Also, the tendency for a greater degree of familiarity to occur in institutions where a high percentage of students live in dormitories suggests that the student who lives at home and commutes to campus has fewer opportunities for developing close relationships with his instructors than does the resident student.

As is evident from Table 28, many of the NORC items have substantial relationships with familiarity. Some of these correlations may be an artifact of the relationship between familiarity and size of the student body, since the proportion of students who can become varsity athletes, participate in musical and dramatic activities, or work on the staff of the school paper is necessarily limited by the number of students at the institution. Perhaps the most interesting implication of the NORC data is that the faculty in the "familiar" environment tend to be highly regarded by the students.

Protestant institutions scored higher on the Familiarity with the Instructor factor than did any other type of institution. Figure 8 compares their scores with the scores for publicly controlled institutions. The very low amount of familiarity with the instructor at public institutions may be attributable in part to their larger average size, although other factors, such as the high proportion of commuters and the existence of large graduate research programs, may also play a role.

The fifth factor from the classroom environment, Organization in the Classroom, is shown in Table 29. This factor, like Extraversion of the Instructor, is correlated with little else except the classroom stimuli that define the factor score: the instructor's assigning seats and taking attendance each day, the class's meeting at a regularly scheduled time and place, and, not surprisingly, the percentage of students who come late to class. It would be interesting to see if the cause-effect relationship suggested by this last item can be demonstrated experimentally by deliberately introducing such practices in classes where they are not now used and by then observing if the proportion of late arrivals is reduced.

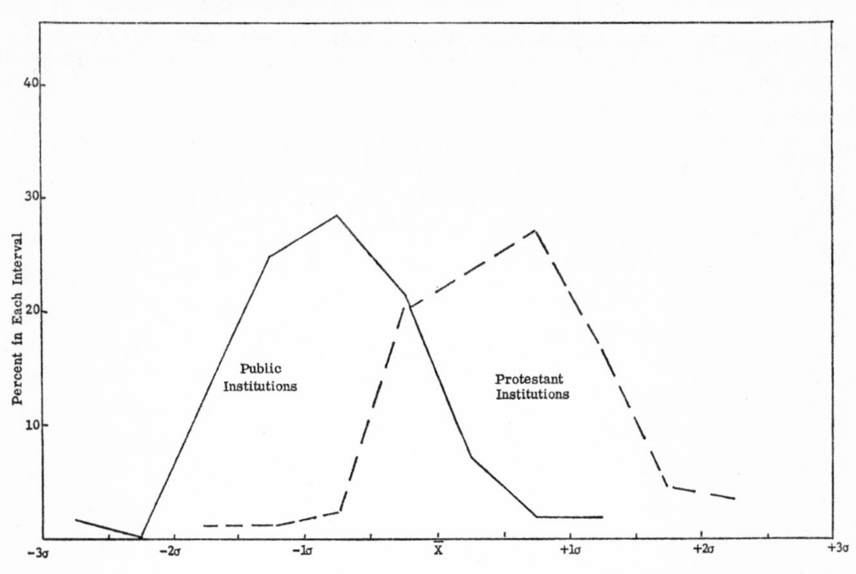

Fig. 8. Scores of Public (N = 56) and Protestant (N = 89) Institutions on Familiarity with the Instructor.

Organization in the Classroom is almost identical to the structure factor identified in an earlier analysis of these same items that used the student as the unit of sampling (Astin, 1965c). This earlier study revealed that the greatest degree of organization exists in accounting and business administration classes and the lowest degree in English and fine arts classes.

Items used to score Organization in the Classroom, unlike those used to score Extraversion of the Instructor, showed a marked diversity among the 246 institutions in their frequencies of occurrence. As we have already noted from Table 24, in some institutions seating is assigned in nearly

Table 29

Organization in the Classroom

Variable	r with Factor Score
A. Correlated Classroom Stimuli	
Students had assigned seating	.88*
Attendance was usually taken every day	.58
(Class met only at a regularly scheduled time and place)	(.46*)
Came late to class	−.69*

* Used in computing the factor score.

every class and attendance is almost always taken, whereas in other institutions these practices are virtually nonexistent. The frequency with which students come late to class also showed considerable diversity, ranging from 21 percent at the lowest institution to 89 percent at the highest, with a median frequency of about 63 percent (see Appendix C). Just one item, "The class met only at a regularly scheduled time and place," showed small variation among institutions, with a limited range of from 83 percent to 100 percent. The restricted variance on this item may account in part for its low correlation with the factor score.

The last identifiable factor from the classroom environment,[2] Severity of Grading, is shown in Table 30. Severity of Grading is defined primarily by the proportion of students who fail a course during their freshman year. As would be expected, the student's average grade during his freshman year has a high negative relationship to this factor. Although it is not immediately apparent how lectures that follow the textbook closely are relevant to severity of grading, an examination of the other correlated student behaviors and personal characteristics provides some possible clues. For example, Table 30 suggests that higher average grades and a smaller number of failing grades are awarded to students who participate in musical, artistic, and dramatic activities and to those students who major in artistic fields such as music, art, speech, and writing. Students in institutions where the grading is relatively easy are also likely to have manifested artistic and literary talent during high school. (The tendency for the grading to be less severe in institutions where a high percentage of students engage in artistic and musical activities has already been mentioned in the previous chapter.) These findings suggest that the correlations of Severity of Grading with the types of lectures given and the nature of written assignments may be attributable to differences in the curricula of those institutions scoring at the extremes on this factor, a conclusion further supported by the results of an earlier

[2] A seventh factor emerged from the analyses of classroom stimuli, although it proved to be difficult to label or interpret. The three items used to score the factor were: cheated on examinations (.79), called a teacher by his first name (.75), and size of the class (.55). Other positively correlated items were father's occupation in the Realistic (technical) class (.53), and "Participated in a drag race" (.50). This factor was negatively correlated with the father's occupation being in the Enterprising class (—.53) and with the institution's being a woman's college (—.50), and also showed negative correlations (in the .60's) with most NORC items pertaining to the socioeconomic background of the students. The factor seems to combine elements of dishonesty, audacity, and low socioeconomic level. It has moderate positive correlations (.42) with each of two factors from the peer environment (Student Employment and Competitiveness versus Cooperativeness), and moderate negative correlations of —.48 and —.42, respectively, with Severity of Policies Against Cheating (see the next chapter) and Organized Dating.

Table 30

Severity of Grading

Variable	R with Factor Score
A. Correlated Classroom Stimuli	
Flunked a course	.92*
Lectures followed the textbook closely	.62*
I usually typed my written assignments	−.75*
Average grade during freshman year	−.66
B. Other Correlated Peer Stimuli	
Musical & Artistic Activity factor	−.58
Played a musical instrument	−.55
Time spent participating in musical, dramatic or artistic activities	−.54
Listened to classical music	−.54
Attended a public lecture	−.51
C. Correlated Student Personal Characteristics	
College should provide career training (NORC)	.59
Prefer to work with things	.53
Pragmatism	.50
Father a professional (NORC)	−.68
College should provide basic education and appreciation of ideas (NORC)	−.64
Father's educational level	−.63
English aptitude (NMSQT)	−.59
Parents' income (NORC)	−.58
Single (NORC)	−.57
Mother's educational level (NORC)	−.56
Home is located in suburbs (NORC)	−.55
Major in Artistic field	−.53
Editor of the high school paper	−.52
Word Usage (NMSQT)	−.51
Won creative writing award in high school	−.51
D. Correlated Aspects of the College Image	
Impersonal	.55
Administration is not really concerned about the individual student	.53
Positive evaluation of the faculty	−.50

* Used in computing factor score.

analysis (Astin, 1965a), which showed clearly that classroom practices vary dramatically as a function of the field of study.

As Table 30 shows, other correlates of Severity of Grading reveal that lower average grades and more failing grades are given in institutions that recruit students who come from less affluent home backgrounds and who are less able academically. (Verbal ability is more highly related to Severity of Grading than is either mathematical or scientific ability.) In short, there seems to be a kind of absolute standard of grading in the higher educational system: the more selective institutions tend to award higher average grades and to fail fewer students than do the less selective institutions. This finding may also help to explain why recent investigations (Lindquist, 1963) have failed to demonstrate that the prediction of academic achievement can be significantly improved by making statistical adjustments for the differential selectivity of high schools and colleges. But even though it might seem from this that subjective weighting of the undergraduate's academic record by employers and by graduate and professional schools is unnecessary, one should remember that the correlation between academic ability and Severity of Grading is far from perfect. Thus, it might be worthwhile to consider using such weighting procedures in those circumstances where the student's record is especially likely to misrepresent his ability (for example, with graduates of highly selective institutions in which few courses are either required or offered in music, art, writing, and related fields).

Severity of Grading is one of the few stimulus factors that shows pronounced differences by geographical region. Figure 9 compares the dis-

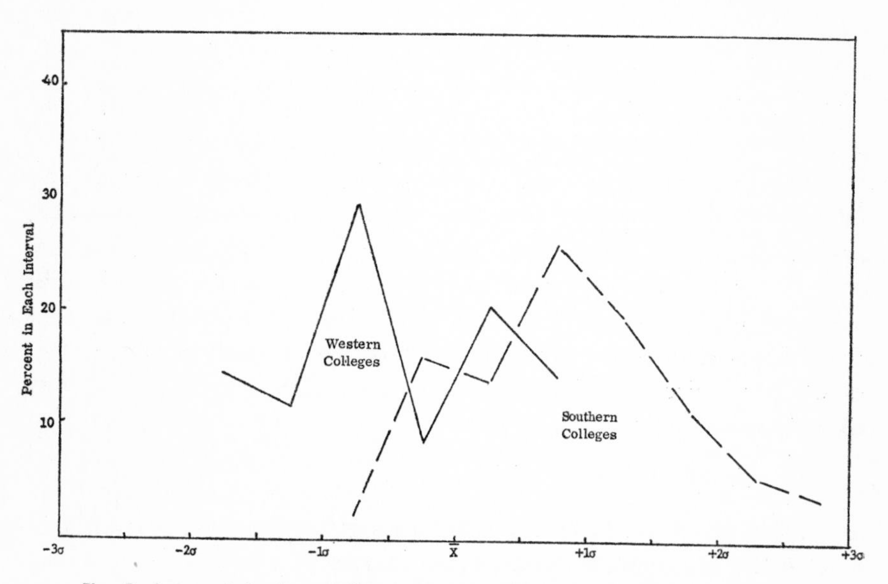

Fig. 9. Scores of Southern Colleges (N = 50) and Western Colleges* (N = 34) on Severity of Grading Practices.

* Includes Southwestern Colleges.

tributions of scores obtained by colleges located in the Southern and the Western region of the country. The relatively high scores of institutions in the South may be a consequence of their lower level of selectivity. The relatively easy grading standards of institutions located in the Western states, however, is more difficult to understand in view of the high concentration of public institutions in these states, since nearly 80 percent of all public institutions have above-average scores on Severity of Grading.

The six factors identified in the analysis of stimuli from the classroom environment clearly involve a diverse set of physical and interpersonal stimuli. Some factors, such as Extraversion of the Instructor and Familiarity with the Instructor, appear primarily to reflect characteristics of the faculty

Table 31

Intercorrelations of the Six Factors from the Classroom Environment

FACTOR	2	3	4	5	6
1. Involvement in the Class	.06	.11	.16	.25	−.09
2. Verbal Aggressiveness		.05	.15	−.20	−.18
3. Extraversion of the Instructor			.13	−.20	−.16
4. Familiarity with the Instructor				−.06	−.26
5. Organization in the Classroom					.12
6. Severity of Grading					

$r_{05} = .12$
$r_{01} = .16$

at the institution. Others, such as Verbal Aggressiveness and Involvement in the Class, are concerned with both student and faculty behavior. Organization in the Classroom seems to involve the administrative practices and the physical characteristics of the class, as well as one aspect of student behavior, coming to class on time. Finally, Severity of Grading appears to depend chiefly on the curriculum and the selectivity of the institution. In short, the findings suggest that the type of classroom experience that confronts the student at any institution consists of a variety of factors, not all of which are directly under the control either of the administration or of the individual professor.

Table 31 shows the intercorrelations of the six classroom environmental factors. Although 10 of the 15 coefficients are statistically significant ($p < .05$), the highest is only −.26. That three of the four largest coefficients involve the Organization in the Classroom factor suggests that environments with more highly organized classes tend to score high on Involvement in the Class and low on Verbal Aggressiveness and Extraversion of the Instructor. It should be stressed, however, that the magnitude of these relationships is small and that the six factors are largely independent.

As we indicated in the previous chapter, one important theoretical and practical consideration in evaluating any new set of factors derived from the analysis of environmental stimuli is their possible redundancy with other factors. Table 32 shows the correlations between the six classroom environmental factors and the 15 factors from the peer environment, together with the multiple correlations between the two sets of factors. The bottom row in Table 32 indicates that two of the classroom environmental factors—Extraversion of the Instructor and Organization in the Classroom—are largely independent of factors in the peer environment. The other four classroom factors show a moderate degree of overlap with the peer environment, but in no case is it sufficient to warrant abandoning any of these factors. Since it is likely that the student's behavior in the classroom will be more or less consistent with his behavior outside the classroom, some overlap is to be expected. Thus, we find that Verbal Aggressiveness in the classroom tends to be associated with Independence and Drinking (versus Religiousness). Similarly, Involvement in the Class is associated with Cohesiveness, Religiousness (versus Drinking), Cooperativeness (versus Competitiveness), and Regularity of Sleeping Habits.

Table 32

Correlations of the Classroom Environment with the Peer Environment

Peer Environmental Factor	Classroom Environmental Factor						Multiple R* from Classroom Environment
	Involvement in the Class	Verbal Aggressiveness	Extraversion of the Instructor	Familiarity with the Instructor	Organization in the Classroom	Severity of Grading	
Competitiveness vs. Cooperativeness	−.44	.13	−.16	−.25	.04	.43	.72
Organized Dating	−.10	.22	.12	−.10	−.07	−.08	.59
Independence	−.40	.55	−.01	.29	−.20	−.18	.73
Cohesiveness	.40	−.19	−.11	.18	.28	.31	.58
Informal Dating	.07	−.21	−.05	.15	−.11	−.11	.50
Femininity	.28	−.12	.11	−.14	−.09	−.25	.58
Drinking vs. Religiousness	−.53	.49	.06	−.12	−.21	−.08	.77
Musical & Artistic Activity	.09	−.03	.17	.42	−.23	−.58	.71
Leisure Time	.05	−.11	−.07	−.10	.06	.32	.33
Career Indecision	−.24	.01	.15	−.03	−.18	−.17	.28
Regularity of Sleeping Habits	.49	−.16	−.06	−.33	.29	.08	.64
Use of the Library	.37	.30	.08	.17	.01	−.22	.51
Conflict with Regulations	.23	.17	−.07	−.20	.18	.08	.49
Student Employment	.11	.03	−.09	.04	.06	.01	.48
Use of Automobiles	−.03	−.16	−.07	−.13	.00	.28	.27
Multiple R from Peer Environment	.77	.67	.27	.67	.37	.66	

* The seventh classroom factor (see footnote 2 p. 61) was included in these step-wise analyses.

SUMMARY

In this chapter, we have examined the characteristics of stimuli associated with the classroom. The diversity among institutions in the frequency of occurrence of various classroom stimuli was considerable, although in some cases not as great as the interinstitutional diversity in stimuli from the peer environment. An analysis of some 49 classroom stimuli revealed six identifiable and independent patterns that differentiated the 246 institutions: Involvement in the Class, Verbal Aggressiveness, Extraversion of the Instructor, Familiarity with the Instructor, Organization in the Classroom, and Severity of Grading.

Extraversion of the Instructor and Organization in the Classroom proved to be largely independent of the 15 factors previously identified in the analysis of stimuli from the peer environment. The other four classroom environmental factors had only moderate relationships with factors from the peer environment.

4

The Administrative Environment

OBTAINING DATA on the administrative environment presented special problems in the design of the Inventory of College Activities. Although students can, obviously, be influenced by the administrative policies of the institution, it is difficult to reduce these rules and regulations to concrete stimuli. Most institutions attempt to communicate the rules to their incoming students by means of college catalogues, student handbooks, and special orientation sessions. We decided against trying to gather the desired data from these diverse sources, on the grounds that they would have no standard method for stating or otherwise defining these rules. Furthermore, we assumed that the college environment is affected less by the formal statement of these rules and regulations than by the way they are implemented.

It seems safe to say that the characteristic administrative practices of the institution are first communicated to the new student through informal interchanges with other students. Thus, significant administrative stimuli would typically take the form of conversations between incumbent and new students or, in some instances, of direct contacts between new students and faculty advisers. Since it is not practicable to monitor this sort of gradual and informal indoctrination, we attempted instead to assess the *consequences* of these experiences by asking a series of structured questions about the student's *perception* of the administrative rules and regulations. Although this decision was not entirely consistent with our earlier definition of the environment, it being impossible to confirm student impressions by independent observation, we attempted to adhere to our definition of *stimulus* as closely as possible by stating each potential student violation in behavioral terms and by stating the administrative actions that might be taken in response in operational terms.

To develop a list of student behaviors that includes most of the potential violations of administrative regulations, we surveyed an assortment of student handbooks and catalogues. This search resulted in the selection of 14 potential student violations:

Coming in from date 10-15 minutes late
Coming in from date 2 hours late
Cheating on examinations
Drinking in student union
Drinking in living quarters
Drinking somewhere off campus
Being drunk
Being alone with a date in your room during the daytime
Being alone with a date in your room at night
Having a date with a faculty member
Staying off campus overnight without permission
Organizing a student demonstration against some administrative policy
Writing off-color stories in a student publication
Participating in a water fight or dormitory raid

In order to reduce the risk of unfavorable public reaction to the mailed questionnaire, the items having to do with the student's sexual behavior were not phrased as frankly as might be desired. We assumed, however, that the existence of curfews and of rules against dates being in dormitory rooms would give some indication of administrative policies on this matter. Homosexual relationships, although a potentially important type of student deviation from administrative policy, was considered too taboo to inquire about, even indirectly.

Our examination of student handbooks and college catalogues indicated that there are four fairly distinct levels of administrative action which can be taken in response to an infraction of the rules. These four levels, in order of increasing severity are:

No policy against this
Reprimand or minor disciplinary action
Major disciplinary action (possible expulsion from college)
Sure expulsion from college

The student was asked to rate the likely consequences of each of the 14 possible infractions as follows: "What action (if any) would be taken by the administration at your college if a student in *your* living quarters were known to have done the following?" A score of "4" was assigned to the item if the student checked "Sure expulsion from college;" a score of "1," if he checked "No policy against this." Scores of "3" and "2" were assigned to the intermediate levels. The severity of any institution's administrative policy with respect to a given infraction consisted of the mean of these scores.[1]

The variation in institutional administrative policies as revealed on these items was greater than the variation for any other group of items in the ICA (see Table 33). This diversity may have occurred in part because we are inquiring here about policies on which, presumably, all the students at an institution will agree. For instance, if a student who is found drinking in the student union is likely to receive a reprimand or some similar minor punishment, 100 percent of the students should check the second alternative; thus the mean score for the institution on this item would be 2.0. Conversely, if there is no policy against drinking in the student union, a mean score of 1.0 should be obtained. In short, we should expect maximum variation among institutional mean scores on items for which there is presumably one correct answer, particularly on those items for which the correct response at a given institution is either "no policy against this" or "sure expulsion from college." Between the two extremes, students may legitimately disagree simply because administrative policies with respect to the infraction are either not fixed or not consistently applied.

Since it is likely that administrative policies about student behavior are applied differently to male and to female students, the problem here was similar to that confronting us in our analyses of students' mode of dress. In the case of the administrative environment, however, it was possible to phrase the items so that they could be answered by both sexes. One major purpose of our analyses was thus to determine if administrative policies concerning the behavior of men and women are comparable enough to permit us to develop a single measure that will apply to both sexes.

Table 33 shows the lowest, the median, and the highest mean scores for the 175 coeducational institutions on each of the 14 potential violations, separately for men and women. The items, which have been ranked roughly in descending order of severity, show clearly the great diversity in administrative policies at different institutions. With the exception of cheating, there is for each of the potential violations at least one institution where no administrative policy against the behavior appears to exist either for the male or for the female students. On the other hand, for each of the 14 potential violations, there is at least one of the 175 institutions where the behavior would draw at least a reprimand. For half of the potential violations, at least one institution considers the behavior sure grounds for expulsion from the college.

[1] Data from commuter students were not used in these analyses.

Table 33

Students' Perceptions of Stimuli in the Administrative Environment: Diversity Among 175 Institutions

Student Behavior	Diversity Among 175 Coeducational Institutions in Severity of Administrative Policies Toward the Behavior*					
	Least Severe		Median		Most Severe	
	Men	Women	Men	Women	Men	Women
Drinking in student union	1.16	1.14	3.44	3.48	3.98	4.00
Drinking in living quarters	1.00	1.05	3.26	3.45	3.96	4.00
Being alone with a date in your room at night	1.11	1.14	3.32	3.50	3.94	3.94
Being drunk	1.13	1.13	2.47	2.79	3.93	3.98
Being alone with a date in your room during the daytime	1.03	1.07	3.10	3.28	3.92	4.00
Drinking somewhere off campus	1.00	1.00	1.79	2.07	3.83	3.81
Cheating on examinations	2.43	2.33	3.03	3.09	3.79	3.93
Participating in a water fight or dormitory raid	1.29	1.29	2.23	2.30	3.26	3.44
Writing off-color stories in a student publication	1.13	1.26	2.02	2.06	2.94	2.98
Staying off campus overnight without permission	1.00	1.10	1.28	3.05	2.92	3.83
Organizing a student demonstration against some administrative policy	1.00	1.02	1.85	1.82	2.85	3.44
Coming in from date 2 hours late	1.00	1.02	1.15	2.71	2.62	3.22
Having a date with a faculty member	1.00	1.00	1.20	1.25	2.13	2.33
Coming in from date 10–15 minutes late	1.00	1.00	1.08	2.00	1.88	2.41

* A score of 4.00 means that 100 percent of the students checked "Sure expulsion from college." A score of 1.00 means that 100 percent of the students checked "No policy against this."

Somewhat contrary to our expectations, the median institutional scores on many items are very similar for men and women, indicating that no "double standard" for certain types of potentially deviant behavior exists. Where sizable differences do occur, however, the consequences are more severe for women than for men. In the analysis of items from the administrative environment, separate mean scores for men and women on each of the 14 items were used, and the median of the 14 correlations between male and female means proved to be .80 (see Appendix G). The relative comparability of administrative policies as they apply to men and to women is further revealed in the factor analytic results described in this chapter.

The factor structure resulting from these analyses was one of the clearest, in its simple structure, of all of the analyses performed in this study. Four distinct factors emerged: severity of administrative policies against (1) drinking, (2) aggression, (3) heterosexual activity, and (4) cheating.[2]

The first factor, Severity of Administrative Policy Against Drinking, is shown in Table 34. This factor is defined primarily by the severity of the administrative policies toward being drunk, drinking off campus, drinking

[2] Diagonal values consisted of the R^2 between each variable and all others. The six components which were retained for rotation accounted for 92.8% of the total communality. (Two of the rotated factors were concerned with disciplinary policies for only one sex.)

Table 34

Severity of Administrative Policy Against Drinking

Variable	r with Factor Score
A. Correlated Administrative Stimuli	
Being drunk (men)	.90*
Drinking somewhere off campus (men)	.90*
Being drunk (women)	.90*
Drinking somewhere off campus (women)	.89*
Drinking in student union (women)	.81
Drinking in student union (men)	.79
Drinking in living quarters (men)	.68
Drinking in living quarters (women)	.60
Writing off-color stories in a student publication (women)	.56
Writing off-color stories in a student publication (men)	.55
B. Correlated Peer Stimuli	
Prayed (not including grace before meals)	.62
Read the Bible	.61
Attended church	.61
Religious articles displayed in the room	.53
Said grace before meals	.53
Said "hello" to students you didn't know	.52
Involvement in the Class factor	.51
Attended Sunday School	.50
Drinking vs. Religiousness factor	−.79
Drank whiskey or other hard liquor	−.73
Drank wine	−.73
Drank beer	−.72
Became intoxicated	−.67
Drank in a bar or club	−.63
Listened to folk music	−.57
Argued with other students	−.56
Saw a foreign movie	−.52
C. Correlated Student Personal Characteristics	
Religious (self-rating)	.64
Intellectualism	−.55
Academic ability (NMSQT Composite)	−.52
Planning to get the Ph.D. degree	−.51
D. Correlated Classroom Characteristics	
Instructor sometimes gave unannounced or "pop" quizzes	.52
Students were permitted to smoke in class	−.61
Instructor was engaged in research	−.51
E. Correlated Physical Stimuli	
Religious articles displayed in the room	.53
F. Correlated Aspects of the College Image	
Victorian	.67
High morale	.67
Campus paper and humor magazine are censored by the administration	.65
Great deal of independence is granted the student	−.71
Liberal	−.68
There is a large group of "avant-garde" students on campus	−.58
G. Correlated Characteristics of the College	
Selectivity	−.51
Nonsectarian	−.51
Private-nonsectarian	−.51

* Used in computing the factor score.

in the student union, and drinking in the living quarters.[3] As indicated by the coefficients in Table 34, the factor loadings for men and women on these four items are essentially the same. The very high loadings show that the administrative policies toward drinking are relatively consistent across institutions, no matter what the circumstances for drinking or the amount consumed may be. There are a few notable exceptions to this generalization, however, particularly in policies concerning drinking on the campus. One large university, for example, forbids drunkenness and drinking in living quarters, but permits beer to be sold to students in the student union.

Severity of Administrative Policy Against Drinking is most closely related to the Drinking versus Religiousness factor identified earlier. This relationship is also manifested in the factor's high positive correlations with specific items involving religious behavior and its high negative relationships with specific items concerning the drinking behavior of students. The tendency for students to drink more in institutions where the policies about student drinking are relatively permissive raises an interesting question concerning possible cause-effect relationships. Do administrative policies directly affect the amount of drinking that goes on, or are they designed rather to accommodate to the level of drinking that is likely to occur because of the types of students recruited? Suffice it to say, this finding represents another problem that has obvious implications for the formulation of administrative policies and practices regarding student conduct and that calls for further research.

Other correlates of restrictions on drinking follow much the same pattern as did the correlates of the Drinking versus Religiousness factor described earlier (Chapter 2). Institutions with relatively severe policies against drinking are likely to be seen as Victorian and as having high morale and as places where the campus paper and humor magazine are censored. Institutions with relatively permissive policies, on the other hand, are often described as liberal and as granting the student a great deal of independence. The permissive institutions also tend to be relatively selective, private, and nonsectarian. Severity of Administrative Policy Against Drinking is more highly related to an institution's being sectarian (.51) than is the Drinking versus Religiousness student behavioral factor (−.42).

[3] In obtaining scores for each of the four administrative factors, the mean score of the highest-loading (starred) items, based on all students (men and women combined), rather than a weighted regression composite, was used. Using a weighted regression composite would have first required refactoring the matrix using all institutions rather than just the coeducational institutions. Tables 34-37 show the rotated factor loading of the administrative items, rather than their correlations with the factor scores.

With respect to policies concerning student drinking, American institutions of higher learning are just about as diverse as it is possible for them to be. The data also indicate that institutions generally regard student drinking as a more serious form of misconduct than any of the other behaviors studied. For example, the means in Table 33 show that the typical (i.e., median) administrative action taken with respect to a student caught drinking either in the student union or in his living quarters is likely to be about midway in severity between a major disciplinary action (possible expulsion from college) and sure expulsion from college.

The second factor identified in these analyses involves severity of policy against student aggression. The correlates of this factor are shown in Table 35. This pattern is defined primarily in terms of the expected reprisals that would follow if a student organized a demonstration against some administrative policy or if he participated in a water fight or dormitory raid. The factor also has moderate relationships with the disciplinary consequences that might be expected for writing an off-color story in a student publication. Once again, the loadings for men and women are very similar. It is interesting to learn that Severity of Administrative Policy Against Aggression is negatively related to the Independence factor from the peer environment; this is also reflected in the findings that students at colleges with relatively permissive policies about aggressive behavior tend to engage in arguments with each other, to drink wine, and to be interested in folk music and foreign movies. Since these students also seem to be more intellectually able than are students in the less permissive environments, we are once again confronted with rival hypotheses to account for these relationships: Does the student at a college with permissive policies toward aggression show more independence simply because he is typically brighter than the student at a less permissive institution, or is his behavior shaped in part by the administrative policy? This problem is related to another: Are administrative policies about student aggression consciously developed according to some explicit educational rationale? Or do they evolve more or less in response to the needs and demands of the particular student body?

The typical classroom in a college where the policies toward student aggression are relatively severe reveals an interesting pattern: lectures tend to follow the textbook closely, and "objective" examinations are preferred over essay exams. These findings suggest that the instructors in these institutions manifest a certain rigidity, a lack of flexibility. Students in these colleges typically believe that the campus paper and humor magazine are censored by the administration and that the students seem very conforming.

Table 35

Severity of Administrative Policy Against Aggression

Variable	r with Factor Score
A. Correlated Administrative Stimuli	
Organizing a student demonstration against some administrative policy (women)	.79*
Participating in a water fight or dormitory raid (women)	.78*
Organizing a student demonstration against some administrative policy (men)	.77*
Participating in a water fight or dormitory raid (men)	.74*
Writing off-color stories in a student publication (women)	.55
Writing off-color stories in a student publication (men)	.53
Severity of Administrative Policy Against Heterosexual Activity Factor	.52
B. Correlated Peer Stimuli	
Listened to folk music	−.61
Independence factor	−.53
Bought a paperback book (not for a class)	−.53
Argued with other students	−.52
Saw a foreign movie	−.51
Time spent studying	−.51
Drank wine	−.51
Talked with another student in a language other than English	−.50
C. Correlated Classroom Stimuli	
Lectures followed the textbook closely	.57
Examinations were usually of the "objective" rather than the "essay" type	.55
Class was taught by a graduate student	.50
D. Correlated Student Personal Characteristics	
Father's occupation in Realistic class	.53
Word Usage (NMSQT)	−.60
Academic ability (NMSQT composite)	−.59
Father's educational level	−.59
Social science reading aptitude (NMSQT)	−.59
Father a professional or executive	−.58
English aptitude (NMSQT)	−.57
Natural science reading aptitude (NMSQT)	−.57
High school grade average	−.54
Father's occupation in Scientific class	−.53
Intellectualism	−.53
Mathematical aptitude (NMSQT)	−.52
Status	−.52
Had poems, short stories, etc. published in high school	−.50
E. Correlated Aspects of the College Image	
Campus paper and humor magazine are censored by the administration	.59
There is a great deal of conformity among the students	.55
Most of the students are of a very high calibre academically	−.56
The intellectual atmosphere is definitely on the theoretical, rather than the practical side	−.52
F. Correlated Characteristic of the College	
Selectivity	−.58

* Used in computing the factor score.

Students in the more permissive institutions, on the other hand, view the intellectual atmosphere as one in which theoretical matters are emphasized over practical matters.

The data shown earlier in Table 33 suggest that administrative policies toward student aggression are, in an absolute sense, less severe than policies toward other kinds of potential infractions. Of course, this finding could be the result of the particular hypothetical infractions that we selected for this study. Of the three forms of student aggression which had high loadings on this factor, participating in a water fight or dormitory raid appeared to represent the most serious infraction. The range of administrative policies toward this particular student behavior is also the greatest, with some institutions viewing it as grounds for possible expulsion. Looking at the median score for the 175 institutions, however, we find that this behavior usually warrants something above a reprimand or minor disciplinary action.

In view of the recent student unrest on many campuses, the range of policies concerning organized demonstrations is of special interest. Although students at some institutions believe that the administration has no policy against their organizing such demonstrations, at other institutions, the students would be subject to possible expulsion from college. Since these data were collected prior to the student demonstrations at the University of California at Berkeley in 1964-65, it might be worthwhile to repeat this study using some of the same institutions, to determine whether the policies or patterns of student behavior have altered.

The third factor identified in the analyses of the administrative environment, Severity of Administrative Policy Against Heterosexual Activity, is shown in Table 36. This factor is defined in terms of the administrative action that would be taken if a student were found alone with a date in his room. At the coeducational colleges, this factor is also closely related to policies concerning women students who return late from dates or who stay off campus overnight without permission. (The fact that, for male students, these two items defined a separate factor in the analyses suggests that where such rules exist for men they are based on policies other than those having to do with heterosexual behavior.) The high relationships of this factor to the policies concerning women who drink in their living quarters indicates that these particular behaviors have certain overtones in the case of women that they do not have in the case of men.

The general pattern of correlations with the Severity of Administrative Policy Against Heterosexual Activity is similar to those found for the two previous factors, although the magnitude of the correlations is generally lower (i.e., much fewer reached $\pm .50$). Students in those colleges where the

Table 36

Severity of Administrative Policy Against Heterosexual Activity

VARIABLE	R WITH FACTOR SCORE
A. Correlated Administrative Stimuli	
Being alone with a date in your room at night (women)	.84*
Being alone with a date in your room during the daytime (women)	.82*
Staying off campus overnight without permission (women)	.82
Being alone with a date in your room at night (men)	.79*
Staying off campus overnight without permission (men)	
Being alone with a date in your room during the daytime (men)	.74*
Coming in from date 2 hours late (women)	.74
Drinking in living quarters (women)	.66
Severity of Administrative Policy Against Aggression Factor	.52
Severity of Administrative Policy Against Drinking Factor	.51
B. Correlated Peer Stimuli	
Prayed (not including grace before meals)	.54
Attended church	.51
C. Correlated Student Personal Characteristics	
Religious (self-rating)	.50
Natural science reading aptitude (NMSQT)	−.59
Mathematics aptitude (NMSQT)	−.56
Academic ability (NMSQT Composite)	−.54
Social science reading aptitude (NMSQT)	−.52
D. Correlated Aspects of the College Image	
Campus paper and humor magazine are censored by the administration	.54
Victorian	.52
Great deal of independence is granted the student	−.58
Liberal	−.51
E. Correlated Characteristic of the College	
Selectivity	−.53

* Used in computing the factor score.

policies concerning heterosexual behavior are relatively severe manifest more religious behavior than do typical students, and they tend to be less able academically. These students often report that their environment is Victorian and believe that the campus paper and humor magazine are carefully censored by the administration. Students in colleges characterized by more permissive policies toward heterosexual activity see their environment as liberal and believe that they are given a good deal of independence.

Being alone with a date in a dormitory room at night seems to be generally considered an infraction as serious as drinking in the student union or drinking in the living quarters. Being alone with a date in the dormitory room during the daytime is regarded as only slightly less serious. The administrative consequences of staying off campus overnight without permission are considerably less serious, although the double standard for men and women is more noticeable for this item than for any other in the table. A pronounced double standard also exists with respect to coming in late from dates. For male students at the typical institution, these behaviors do not seem to be regarded as infractions of the rules, although some institutions do have policies against them. The diversity in administrative policies with respect to all of these potential infractions—particularly having dates in living quarters—is once again considerable. However, had it been possible to obtain reports about behavior of a much more explicitly sexual nature, administrative policies may have proved to be generally more severe and more homogeneous from one institution to another.

The fourth and last factor identified in the analyses of the administrative environment, Severity of Administrative Policy Against Cheating, is shown in Table 37. Once again, the relative severity of the policies is similar for male and female students. The other correlates of this factor reflect the relationship with a factor from the peer environment, Student Employment. Administrative policies toward cheating are more permissive in institutions where a relatively high proportion of the students work during the school year. The fact that the rate of reported cheating is negatively related to the severity of administrative policy against cheating may be very significant. One could interpret this to mean that the policies against cheating do indeed work and that the best way to reduce the amount of cheating that

Table 37

Severity of Administrative Policy Against Cheating

Variable	r with Factor Score
A. Correlated Administrative Stimuli	
Cheating on examinations (women)	.87*
Cheating on examinations (men)	.85*
B. Correlated Peer Stimuli	
Cheated on an examination	−.52
Time spent working for pay	−.52
Regularly employed during the school year	−.50
C. Correlated Student Personal Characteristics	
Father's occupation in Enterprising Class	.54
Father's occupation in Realistic Class	−.50

* Used in computing the factor score.

goes on is to stiffen the penalties. We must again recognize, though, that alternative interpretations of this finding could be given; for example, it could be argued that colleges with severe policies against cheating are more likely to recruit students who are less inclined to cheat. However, the fact that only a few student personal characteristics were correlated with this factor renders this particular interpretation less tenable. In any case, the validity of this causal interpretation should be explored in future research.

The data in Table 33 show that administrative policies toward cheating on examinations are typically somewhat less severe than are the policies concerning drinking and heterosexual behavior: The median response for the 175 coeducational institutions is that major disciplinary action (possibly expulsion) would result. Unlike the other potential student infractions, however, cheating is viewed as a violation of policy even at the most permissive institutions (where it is usually regarded as a minor infraction). In short, these findings indicate that the policy concerning cheating on examinations is less variable across institutions than are the policies concerning various other types of infractions of the rules.

Table 38 shows the intercorrelations among the four factors from the administrative environment. Colleges appear to be moderately consistent in the severity of their policies toward drinking, aggression, and heterosexual activity. But their policies concerning cheating seem to be relatively independent of their other policies. Apparently, they are based on a different set of values or premises than are the policies about drinking, aggression, and heterosexual behavior.

The correlates of the first three administrative factors shown in Tables 34, 35, and 36 indicate that the more selective institutions tend to have relatively permissive policies with respect to drinking, aggression, and heterosexual activity. This finding is further reflected in the significant correlations of student aptitude scores with all three factors.

Table 38

Intercorrelations of the Four Factors from the Administrative Environment

FACTOR	2	3	4
Severity of Administrative Policies Against:			
1. Drinking	.44	.51	−.15
2. Aggression		.52	−.16
3. Heterosexual Activity			.13
4. Cheating			

The relationships of these four factors with the factors identified in the peer environment and the classroom environment are shown in Table 39. The relatively high multiple correlation coefficients in the last row of Table 39 reveal that the information contained in the administrative factors is to some extent redundant with the information contained in the peer factors and classroom factors. Nevertheless, the fact that the squared multiple correlation coefficients are considerably smaller than the reliabilities shown in

Table 39

Correlations of the Administrative Environment with the Peer and Classroom Environments

(N=238 Resident Colleges)

Factor	Severity of Administrative Policy Against:			
	Drinking	Aggression	Heterosexual Activity	Cheating
A. Peer Environment:				
Competitiveness vs. Cooperativeness	−.38	.07	−.15	.07
Organized Dating	−.33	−.19	−.13	.39
Independence	−.41	−.53	−.36	.30
Cohesiveness	.49	.38	.43	−.10
Informal Dating	.04	.05	.06	−.33
Femininity	.04	.07	.00	−.13
Drinking vs. Religiousness	−.79	−.48	−.45	.27
Musical & Artistic Activity	−.02	−.42	−.29	−.16
Leisure Time	−.04	.22	.17	−.04
Career Indecision	−.13	−.13	−.15	−.05
Regularity of Sleeping Habits	.36	.31	.35	−.19
Use of the Library	.11	−.06	.17	.05
Conflict with Regulations	.13	.15	.40	.15
Student Employment	−.08	.05	−.09	−.48
Use of Automobiles	−.10	.19	.01	−.10
B. Classroom Environment:				
Involvement in the Class	.51	.24	.44	−.11
Verbal Aggressiveness	−.25	−.40	−.13	.27
Extraversion of the Instructor	−.12	−.06	−.08	.04
Familiarity with the Instructor	.10	−.29	−.24	−.06
Organization in the Classroom	.28	.20	.23	.05
Severity of Grading Practices	.10	.44	.34	.16
Multiple R from the Peer & Classroom Environments	.84	.73	.75	.69

Appendix F indicates that each of these four factors contains a significant amount of information not included in the other factors.

In general, the patterns of relationships are consistent with the suggested meaning of the factors. The patterns for the policies toward drinking, aggression, and heterosexual activity have many similarities. For example, those institutions with relatively severe policies concerning these three types of student behaviors tend also to be high on religiousness, cohesiveness, involvement in the class, organization in the classroom, and regularity of sleeping habits. A high degree of religiousness and a low amount of drinking is especially likely to be found at institutions where the policies toward student drinking are relatively severe. Those institutions that have relatively severe policies toward student aggression are characterized by little student independence, a lack of verbal aggressiveness in the classroom, and rather strict grading practices (i.e., a high percentage of students who fail a course). Conflict with regulations is more likely to occur in those institutions where the policies toward heterosexual behavior are relatively severe. The pattern of relationships with policies toward cheating is very different: severe policies toward cheating are associated with organized dating, independence, drinking, and verbal aggressiveness in the classroom. Permissive policies toward cheating are associated with student employment and informal dating. These relationships are generally lower than those found for the first three administrative factors.

OTHER ADMINISTRATIVE POLICIES AND PRACTICES

Additional information about the administrative environment was obtained by means of a questionnaire sent to administrative officers in each of the 246 institutions (see Appendix E). In most cases, it went either to a Dean of Students or to a Dean of Men or Women, although in some instances it was completed by the Academic Dean or Dean of Admissions. After three follow-up reminder letters to nonrespondents, 240 questionniares were returned. Of these, 232 were from the noncommuter colleges for which we had the student data on administrative policies.

These questionnaires were sent to administrators for two major reasons: to get factual information on certain administrative policies and to learn the administrators' judgments concerning the nature of certain administrative practices. The questionnaires thus contained 18 items concerning administrative policies (e.g., Are students permitted to keep their own automobiles on campus?), and 12 items in which the administrator was asked to judge what administrative action would be taken in certain hypothetical situations. The latter set of items included several taken verbatim from the corresponding section on the ICA.

Only three of the factual items from the administrators' questionnaire produced correlations equal to or greater than .40 with any of the environmental factors. The factors which have the highest correlations with these three administrative policies are shown in Table 40. Institutions which permit national social fraternities and sororities to function on campus tend to

Table 40

Environmental Correlates of Three Administrative Practices
(N=232 Institutional Administrators)

Administrative Practice	r	Environmental Factor
National social fraternities and sororities exist on campus	.45	Competitiveness vs. Cooperativeness
	.35	Drinking vs. Religiousness
	.34	Spread of the Campus*
	.32	Severity of Grading Practices
	−.44	Involvement in the Class
Atheists would not knowingly be hired on the faculty	.59	Severity of Administrative Policy Against Drinking
	.50	Cohesiveness
	.49	Involvement in the Class
	.43	Severity of Administrative Policy Against Heterosexual Activity
	−.53	Drinking vs. Religiousness
Chapel attendance is compulsory	.48	Severity of Administrative Policy Against Drinking
	.45	Cohesiveness
	−.43	Drinking vs. Religiousness
	−.41	Spread of the Campus*

* See Chapter 5.

have environments characterized by competitiveness, drinking, large campuses, and severe grading practices. Institutions that do not have national social fraternities and sororities tend to manifest a high degree of involvement in the class.

Colleges with a policy against hiring atheists on the faculty tend to have relatively severe policies against both drinking and heterosexual activity and to show a good deal of cohesiveness and involvement in the classroom. At such colleges, the amount of student drinking is small and the amount of religious behavior great. A similar pattern of environmental characteristics is found in institutions that require compulsory chapel attendance;

such institutions are likely to be relatively small compared with institutions where such attendance is not compulsory.

The judgment of individual administrators concerning the probable disciplinary consequences of various student infractions had only modest relationships with the four disciplinary factors. However, the pattern of relationships was consistent with the suggested meaning of these factors. Table 41 shows the correlations between the four administrative factors and four items—each corresponding to one of the four administrative factors—selected from the administrator's questionnaire. The order of the question-

Table 41

Correlations Between the Administrative Environment and Administrators' Judgments

(N=232 Institutional Administrators)

Administrator's Judgment of Probable Severity of Punishment for:	ICA Factor Score for Severity of Administrative Policy Against:			
	Drinking	Aggression	Heterosexual Activity	Cheating
Being drunk	*.55*	.32	.19	.01
Participating in a water fight or dormitory raid	.23	*.38*	.23	.15
Staying off campus overnight without permission	.16	.17	*.34*	−.18
Cheating on examinations	−.20	.02	−.06	*.36*

naire items (potential student infractions) and administrative factors in Table 41 is the same, so that the diagonal values in the matrix represent the correlations between each item and its corresponding factor. Although the correlations are generally quite low, the highest correlation in each column and row of Table 41 is in every case located in the diagonal cell of the matrix. In other words, the administrators' judgments are most highly correlated with the most appropriate disciplinary factor score.

These findings suggest that the administrative factor scores as defined by aggregated student judgments are significantly consistent with the opinions of individual administrators concerning disciplinary practices, but the relationships are generally much lower than might be expected, considering that identical items were used. The most likely explanation for these low relationships is that some kinds of judgments made by individual observers are notoriously unreliable. It would be useful in future studies to examine the opinions of several administrators at each institution in order to obtain a more accurate picture of the administrative practices as perceived by persons other than the students.

SUMMARY

In this chapter, we have attempted to develop measures of the administrative practices of undergraduate institutions with respect to potential student infractions of the rules. Since it is difficult to reduce the administrative practices of an institution to concrete stimuli that can be observed and directly reported, we chose instead to rely on the students' judgments concerning the probable administrative action that would be taken in response to a number of specific student behaviors.

Analyses of the students' perceptions of the administrative policies revealed four distinct patterns: Severity of Administrative Policies Against Drinking, Against Aggression, Against Heterosexual Activity, and Against Cheating. With the exception of cheating, which was considered to be an infraction of the rules at even the most permissive institutions, the range of administrative practice among the 175 coeducational institutions studied ran nearly the entire gamut from complete acceptance to sure expulsion from college. The policies of various institutions concerning drinking, sexual behavior, and aggressive behavior were generally consistent, as is indicated by an average correlation of approximately .50 among these three factor scores. Policies toward cheating, however, were largely independent of policies toward the other three types of infractions, indicating that the rationale used in developing a policy toward cheating is different from the rationale for developing policies toward other types of infractions.

Reports on disciplinary practices obtained from individual administrators tended to agree with the students' impressions as measured by the four factor scores.

5

The Physical Environment

ALTHOUGH THE PHYSICAL facilities and environments of higher educational institutions greatly concern most administrators, researchers have paid little attention to this potentially important area of environmental stimuli. When discussing the "physical" environment of an institution, one normally thinks of dormitories, laboratories, the library, and other facilities directly connected with student life or with the academic program of the institution. On a broader level, however, the physical environment involves the way in which these facilities are arranged with respect to each other and their general environmental context, including the surrounding town and community and the climate of the particular geographic region. Any or all of these physical characteristics of the college environment can affect the progress and development of the college student.

While it would have been desirable to obtain information on all aspects of the physical environment, considerations of cost and other logistical matters necessarily limited the amount and type of information collected to four broad categories: the type of college town (size and location); the climate; the geographic arrangement of various buildings on the campus and in the town; and the characteristics of the students' living quarters. A total of 37 variables within these four broad categories of physical stimuli were selected for study:

A. Location of College
   1. Large city (population 500,000 or more)
   2. Medium-size city (population 100,000-500,000)
   3. Suburb of large or medium-size city
   4. Town or small city (population less than 100,000)

B. Climate of College Community
   5. Percent of students reporting that the weather is the same as the weather in their hometown
   6. Percent of students reporting that the weather is colder than the weather in their hometown

C. Geographic Arrangement of Campus and College Town
   ("How long did it take you to get from your living quarters to the

following places [indicate traveling time in minutes by the means you usually use; e.g., if you walked, give walking time; if you usually drove, give driving and parking time, etc.]")

7. Library
8. Student union
9. Your most distant classroom
10. Nearest restaurant or snack bar
11. Closest place where you could visit and talk with people of your own age of the opposite sex
12. Nearest bar that served alcoholic beverages to students
13. Nearest movie theater

D. Students' Living Quarters

("Where did you live during your freshman year at college?")

14. Dormitory
15. Fraternity or sorority house
16. Private room or apartment
17. At home

---

18. Median number of students living in the same residence
19. Median number of roommates

("Which of the following did you have displayed in your room at college?")

20. Pennants
21. Souvenirs from dates (programs, flowers, favors, etc.)
22. Cartoons or jokes
23. Scientific models
24. Pin-ups
25. Schedule
26. Abstract painting
27. Other painting or drawing
28. Sports trophies
29. Photographs of friends
30. Religious articles
31. None of these

---

32. In your living quarters, did you have a housemother, dorm counselor, or head resident?

("How would you describe this person?")

33. Friendly
34. Strict, but fair
35. Strict almost to the point of being ruthless
36. Listened to your problems
37. Permissive

The large number of items concerning the characteristics of the students' living quarters was considered important, because the resident student normally spends a rather large proportion of his total time at college in his living quarters. Students who reported that they lived at home during their freshman year were requested not to answer the specific questions about living quarters; therefore, this information was based only on the reports of those students who lived away from home. (The eight commuter colleges were thus excluded from these analyses.) Similarly, those students who did not have a housemother or some other supervisory person were asked to skip the relevant section of the questionnaire.

We felt that the most important aspect of the geographic arrangement of the campus would be the traveling time required for the student to go from his living quarters to a particular building. Perhaps we should have included other buildings (e.g., laboratories, dining halls), but we attempted to limit the list to those buildings that are likely to be found on every campus and in every campus town.

Although it would have been desirable to include items on the nature of the library, classroom, and laboratory facilities of the institution, such information was not available at the time of the study. Previous analyses (Astin, 1962a) have shown that the general quality of these facilities is highly related to such characteristics as the prestige of the institution and its expenditures per student for educational and general purposes.

DIVERSITY IN PHYSICAL ENVIRONMENTS OF COLLEGES AND UNIVERSITIES

Table 42 shows the range among the 238 noncommuter institutions in the characteristics covered by 21 items concerning the physical environment. Once more extraordinary diversity among institutions is manifested. For example, although the typical resident freshman student lives in a dormitory with nearly 240 other freshmen, freshmen at some institutions live in residences which average as few as seven residents in all. Also, the median number of roommates varies from none to nearly six, with the typical institution housing between two and three students to a room. The rooms themselves are diverse in the quality and quantity of articles displayed. For example, the room of an average student at a typical institution contains a schedule, souvenirs from dates or parties, photographs of friends, and cartoons and jokes. Items such as pin-ups, abstract paintings, and religious articles are not apt to be displayed, although at some institutions they are on view in the large majority of the students' rooms. Conversely, virtually all of the articles in the list are likely to be absent from the rooms of most students at certain institutions.

Table 42

Stimuli in the Physical Environment: Diversity Among 238 Institutions*

Item	Scores for		
	Lowest Inst.	Median Inst.	Highest Inst.
Median number of students living in the same residence	7	239	396
Median number of roommates	0.0	2.4	5.7
Displays on walls of room:			
Schedules	35.7	81.0	99.9
Souvenirs from dates	6.1	61.3	95.6
Religious articles	4.0	24.3	95.7
Photographs of friends	24.6	65.2	91.5
Cartoons or jokes	16.1	57.8	79.7
Pin-ups	0.0	16.0	54.0
Abstract painting	0.9	18.4	60.2
Other painting or drawing	0.0	44.8	91.4
Housemother or dorm counselor in living quarters	7.2	96.4	100.0
Description of housemother:**			
Listened to your problems	7.7	53.2	83.6
Strict, but fair	7.7	45.3	78.9
Permissive	0.0	5.4	45.3
Median travel time (in minutes) from living quarters to:			
Nearest bar serving liquor to students	5.2	15.2	51.2
Nearest place where a date can be found	1.6	3.8	40.8
Nearest movie theater	4.6	15.5	35.8
Most distant classroom	4.2	6.7	16.0
Student union	1.0	4.5	15.8
Library	2.1	5.1	15.1
Weather in student's hometown same as at college	10.5	56.3	100.0

* Based only on observations of resident students.

** Based only on reports of students who lived in a residence where a housemother, dorm counselor, or head resident also lived.

Data in Table 42 show clearly that nearly all of the students at the typical institution live in a residence where there is also a housemother, head counselor, or similar supervisory person. Nevertheless, at some institutions, supervisory personnel are missing from most residences. Where these personnel do exist, they are typically described as being willing to listen to the students' problems, but as *not* being permissive. Despite these trends, there is still a considerable diversity among institutions in how students perceive this supervisory person.

Within the sample of 238 institutions, there were large variations in the proximity of the students' living quarters to various campus buildings, and, in particular, to various places in the college town. The average student at a typical institution takes about seven minutes to go from his living quarters to his most distant classroom, although at some institutions this trip typically takes about 16 minutes. On the average, the student union and the library tend to be about five minutes away from the students' living quarters, although the range for student unions varies from one minute to nearly 16 minutes and the range for libraries varies from two minutes to 15 minutes. The nearest bar serving liquor to students is typically located about 15 minutes away from the students' living quarters, although at some colleges it is nearly an hour away. Somewhat surprisingly, the pattern for the nearest movie theater is similarly diverse, although the highest median travel time—nearly 36 minutes—is not quite as extreme. Although dates are usually located nearby (typically the student has to travel about four minutes to find a person of the opposite sex to visit and talk with), at certain institutions dates can be found only after traveling for nearly three-quarters of an hour. Clearly, the time and effort required to attend a movie, buy a drink, or find a date varies markedly among institutions.

PATTERNS OF PHYSICAL STIMULI

Because of the large number of items concerning the students' living quarters, the four disciplinary factors discussed in the previous chapter were included in the analysis of intercorrelations among the 37 items concerning the physical environment.[1] The results were generally disappointing, in that many of the factors either were difficult to interpret or were the consequence of artifacts in the original 37 variables.[2] The two interpretable factors emerging from this analysis were labeled Spread of the Campus and Friendliness of the Dorm Counselor or Housemother.

Table 43 shows the correlates of the first interpretable factor, Spread of the Campus, which reflects primarily the distance, in traveling time, re-

[1] Since only the resident students provided data upon which these four disciplinary factors were based, it was felt that these four factors would provide appropriate "marker variables" for the analyses of physical stimuli.

[2] The component analysis was performed on a matrix in which the squared multiple correlation of the variable with all others was used as the diagonal value. Eigenvalues of at least 1.0 were associated with the first ten components. These components, which accounted for 92.6 percent of the total communality, were retained for rotation. Rotating fewer factors did not produce any appreciable improvement in the interpretability of the results. Three of the factors (VII, VIII, and IX) appeared to be artifacts of the four experimentally dependent measures of type of community; another factor (X) appeared to be an artifact of the sex ratio in the student body; and four factors (I, II, III, and V) appeared to be uninterpretable factors for which no reliable estimate of the factor score could be obtained.

Table 43

Spread of the Campus

Variable	r with Factor Score
A. Correlated Physical Stimuli	
Travel time to most distant classroom	.95*
Travel time to library	.86*
Travel time to student union	.82*
B. Correlated Aspects of the College Image	
Most students are more like "numbers in a book"	.57
Campus is too big	.52
Faculty seem to be interested more in research than in teaching students	.51
Faculty go out of their way to help the student	−.52
C. Correlated Characteristics of the College	
Size of the entering class	.67
University	.57
Liberal Arts College	−.53

* Used in computing factor score.

quired for the student to go from his dormitory to his most distant classroom, to the library, and to the student union. As we have already seen from Table 43, the absolute differences in these items among institutions are considerable. Students on the larger campuses tend to feel that they are treated like "numbers in a book," that the campus is too big, and that the faculty seem to be more interested in research than in teaching. Students on the more compact campuses, on the other hand, are inclined to report that the faculty go out of their way to help the student. Not surprisingly, Campus Spread is substantially correlated (.67) with the size of the entering class. Similarily, the campuses of universities tend to be much larger than the campuses of other types of institutions, particularly liberal arts colleges.

These correlates are in many ways consistent with the popular stereotype of the impersonal multiversity. However, it is important to note that the geographic spread of the campus itself is not related to the distances that students have to travel to go from their living quarters to various parts of the college town (movie theaters, bars, etc.). Moreover, there were no observable trends in the relationship between Spread of The Campus and type of town in which the college was located. However, Spread tended to be related to the percentage of students who lived in fraternity houses (r =

.41) and to the number of students who lived in the same residence (r = .31).

Interestingly, this factor is largely independent of the many stimulus items concerning the peer environment, the classroom environment, and the administrative environment. This finding is consistent with the earlier study of student inputs involving these same students (Astin, 1965d), in which size of the student body was found to be unrelated to such traits as intellectualism, estheticism, status, masculinity, leadership, and pragmatism. This relative independence indicates that the effects of Spread of the Campus on student development will be somewhat easier to detect in controlled longitudinal studies than will the effects of many of the other environmental factors, since the confounding of student input characteristics and Spread is relatively small. To put it more simply: the larger campuses

Table 44

Friendliness of the Dorm Counselor or Housemother

Variable	r with Factor Score
A. Correlated Ratings of the Housemother	
Friendly	.92*
Listened to your problems	.81*
Strict, almost to the point of being ruthless	−.78*

* Used in computing factor score.

do not seem to enroll student bodies that differ appreciably from those enrolled by the smaller campuses.

The second interpretable factor from the physical environment was identified as Friendliness of the Dorm Counselor or Housemother (see Table 44). The correlates of this factor, which include only the three items that were used to define it, are self-explanatory. Surprisingly, the four disciplinary factors had very low relationships with the factor.

Table 45 shows the correlations of Spread of the Campus and Friendliness of the Dorm Counselor or Housemother with the 25 factors identified in the three previous chapters. The multiple correlations (given in the last row of Table 45) indicate that Campus Spread is only moderately related to these previously identified factors and that Friendliness of the Dorm Counselor or Housemother has only a negligible relationship with them. In spite of these relatively low correlations, the larger ones are generally consistent with our interpretation of these two factors from the physical envi-

Table 45

Correlations of the Physical Environment with the Peer, Classroom, and Administrative Environments

Factor	Physical Environmental Factor: Spread of the Campus	Friendliness of Housemother or Dormitory Counselor
A. Peer Environment:		
Competitiveness vs. Cooperativeness	.27	−.01
Organized Dating	.19	−.06
Independence	−.15	.08
Cohesiveness	−.24	−.19
Informal Dating	.14	−.03
Femininity	.16	−.07
Drinking vs. Religiousness	.18	.07
Musical & Artistic Activity	−.16	.21
Leisure Time	.16	−.20
Career Indecision	.07	.10
Regularity of Sleeping Habits	−.12	−.09
Use of the Library	−.19	.03
Conflict with Regulations	−.03	−.23
Student Employment	−.11	.09
Use of Automobiles	.05	.08
B. Classroom Environment:		
Involvement in the Class	−.36	−.09
Verbal Aggressiveness	−.18	.12
Extraversion of the Instructor	−.08	−.02
Familiarity with the Instructor	−.43	.16
Organization in the Classroom	−.15	−.12
Severity of Grading	.19	−.21
C. Administrative Environment:		
Severity of Administrative Policy Against:		
Drinking	−.22	−.10
Aggression	.15	−.23
Heterosexual Activity	−.08	−.32
Cheating	−.02	−.10
Multiple R from above factors	.65	.39

ronment. The larger institutions, for example, tend to have peer environments that are relatively competitive. The peer environments of the smaller institutions, on the other hand, tend to be more cooperative and cohesive. In particular, the smaller institutions manifest a distinctive pattern of classroom environmental stimuli—involvement in the class and familiarity with the instructor—which is probably a result of the tendency for geographically smaller institutions to have smaller classes.

The pattern of correlations with Friendliness of the Dorm Counselor or Housemother is also consistent with the meaning of this factor, although the correlations are very small. At institutions where the housemother or dorm counselor is regarded as relatively unfriendly, for example, there tends to be a higher degree of conflict with the regulations, more severe grading practices, and more severe administrative policies concerning the students' heterosexual behavior and aggression.

The relatively unproductive factor analysis of stimuli from the physical environment may have been caused in part by the heterogeneous nature of the original 37-item pool. Thus, it is to be expected that distinctive patterns of physical stimuli will be difficult to identify when one looks at such diverse sources as demographic characteristics (type of town), location of the campus and town buildings with respect to the students' living quarters, climate, and characteristics of living quarters. In future research on the college environment, it may be desirable to explore further the physical environment by identifying a larger number of stimuli in each of these categories. It seems likely, for example, that distinctive patterns of the demographic characteristics of the town and community in which the college is located could be identified if more detailed information about the nature of the college town were used. This additional information might include data on the relationships between the townspeople and the college students, between the townspeople and the administration, and so forth. It might also be wise to include information about the economic relationships between the college community and the surrounding town.

Certain clues to the importance of these demographic characteristics are provided by the correlations between them and the factors previously identified in the analyses of the peer, classroom, and administrative environments. Colleges that are located in small towns, for example, tend to have peer environments characterized by cohesiveness ($r = .39$), a large amount of leisure time ($r = .28$), and a low rate of drinking ($r = -.22$). Their classroom environments are usually characterized by a high degree of familiarity with the instructor ($r = .32$) and a low rate of verbal aggression ($r = -.22$). The small-town college's administrative environment is often marked by relatively severe policies concerning student drinking ($r = .21$). Although these relationships are generally low, they nevertheless indicate that the demography of institutions may have some significance in terms of the pattern of environmental stimuli that the student is likely to encounter.

SUMMARY

In this chapter, we have attempted to examine some of the stimuli from the physical environments of the 238 noncommuter institutions in our sample. An examination of 37 different stimuli once again demonstrated a remarkable degree of diversity within the sample. The factor analysis of the intercorrelations among these items revealed only two interpretable factors: Spread of the Campus, which relates primarily to the distance of various buildings from the students' living quarters, and Friendliness of the Dorm Counselor or Housemother, which relates to the students' perceptions of the supervisory person in their living quarters. Spread of the Campus overlaps only moderately with the factors previously identified in the analysis of stimuli from the peer, classroom, and administrative environments. Friendliness of the Dorm Counselor or Housemother had even less overlap with these other factors. It was concluded that additional studies of the physical environments of higher educational institutions should include much more detailed information concerning the physical facilities and demography of the institution.

6

The College Image

THE PRECEDING FOUR chapters have presented some of the principal patterns of stimuli that differentiate among college environments. In describing these patterns, we have attempted to utilize the student primarily as an *observer* of the stimuli in his environment. In the current chapter, however, we view the student not merely as an objective observer but as an *interpreter* of his college environment.

The student's subjective interpretation or impressions of his college environment depend not only on the particular patterns of environmental stimuli to which he is exposed, but also on his values, attitudes, abilities, previous experiences, and other personal characteristics. In one sense, the student's "image" of his college environment at a given point in time is simply his subjective response to a particular set of environmental stimuli; in another sense, it is a potentially important frame of reference for interpreting and responding to new stimuli. Thus, the student's image of his college is both a response to his environment and a potential determinant of his future responses.

The students' perceptions of their colleges were assessed by means of 75 items from the Inventory of College Activities. The largest subgroup consisted of 35 items similar to those used in the CCI, CUES, and other instruments designed to measure the student's perception of his environment (see Chapter 1). Some examples of these items are:

> Being in this college builds poise and maturity.
> There isn't much to do except go to class and study.
> The faculty seem to be interested more in research than in teaching students.

Students were instructed to "Answer each of the following [yes or no] as it applies to your college." Scores for a given college on each item consisted of the percentage of students who responded "yes."

A second group of items, which consisted of 17 adjectives (e.g., intellectual, snobbish, competitive), was preceded by the following question: "To what extent does each of the following describe the psychological *climate* or *atmosphere* at your college?" Students were asked to indicate for each adjective whether it was very descriptive, in between, or not at all descriptive.

A third group of 20 items was designed to determine whether the student was satisfied with various aspects of his freshman college year: e.g., his freedom in selecting courses, amount of social life, amount of intellectual activity, number of personal contacts with the faculty. Students were given the following instructions: "All in all, in terms of your own needs and desires, how much of the following did you receive during your freshman year?" There were three possible alternatives: too much or too many, just about the right amount, not enough.[1]

The final three items concerning the student's subjective impressions of his college are shown below:

1. Is your average grade [during the freshman year in college] a fair indication of your ability? (Five-point scale, ranging from "It grossly under-represents my ability" to "It grossly over-represents my ability.")
2. Have you ever felt "out of place" at this college? (Four-point scale: "Yes, all of the time"; "Yes, frequently"; "Yes, but only occasionally"; "No, never.")
3. "What is your over-all evaluation of your college so far?" (Five-point scale: "Very satisfied"; "Satisfied"; "On the fence"; "Dissatisfied"; "Very dissatisfied.")

The score for a given college on each of these last 40 items consisted of the median score obtained by all students reponsing to the item.

DIVERSITY IN THE COLLEGE IMAGE

Table 46 shows the scores for the lowest, median, and highest of the 246 institutions on selected items concerning the student's perception of his college environment. The range of scores on these items reveals that the perceptions of students at different colleges are as diverse as the environmental stimuli discussed in the preceding chapters. An inspection of the middle column of data in Table 46 (median institutional scores) indicates the general direction of scores for the entire sample. For example, students at the median or typical institution are inclined to feel that both the faculty and the upperclassmen go out of their way to offer help and that they are granted a good deal of independence. These students are *not* apt to feel

[1] These items have been adapted from a pool of items originally used in student studies conducted at Yale University.

Table 46

The College Image: Diversity Among 246 Institutions

Item	Scores for:		
	Lowest Inst.	Median Inst.	Highest Inst.
Percentages of students answering "yes":			
Students are under a great deal of pressure to get high grades	0.0	37.8	89.1
Upperclassmen go out of their way to help new students	23.5	67.6	98.7
It's important socially to be in the right club or group	0.0	29.5	90.0
Athletes are given special privileges	0.0	25.6	86.2
Faculty go out of their way to help the student	35.4	81.1	100.0
Most students are more like "numbers in a book"	0.0	6.7	79.5
There is a great deal of conformity among the students	3.1	59.5	92.9
Great deal of independence is granted the student	3.5	79.7	100.0
Student publications often openly ridicule the administrative policies	0.0	34.8	96.0
*Mean Score:**			
Intellectual	1.69	2.24	3.00
Sophisticated	1.31	1.72	2.73
Social	1.37	2.17	2.86
Liberal	1.31	2.23	2.95
Arty	1.21	1.67	2.63

* Based on a three-point scale: 3-"very descriptive"; 2-"in-between"; 1-"not at all descriptive."

that they are under a great deal of pressure to get high grades, that student publications openly ridicule the administration, that it is important socially to be in the right club or group, that athletes are given special privileges, or that they are treated like "numbers in a book." However, these general trends should not obscure the fact that students at certain of the 246 institutions perceive their college environments quite differently.

The second set of items shown in Table 46 comprises those adjectives which show the greatest variation in mean scores among institutions. Although it is not surprising to find that some institutions are rated as intellectual by all of their students, we did not expect that a substantial proportion of students at certain institutions would consider this adjective to be not at all descriptive of their college environment.

Since all of the student observers at an institution were presumably rating the same environment, it seemed reasonable to suppose that the distribution of the 246 institutional mean scores on each item would be bimodal—that is, that the majority of students at each college would agree that the item either did or did not accurately describe the environment. An examination of the distribution of mean scores does not, however, support this expectation. On the contrary, most of the distributions were relatively unimodal and symmetrical. Thus, instead of finding a high degree of commonality in the perceptions of the students at a college, we frequently encounter great disagreement, perhaps because not every student at an institution is exposed to exactly the same pattern of environmental stimuli. The particular stimuli which impinge upon him may vary, depending, for example, on the characteristics of his roommate, the particular professors who happen to be assigned to teach his courses, and—as we have already seen in Chapter 3—the type of curriculum in which he is enrolled. Still more important a determinant of the student's perception, perhaps, is the frame of reference from which he views the various environmental stimuli. What one student may feel as heavy pressure to get high grades, for example, may be perceived by another student at the same college as normal and appropriate academic standards. Although the research reported here is concerned primarily with the commonalities in student perceptions of their college environment, it is important to recognize that at only a few institutions are the students unanimous or nearly unanimous in their responses to most items,

Table 47 shows the range of scores and the median scores for the 246 institutions on each of the 20 items describing the students' sources of satisfaction or dissatisfaction with their college. In a sense, these data can be regarded as documentation of the American college freshman's over-all reaction to specific aspects of his freshman year. A mean score near 2.00 means that the average student at the institution felt that he had received just about the right amount of whatever is described in the item. Higher scores (the highest possible being 3.00) indicate that the students feel that they received not enough during their freshman year; a mean score below 2.00 (the lowest possible being 1.00) indicates that the students feel that they had received too much or too many. Although there is extensive variation between items and also among institutions on given items, students are inclined to report that they have received an inadequate amount. Because most of the 20 items refer to positive attributes of the college, this trend is probably to be expected.

Freshmen students appear to be best satisfied with the number of friends that they had and with the frequency of their personal contacts with classmates. Both mean scores here are very close to 2.00, and variation among institutions is quite small. Although the median institutional scores on "examinations on course material" and "liberal studies not closely related to

Table 47

Mean Satisfaction Scores* of Students at 246 Institutions

Item	Range of Mean Scores:		
	Lowest Inst.	Median Inst.	Highest Inst.
Personal direction in studies and in course selection	2.03	2.22	2.53
Freedom in course selection	1.68	2.15	2.72
Opportunity for classroom discussion	1.99	2.16	2.41
Social life	1.89	2.24	2.84
Extracurricular activity	1.64	2.23	2.50
Intellectual activity	1.95	2.23	2.46
Personal contacts with classmates	1.86	2.07	2.29
Personal contacts with faculty	2.11	2.37	2.83
Time for social activity	1.95	2.24	2.89
Time for extracurricular activity	1.95	2.30	2.66
Time for intellectual activity	1.95	2.25	2.54
Work required of you in courses	1.65	2.00	2.50
Outlets for creative activities	2.09	2.41	2.65
Occupational or professional preparation	2.04	2.36	2.59
Liberal studies not closely related to any occupation	1.77	2.02	2.56
Examinations on course material	1.89	2.06	2.59
Dates	2.06	2.28	2.89
Friends	1.96	2.10	2.22
Sleep	2.17	2.50	2.76
Exercise	1.68	2.38	2.76

* Based on a three-point scale: 3-"not enough;" 2-"just about the right amount;" 1-"too much or too many."

Note: A mean score near 2.00 indicates that the typical student feels that the institution provides "just the right amount." A mean score near 3.00 indicates that most students feel that there is "not enough." A mean score near 1.00 means that most of the students feel that there is "too much."

any occupation" are also very close to 2.00, the variation among the 246 institutions is extensive. This finding indicates that, even though students at the typical institution are very well satisfied with the number of examinations and the number of liberal studies required, at some institutions many students feel that they have not been given enough, and at others they feel that too many have been required.

Students at most institutions seem to feel that they have not had enough sleep, exercise, occupational or professional preparation, outlets for creative activities, and personal contacts with faculty. Every institution in the sample had a mean score greater than 2.00 on each of these items, with the exception of "exercise," where one institution—a military academy—had a mean score in the direction of "too much." The greatest variation among institutions was in the degree of satisfaction reported by students on freedom in course selection, extracurricular activity, intellectual activity, time for social activity, work required in courses, and dates. While the scores for most of the institutions were in the direction of "not enough" on these items, there were at least a few institutions where the mean tended toward "too much or too many" on every item except "dates."

The range of institutional mean scores on the over-all evaluation of the college was from 3.4 (midway between "on the fence" and "satisfied") and 4.6 (midway between "satisfied" and "very satisfied"), with a median score of 4.2

In summary, these results suggest that most students at most institutions are relatively well satisfied with many aspects of their freshman college year. However, this general conclusion should be tempered by a recognition that degrees of reported satisfaction varied considerably among the 246 institutions and that students at several institutions reported moderate and even substantial dissatisfaction with certain areas.

DIMENSIONS OF THE COLLEGE IMAGE

Eight identifiable factors emerged from the analysis of correlations among the 75 items concerning the students' subjective impressions of their colleges.[2] The first college image factor, Academic Competitiveness, is shown in Table 48. The degree of Academic Competitiveness is defined primarily in terms of the perceived pressures for high grades and the perceived competitiveness among the students. Students at colleges with highly competitive images are likely to see their fellow students as being very able academically and as feeling that their college is superior to other colleges. Students at these institutions also feel that their college has an outstanding reputation nationally and that its environment is both tense and enterprising. In contrast, students at colleges with less competitive images feel that intellectual activity is low, that not enough work is required in class, and that the environment is carefree.

The several student behaviors and personal characteristics that correlate highly with Academic Competitiveness indicate that this college image factor has some basis in fact. To illustrate, one student behavior, median num-

[2] Diagonal values consisted of the highest correlation. At least 1 percent of the total communality was accounted for by each of the first 11 components. However, the most interpretable simple structure was obtained by rotating the first eight components, which accounted for 94.6 percent of the total communality. The communalities for the 75 items across the eight rotated factors were fairly high. Fifty-six of the 75 items had communalities exceeding .50, and nearly half of the items had communalities exceeding .70. Of the seven items with communalities less than .40, three were concerned with the students' degree of satisfaction with specific aspects of their college experience; two others of these seven items were concerned with the students' impressions of the college library.

Table 48

Academic Competitiveness

Variable	r with Factor Score
A. Correlated Aspects of the College Image	
Students are under a great deal of pressure to get high grades	.95*
There is keen competition among most of the students for high grades	.92*
Competitive	.82
Most of the students are of a very high calibre academically	.80*
Intellectual	.77
This college has an outstanding reputation nationally	.68
Students have a sense of superiority with regard to most other colleges	.68
Calibre of students (NORC)	.63
Evaluation of curricular offerings (NORC)	.60
Tense	.60
Enterprising	.59
Professional standing of faculty (NORC)	.51
Students value having a good time (NORC)	−.73
Students value getting along with people (NORC)	−.69
Not enough intellectual activity	−.63
Carefree	−.61
Not enough work required in class	−.53
B. Correlated Peer Stimuli	
Hours per week spent studying	.85
C. Correlated Student Personal Characteristics	
Percent planning graduate work	.63
Value being original (NORC)	.63
Major in Scientific field	.59
High school grades	.59
Vocational choice in Scientific class	.57
Took NMSQT test in high school	.57
Intellectualism of entering class	.55
Placed in a state science contest in high school	.54
Intelligent (self-rating)	.54
Natural science reading aptitude (NMSQT)	.53
Academic ability (NMSQT composite)	.52
Mathematics aptitude (NMSQT)	.52
Social science reading aptitude (NMSQT)	.52
Family income (NORC)	.51
Planning to get a graduate degree	.51
Percent Merit Scholars in student body	.51
Planning to get a Ph.D. degree	.51
Parents influenced plans (NORC)	−.67
Adviser influenced plans (NORC)	−.64
Value getting along with people (NORC)	−.62
D. Correlated Characteristics of the College	
Selectivity	.59

* Used in computing the factor score.

ber of hours per week that freshman students spend studying, correlated .58 with Academic Competitiveness. Students in colleges with highly competitive images also manifest a pattern of personal characteristics that is consistent with the interpretation of the factor: They have high academic ability, high aspirations for educational attainment, and an interest in science. Their colleges enroll large proportions both of Merit Scholars and of students who made high grades in secondary school. As is to be expected, colleges with high scores on Academic Competitiveness tend to be relatively selective.

The NORC items correlating highly with this factor are remarkably similar in content to the ICA items just mentioned. For example, Academic Competitiveness is positively correlated with the rated academic calibre of the students and with the students' high evaluation of the curricular offerings. Similarly, it is negatively correlated with the extent to which the students say that the students value having a good time and getting along with people. As for the personal characteristics of the students as revealed by the NORC items, Academic Competitiveness is positively correlated with assigning a high value to being original and with the average income of the students' parents.

While these findings suggest that the students' perceptions of the degree of Academic Competitiveness at their college has some basis in reality, the correlations of this factor with time spent in studying and with the students' level of academic ability and academic motivation are only moderate. It might be worthwhile in future research to try to identify the factors that account for the development of a college image which is not entirely consistent with the objective realities.

Of the various types of institutions, technological institutions and teachers colleges show the greatest discrepancies from the typical college (see Figure 10). Whereas all the technological institutions had above-average scores on Academic Competitiveness, none of the teachers colleges scored above the institutional average.

The second college image factor, Concern for the Individual Student, is shown in Table 49. This factor accounted for more of the variance (10 percent) among the 75 college image items than did any of the other seven image factors. Concern for the Individual Student is positively associated with the extent to which freshmen see the faculty and the upperclassmen as going out of their way to help students. Colleges which are viewed as having relatively great concern for the individual student tend to be rated as warm, friendly, and high in morale. Their students spend a fairly large

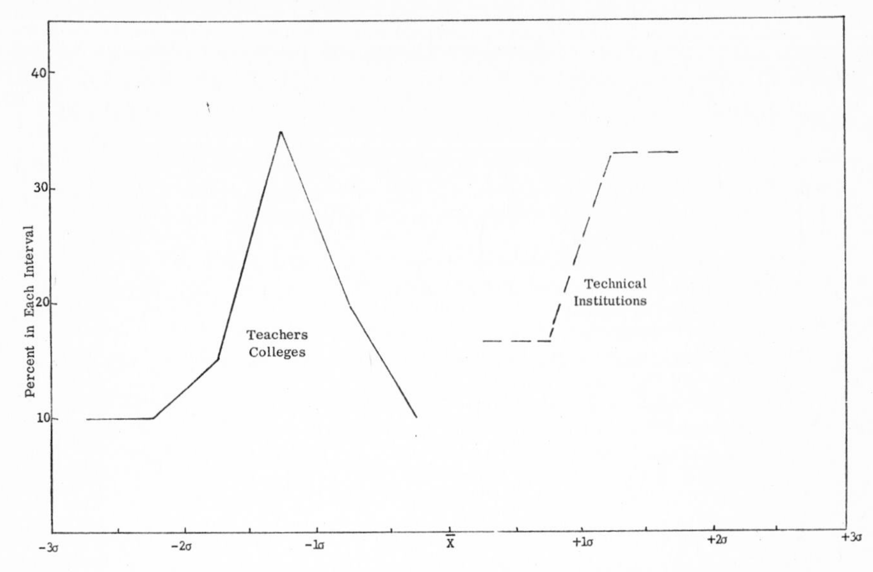

Fig. 10. Scores of Teachers Colleges (N = 20) and Technical Institutions (N = 6) on Academic Competitiveness.

Table 49

Concern for the Individual Student

Variable	R with Factor Score
A. Correlated Aspects of the College Image	
Faculty go out of their way to help the student	.84
Upperclassmen go out of their way to help new students	.81
Warm	.78*
College should provide basic education and appreciation of ideas (NORC)	.66
It is a friendly campus	.61
High morale	.54
Positive evaluation of the faculty (NORC)	.53
Most students are more like "numbers in a book"	−.94*
Administration is not really very concerned about the individual student	−.80
I felt "lost" when I first came to the campus	−.73*
Faculty seem to be interested more in research than in teaching students	−.73
College should provide career training (NORC)	−.67
Not enough personal direction in studies and in course selection	−.63
Not enough personal contacts with faculty	−.62
Athletes are given special privileges	−.50
Campus is too big	−.50

* Used in computing the factor score.

Table 49 (Continued)

Variable	r with Factor Score
B. Correlated Peer Stimuli	
Hours per week spent participating in musical, dramatic, or artistic activities	.65
Participated in informal group singing	.63
Participated in music and dramatic arts (NORC)	.63
Participated in varsity athletics (NORC)	.63
Attended a student stage play	.61
Number of students called by their first names	.56
Worked on the school paper (NORC)	.56
Sang in a choir or glee club	.51
Said "hello" to students you didn't know	.50
Discussed religion with other students	.50
Musical & Artistic Activity factor	.50
Competitiveness vs. Cooperativeness factor	−.61
C. Correlated Classroom Stimuli	
Instructor knew me by name	.57
D. Correlated Physical Stimuli	
Spread of the Campus factor	−.55
E. Correlated Student Personal Characteristics	
Pragmatism of entering class	−.54
Major in Realistic field	−.51
Vocational choice in Realistic class	−.50
F. Correlated Characteristics of the College	
Liberal arts college	.66
Size of entering class	−.71
University	−.62
Public control	−.50

amount of time participating in musical, dramatic, and artistic activities, and they tend to be cooperative rather than competitive in their interpersonal relations. Instructors in these colleges are more likely to know their students by name than are instructors in colleges where concern for the individual student is low.

Colleges that are seen as showing little concern for the individual student are best typified by the item "Most students are more like 'numbers in a book'." Students at these institutions report that they felt lost when they first came to the institution, that the faculty is more interested in research than in teaching, that athletes are given special privileges, and that the campus is too big. Furthermore, they tend to feel that they have not had enough personal direction in their studies and course selection and that their personal contact with faculty members has been insufficient.

The degree of perceived concern for the individual student tends to be much higher at liberal arts colleges than at universities, partly, perhaps, because of the substantial negative correlation of Concern for the Individual Student with size of enrollment and physical size. Indeed, it is likely that differential institutional size mediates many of the correlations shown in Table 49.

The third factor identified in the analysis of the college image, School Spirit, is shown in Table 50. Environments which are seen as being high in school spirit are perceived as fostering poise and maturity and as having high morale. Students at such institutions also report that they are relatively well satisfied with their over-all experience during the freshman year. Institutions low in school spirit, on the other hand, have student bodies that are rated as apathetic and not well-rounded. Students at such institutions are also inclined to feel that there is little to do except to go to class and study.

These interpretations are confirmed by the NORC items that have high correlations with the factor. Institutions that are rated high in school spirit, for example, tend to have students whose loyalty to the institution is judged to be relatively strong. Institutions attended by high percentages either of commuter students or of students who live in large cities tend to be rated low in school spirit.

Table 50

School Spirit

Variable	r with Factor Score
A. Correlated Aspects of the College Image	
Being in this college builds poise and maturity	.81*
High morale	.63
Over-all satisfaction with the college	.60
Facilities for research (NORC)	.50
Student body is apathetic and has little "school spirit"	−.79*
Students are not well-rounded	−.56
There isn't much to do except go to class and study	−.53*
B. Correlated Student Personal Characteristics	
Institutional loyalty is strong (NORC)	.63
Home is located in large city (NORC)	−.54
Lived at home during freshman year (NORC)	−.51

* Used in computing the factor score.

The fourth factor identified in the analysis of students' perceptions of their college environment, Permissiveness, is shown in Table 51. Permissiveness is best characterized by the adjective "liberal." Institutions that are perceived as highly permissive seem to allow the student a good deal of independence and to have a faculty which is liberal in interpreting regulations. Classes are described as being very informal, and the intellectual atmosphere is rated as more theoretical than practical. Finally, students at highly permissive institutions are seen as tending to be avant-garde and to be relatively unconcerned with their personal appearance. These last two correlations suggest that permissiveness may be connected with the amount of student protest and student activism on the campus. Although these data were collected before the advent of the Berkeley Free Speech Movement and similar student protest demonstrations, a recent study (Astin, 1967) shows that Permissiveness correlates .40 with the total amount of student protest during the 1964-65 academic year as reported by representatives of these institutions (Peterson, 1966; Sasajima, Davis & Peterson, 1967).

The rate of drinking among freshmen attending permissive institutions is rather high. The students are also likely not to be religious and to describe themselves as unconventional. They are, however, inclined to give a favorable rating to the course offerings, the facilities for research, and the professional standing of their faculty.

Institutions that are perceived as low in permissiveness tend to be called "Victorian" by the students. The students at such institutions are inclined to feel that the college paper and humor magazine are censored and that the campus is pervaded by a narrow political point of view. They are also more likely than students at permissive institutions to pray, to attend church, and to rate themselves as religious.

Permissiveness has moderate negative correlations with Severity of Administrative Policies Against Aggression and Against Heterosexual Activity and a large negative correlation with Severity of Administrative Policy Against Drinking. These findings reveal once more that there is substantial agreement between the objective characteristics of the institution, on the one hand, and its image, on the other, though the extent of correspondence is far from perfect.

The fifth college image factor, Snobbishness, is shown in Table 52. Colleges with high scores on this factor tend to be rated as snobbish and sophisticated; their students are inclined to say that the intellectual atmosphere is theoretical rather than practical and that there is a large group of avant-garde students on campus (two correlates which suggest that this fac-

Table 51

Permissiveness

Variable	r with Factor Score
A. Correlated Aspects of the College Image	
Liberal	.94*
Great deal of independence is granted the student	.83
Faculty is usually liberal in interpreting regulations and treats violations with understanding and tolerance	.68
Classes are usually run in a very informal manner	.65*
Students here are not particularly concerned about their personal appearance	.59
Positive evaluation of course offerings (NORC)	.59
There is a large group of "avant-garde" students on campus	.58
Professional standing of the faculty (NORC)	.56
Facilities for research (NORC)	.56
Intellectual atmosphere is definitely on the theoretical, rather than the practical side	.53
Victorian	−.81*
Campus paper and humor magazine are censored by the administration	−.68
There is a narrow political point of view on campus	−.54
B. Correlated Peer Stimuli	
Drinking vs. Religiousness factor	.67
Became intoxicated	.61
Drank wine	.59
Drank beer	.56
Drank whiskey or other hard liquor	.55
Overslept and missed a class or appointment	.54
Argued with other students	.52
Went to a foreign movie	.52
Prayed (not including grace before meals)	−.64
Attended church	−.61
Said grace before meals	−.55
Read the Bible	−.53
C. Correlated Classroom Stimuli	
Students permitted to smoke in class	.63
D. Correlated Administrative Stimuli	
Severity of Administrative Policy Against Drinking factor	−.70
Severity of Administrative Policy Against Heterosexual Activity factor	−.58
Severity of Administrative Policy Against Aggression factor	−.50
E. Correlated Student Personal Characteristics	
Religion none (NORC)	.66
Unconventional (self-rating) (NORC)	.65
Very nonreligious (self-rating) (NORC)	.64
Religious (self-rating)	−.61
Very religious (NORC)	−.52

* Used in computing the factor score.

Table 52

Snobbishness

Variable	r with Factor Score
A. Correlated Aspects of the College Image	
Snobbish	.76*
Felt "out of place" at this college	.61
Sophisticated	.58
Intellectual atmosphere is definitely on the theoretical, rather than the practical side	.58
There is a large group of "avant-garde" students on campus	.56
Practical-minded	−.88*
Realistic	−.75*
B. Correlated Peer Stimulus	
Went to a foreign movie	.50
C. Correlated Student Personal Characteristics	
Father's educational level	.58
Status of entering freshman class	.57
Father a professional or executive	.57
Father's occupation in Scientific class	.56
Prefer to work with people (NORC)	.56
Father's occupation in Enterprising class	.55
Father's occupation in Realistic class	−.58

* Used in computing the factor score.

tor might also be called "Intellectual Snobbery" or perhaps "Highbrow-ism").

The extent to which students are likely to report that they feel out of place at the college is also positively related to snobbishness, which is, in fact, the only college image or college environmental factor even moderately related to this item.

The only stimulus item from the peer environment correlating as much as .50 with Snobbishness is the percentage of students who reported attending foreign movies during their freshman year. The correlated student personal characteristics indicate that there is a tendency for students from the higher socioeconomic levels to attend the more snobbish institutions. Snobbishness is positively correlated with the level of the father's education, the status (parents' educational level) of the entering freshman class, and the percentage of fathers who are professionals or executives.

Institutions that are rated low in snobbishness are likely to be seen as practical-minded and realistic. The students' fathers are relatively likely to be employed in Realistic occupations (mostly skilled trades).

The sixth college image factor, Emphasis on Athletics, is shown in Table 53. This factor is defined primarily by the extent to which the students report that athletics are overemphasized and athletes given special privileges. Students attending athletically-minded institutions spend a relatively large amount of time watching sports events.

Students attending institutions which are not perceived as heavily emphasizing athletics are inclined to report that they did not get enough exercise during their freshman year. They also tend to be above average in verbal ability. This last finding appears to be a consequence of two factors: The brighter students are usually less interested in athletics, and women generally have more verbal ability and less interest in athletics than men do.

Table 53

Emphasis on Athletics

Variable	r with Factor Score
A. Correlated Aspects of the College Image	
Athletics are overemphasized here	.70*
Athletes are given special privileges	.57*
There isn't much to do except go to class and study	.55
Not enough exercise	−.62*
B. Correlated Peer Stimuli	
Time spent watching athletic events (intercollegiate or intramural)	.54
C. Correlated Student Personal Characteristic	
Word usage (NMQT)	−.52

* Used in computing the factor score.

The correlation between Emphasis on Athletics and the percentage of students who report that there is little to do except go to class and study is puzzling; in part, it may reflect the students' dissatisfaction with the college that emphasizes athletics (Emphasis on Athletics had a modest negative correlation of −.28 with the students' over-all evaluation of their college).

The seventh factor identified in the analyses of students' perceptions of their college environment, Flexibility of the Curriculum, is shown in Table 54. Note that all four of the items listed in the table are concerned with the college image; none of the items pertaining to environmental stimuli or

Table 54

Flexibility of the Curriculum

Variable	r with Factor Score
A. Correlated Aspects of the College Image	
Not enough outlets for creative activities	−.74*
Not enough freedom in course selection	−.73*
Too much work required in courses	−.55*
Not enough time for extracurricular activity	−.51

* Used in computing the factor score.

student personal characteristics correlated as much as .50 with this factor. Institutions perceived as inflexible in their curricula are seen by the freshmen as requiring too much work in courses, and as not offering enough in the way of outlets for creative activity, freedom in course selection, and time for extracurricular activities. Two other items which produce correlations approaching .50 may be of interest: Flexibility of the Curriculum correlated .46 with the percentage of students who reported that they "took a course over and above requirements" and −.43 with the item "There are too many required courses here." Flexibility of the Curriculum also correlated −.41 with an institution's being located in the northeastern region of the United States. Apparently, freshmen attending institutions in this region are inclined to feel that too many courses are required and that they are not given enough freedom to select their own courses of study.

The highest scores on Flexibility of the Curriculum were obtained by public institutions, and the lowest scores were obtained by Roman Catholic institutions (see Figure 11). Thus, 61 percent of the public institutions and only seven percent of the Roman Catholic institutions obtained above-average scores on this factor.

Table 55 shows the last factor identified in these analyses, Emphasis on Social Life, a factor obviously concerned with the extent to which the students feel that the social aspects of their life at college is stressed. Institutions with high scores are rated as social and carefree and as overemphasizing the students' social life. Their students are likely to feel that it is important to belong to the right club or group, that fraternity and sorority life is overemphasized, that there is a great deal of conformity among the students, and that the amount of intellectual activity on the campus is too low. In contrast, students attending institutions which are seen as giving less emphasis to social life are likely to complain that they do not have enough

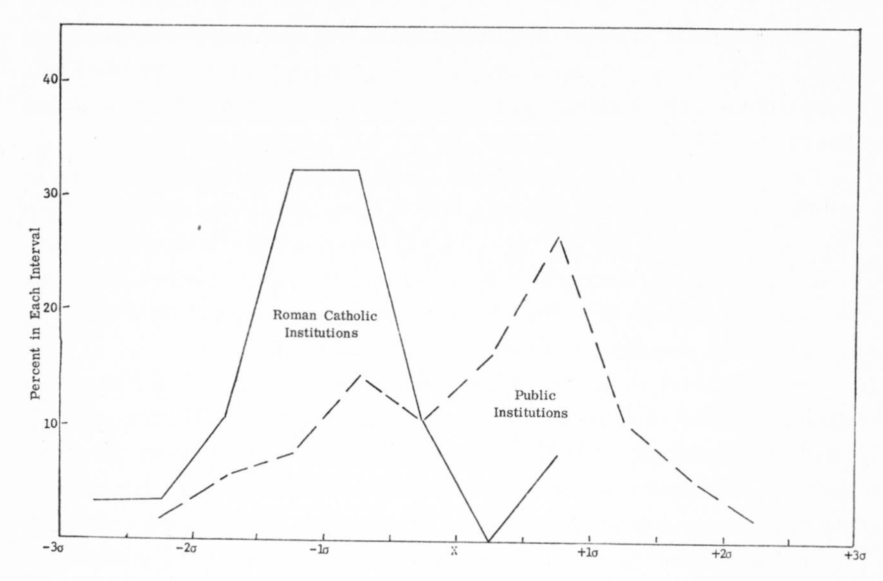

Fig. 11. Scores of Public (N = 56) and Roman Catholic (N = 28) Institutions on Flexibility of the Curriculum.

social life or time for social activities or dates, and that there is not much to do except to go to class and study. Although the rating of the environment as not providing enough "personal contacts with classmates" entered into the computation of the factor score with a small negative weight, its correlation with the factor score was only −.40.

Table 55

Emphasis on Social Life

VARIABLE	R WITH FACTOR SCORE
A. Correlated Aspects of the College Image	
Social	.93*
Social activities are overemphasized	.81
It's important socially to be in the right club or group	.64
Students value having a good time (NORC)	.64
Carefree	.63
There is too much emphasis on fraternities and sororities	.60
Not enough intellectual activity	.53
There is a great deal of conformity among the students	.52
Not enough social life	−.89*
Not enough time for social activity	−.68
Not enough dates	−.61
There isn't much to do except go to class and study	−.55
(Not enough personal contacts with classmates)	(−.40*)

* Used in computing the factor score.

The moderate positive correlation of .51 between Emphasis on Social Life and the frequency with which students reported that they went to a party during their freshman year indicates that this college image factor has some basis in fact.

The various types of institutions show an interesting configuration of scores on Emphasis on Social Life (see Figure 12). Three-fourths of both the universities and the teachers colleges scored above the over-all institutional mean on this factor, although there was much more variation within the university group. By contrast, every one of the technological institutions scored at least one standard deviation below the mean.

The intercorrelations among the eight measures of the college image are shown in Table 56. Most of the correlations are quite small, with only one coefficient exceeding .30. The largest coefficients are, however, consistent with the definitions of the image factors. Academic Competitiveness, for example, is negatively related both to Emphasis on Athletics and to Emphasis on Social Life. Although these coefficients and several of the others are statistically significant, their relatively small size indicates that these eight variables can be regarded as relatively independent measures of the college image.

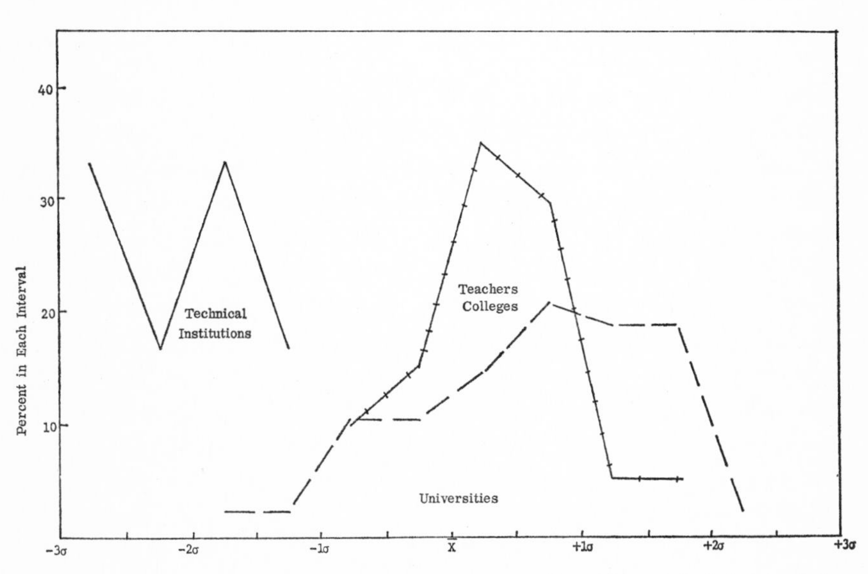

Fig. 12. Scores of Universities (N = 48), Teachers Colleges (N = 20), and Technical Institutions (N = 6) on Emphasis on Social Life.

Table 56

Intercorrelations of the Eight Factors of the College Image

Image Factor	2	3	4	5	6	7	8
1. Academic Competitiveness	.07	.08	.09	.12	−.29	−.11	−.32
2. Concern for the Individual Student		.18	−.13	−.17	−.15	−.05	−.20
3. School Spirit			−.08	−.27	−.25	.12	.20
4. Permissiveness				.21	−.12	.17	.12
5. Snobbishness					−.13	.01	.08
6. Emphasis on Athletics						.09	−.05
7. Flexibility of the Curriculum							.17
8. Emphasis on Social Life							

THE RELATIONSHIP BETWEEN THE COLLEGE IMAGE AND THE COLLEGE ENVIRONMENT

A casual inspection of these results suggests that very few, if any, of the image factors can be directly matched on a one-to-one basis with the environmental stimulus factors described in the earlier chapters. This observation is supported by the data given in Table 57, which shows the correlations between each of the eight image factors and the 27 factors derived from the analyses of environmental stimuli. The last column in Table 57 shows the multiple correlation coefficients between each environmental factor and the eight college image factors; the last row in the table shows the multiple correlations between each image factor and the 27 environmental factors. Two of the image factors—Concern for the Individual Student and Permissiveness—seem to overlap substantially the environmental factors, but the other six have only a moderate degree of overlap. In general, the environmental factors receiving the greatest weights in each multiple regression solution are consistent with the meaning of the image factor which is used as the dependent variable. For example, in the equation for estimating Concern for the Individual Student, large positive weights are assigned to Musical and Artistic Activity, Involvement in the Class, and Familiarity with the Instructor. Negative weights (indicating lack of concern for the student), on the other hand, are assigned to Competitiveness (versus Cooperativeness), Severity of Grading Practices, and Spread of the Campus.

The peer environments of institutions perceived by the students as relatively permissive tend to manifest independence, competitiveness, and drinking. Students in colleges that are perceived as relatively restrictive tend to be cohesive and to have regular sleeping habits; their classes inspire involvement and are organized. The college with a relatively restrictive image, as we have already seen, tend to have rather severe policies against drinking, heterosexual activity, and aggression.

The fact that Academic Competitiveness was not correlated even as much as .40 with any environmental factor was surprising, since the folklore of higher education suggests that this is one of the principal differentiating characteristics of the college environment. An analysis of a wide range of environmental stimuli, however, failed to reveal any factor that is comparable or parallel to the image of Academic Competitiveness. Nevertheless, those environmental factors that have the highest correlations with Academic Competitiveness appear to be consistent with the meaning of this image factor, which correlates positively with Independence and negatively with Leisure Time and Severity of Administrative Policies Against Aggression.

College environments that are seen as snobbish tend to have independent, verbally aggressive students who go in for a relatively large amount of drinking and organized dating, and their administrative policies about cheating tend to be rather strict. Institutions seen as low on snobbishness, on the other hand, tend to manifest a high degree of cohesiveness, regularity of sleeping habits, and class involvement. Their administrative policies concerning drinking, heterosexual activity, and aggression are relatively severe.

Emphasis on Athletics produced one of the most interesting patterns of correlations with the environmental factors. Institutions that seem to their students to overemphasize athletics tend to have cohesive student bodies, to give students a large amount of leisure time, and to grade severely.

These results indicate that the pattern of factors emerging from the student's perceptions of the college environment is qualitatively different from the pattern of factors based on observable environmental stimuli. Although there is, of course, some degree of redundancy across the two domains, most of the factors in one domain are sufficiently independent of factors in the other domain to justify the assumption that the college image and the college environment involve somewhat different aspects of institutional differences.

It is difficult to explain why we failed to find college image factors that can be directly matched with corresponding factors from the environment. That these college image factors have *some* "validity," in that they correlate with certain environmental stimuli, is clear from the results shown in

Table 57

Correlations of the College Image with the College Environment

Environmental Factor	Image Factor								Multiple R from the College Image
	Academic Competitiveness	Concern for the Individual Student	School Spirit	Permissiveness	Snobbishness	Emphasis on Athletics	Flexibility of Curriculum	Emphasis on Social Life	
Peer Environment:									
Competitiveness vs. Cooperativeness	−.05	−.61	−.25	.35	.04	.25	−.05	.14	.63
Organized Dating	.02	.02	.16	.17	.32	−.13	.05	.38	.54
Independence	.34	.12	−.22	.40	.35	−.03	−.15	−.16	.63
Cohesiveness	−.25	.20	.04	−.37	−.41	.43	.03	.17	.64
Informal Dating	−.28	.05	−.10	.03	−.04	−.01	.29	.30	.54
Femininity	−.23	.15	.16	−.10	.07	−.23	.19	.21	.29
Drinking vs. Religiousness	.16	−.24	−.15	.67	.41	−.19	−.02	.13	.76
Musical & Artistic Activity	.23	.50	.17	.10	.14	−.24	.26	−.21	.59
Leisure Time	−.31	−.22	−.02	.10	−.03	.32	.20	.39	.45
Career Indecision	.19	.01	.10	.10	.15	−.29	.14	−.01	.31
Regularity of Sleeping Habits	−.26	.03	.16	−.42	−.42	.07	−.12	−.17	.59
Use of the Library	−.08	.24	.06	−.10	.11	−.08	−.07	−.08	.40
Conflict with Regulations	−.12	.11	.17	−.27	−.13	−.11	−.22	.12	.44
Student Employment	−.20	.03	−.06	.08	.22	.04	.15	−.08	.39
Use of Automobiles	−.29	−.18	−.06	.03	.14	.13	.12	.21	.29
Classroom Environment:									
Involvement in the Class	−.27	.44	.13	−.45	−.33	.13	−.07	−.12	.62

Table 57 (Continued)

Environmental Factor	Image Factor								Multiple R from the College Image
	Academic Competi-tiveness	Concern for the Indi-vidual Student	School Spirit	Permis-siveness	Snob-bishness	Emphasis on Athletics	Flexibility of Curricu-lum	Emphasis Social Life	
Verbal Aggressiveness	.19	.17	−.08	.28	.30	−.19	−.21	−.08	.61
Extraversion of the Instructor	.22	.11	.15	.13	−.04	−.15	.11	−.12	.27
Familiarity with the Instructor	.09	.42	−.16	.13	.05	.08	−.16	−.16	.60
Organization in the Classroom	−.23	.03	−.02	−.38	−.20	.20	−.08	.02	.40
Severity of Grading	−.24	−.45	−.12	−.10	−.23	.38	−.08	.26	.60
Administrative Environment:									
Severity of Administrative Policy Against:									
Drinking	−.12	.23	.14	−.70	−.30	.20	−.06	−.11	.75
Aggression	−.35	−.29	.10	−.50	−.31	.25	.02	.23	.66
Heterosexual Activity	−.26	−.02	.08	−.58	−.24	.16	−.20	.13	.59
Cheating	.14	−.05	.00	.04	.31	−.09	−.27	.02	.46
Physical Environment:									
Spread of the Campus	−.03	−.55	−.02	.06	.12	.00	.10	.23	.60
Friendliness of the House-mother or Dorm Counselor	.21	.12	.05	.19	.06	−.20	.09	−.14	.29
Multiple R from the College Environment	.64	.84	.49	.79	.66	.55	.66	.69	

Tables 48-55. The perceived Permissiveness of the college, for example, was substantially related to the amount of student drinking and negatively related to the amount of religious activity and to the severity of the administrative policies against student drinking, heterosexual activity, and aggression. Similarly, the degree of Concern for the Individual Student, as perceived by the students, was negatively related to the physical size of the institution, and perceived Emphasis on Social Life was positively correlated with the frequency of Organized Dating and of Informal Dating, and the amount of Leisure Time. Also, we have previously noted that the perceived degree of Academic Competitiveness was moderately related to the amount of time that the students spend in studying. The point to emphasize here is that these relationships are far from perfect, and that at many institutions the student's impression of the college seems significantly discrepant from the objective environmental stimuli that we would expect to determine these perceptions.

We have already suggested that the students' personal biases and expectations may distort their perceptions of the college environment, although the fact that we are dealing here with the *modal* or pooled perceptions of all the students at the institution should compensate for individual biases. One possible explanation is that the modal student perceptions at some colleges are systematically biased because of certain personal prejudices or other personal characteristics that are shared by most of the students who enroll. Another possibility is that the image of the college is something that develops gradually, and that it is transmitted from incumbent upperclassmen to incoming freshmen more or less informally by word of mouth. Although these images may initially have been based on the external realities of the institutional environment, there is necessarily a considerable time lag between changes in the external environment (alpha press) and the perceptions of this environment (beta press). Thus, even though an institution may deliberately institute major changes in its environment, its image may be naturally resistant to any change.

This hypothetical explanation of the discrepancies between the college image and the college environment has certain implications for future research and practice. It should be possible to test it empirically, for example, by determining if the degree of congruence between the college image and the college environment is lowest for those institutions whose environments have undergone recent change. Furthermore, if these assumptions prove valid, administrators who are interested in changing their college's image might want to consider reducing or even cutting off communication between the incoming student body and the incumbent upperclassmen. In developing their perceptions of the environment, new students would thus be forced to look at the external realities.

SUMMARY

In this chapter we have attempted to analyze the image of the institution as revealed by the students' perceptions of their college environments. An analysis of 75 items concerning the student's impressions revealed eight relatively independent dimensions of the college image: Academic Competitiveness, Concern for the Individual Student, School Spirit, Permissiveness, Snobbishness, Emphasis on Athletics, Flexibility of the Curriculum, and Emphasis on Social Life.

Although the relationships between these eight image factors and the 27 measures of the college environment described in the earlier chapters tend to confirm the interpretations of the image factors, the moderate degree of overlap found between the two domains suggests that the college image and the college environment are related to somewhat different aspects of institutional variation. Some possible interpretations of these discrepancies were discussed.

7

Summary and Implications of the Study

THE PURPOSE OF THIS STUDY was to identify and measure some of the important differences among college environments. A major impetus toward undertaking this project was the need to document more systematically the great diversity in the American higher educational system and to comprehend more fully what this diversity implies for student development. It was assumed that the results would contribute to an understanding of why institutions differ in their impact on the student and, ultimately, to our knowledge of how to select students and to structure college environments so as to increase the benefits of higher education.

In contrast to previous research on college environments, we viewed the environment as an array of potential "stimuli," defining this term as any behavior, event, or other observable characteristic of the institution which is capable of changing the student's sensory input, and whose existence or occurrence can be confirmed by independent observation. A list of 275 such stimuli was developed, covering four different areas: the peer environment, the classroom environment, the administrative environment, and the physical environment. This list was incorporated as part of a questionnaire, the Inventory of College Activities, which was completed by some 30,570 students at 246 institutions at the end of their freshman year. Each institution averaged approximately 125 student observers.

Variations among the environments of the 246 institutions were measured in terms of the students' reports about the relative frequency of occurrence of each of the 275 stimuli. For many of these, the diversity within the sample of institutions was indeed remarkable, ranging from very frequent occurrence at some institutions to virtual nonoccurrence at others. These variations in environmental characteristics suggest that the types of changes that take place in the student during the undergraduate years may be highly dependent on the type of institution he attends. Correlations between certain environmental stimuli and other features of the institution and of the student suggested a variety of hypotheses about some of these environmental effects, but it will be necessary to conduct an extensive series of longitudinal studies in order to test them empirically.[1]

[1] Several of these hypotheses are currently being explored in the Cooperative Institutional Research Program of the American Council on Education (Astin, Panos, and Creager, 1966, 1967a, 1967b).

Factor analyses of the correlations among the various stimulus items, in which the institution was used as the sampling unit, revealed some 27 patterns of environmental stimuli that differentiate among institutions. These 27 environmental factors, which account for the bulk of the information contained in the original pool of 275 stimuli, are listed below:

A. The Peer Environment
   1. Competitiveness vs. Cooperativeness
   2. Organized Dating
   3. Independence
   4. Cohesiveness
   5. Informal Dating
   6. Femininity
   7. Drinking vs. Religiousness
   8. Musical & Artistic Activity
   9. Leisure Time
   10. Career Indecision
   11. Regularity of Sleeping Habits
   12. Use of the Library
   13. Conflict with Regulations
   14. Student Employment
   15. Use of Automobiles

B. The Classroom Environment
   16. Involvement in the Class
   17. Verbal Aggressiveness
   18. Extraversion of the Instructor
   19. Familiarity with the Instructor
   20. Organization in the Classroom
   21. Severity of Grading

C. The Administrative Environment
   22. Severity of Administrative Policy Against Drinking
   23. Severity of Administrative Policy Against Aggression
   24. Severity of Administrative Policy Against Heterosexual Activity
   25. Severity of Administrative Policy Against Cheating

D. The Physical Environment
   26. Spread of the Campus
   27. Friendliness of the Dorm Counselor or Housemother

A similar analysis of 75 items concerning the student's impressions of his college environment yielded an additional eight measures of the college image. These image factors, which are only moderately related to the 27 environmental stimulus factors, are shown below:

1. Academic Competitiveness
2. Concern for the Individual Student
3. School Spirit

4. Permissiveness
5. Snobbishness
6. Emphasis on Athletics
7. Flexibility of the Curriculum
8. Emphasis on Social Life

In the sections that follow, we shall attempt first to use these 35 factors as a basis for describing the environmental characteristics of different types of institutions and then to summarize some of the implications that the findings have for educational administration, classroom teaching, counseling, and educational research.

ENVIRONMENTAL CHARACTERISTICS OF DIFFERENT TYPES OF INSTITUTIONS

Higher educational institutions are traditionally viewed as being of certain administrative types: liberal arts college or university, publicly controlled or privately controlled, and so on. Because these categories are used so frequently in administration and guidance, it may be useful to summarize the patterns of environmental variables that characterize the more familiar institutional types. In particular, it would be helpful to determine if the institutions within certain administrative categories are relatively homogeneous with respect to given environmental characteristics.

For this analysis, five broad administrative classifications have been selected: type of curriculum (university, liberal arts college, teachers college, or technological institution), type of control (public, private nonsectarian, Roman Catholic, or Protestant), geographic region (Northeast, Midwest, Southeast, or West and Southwest), race (predominantly Negro or non-Negro), and sex (coeducational, men's, or women's). We shall summarize the distinctive environmental features of these specific types of institutions within each of these five taxonomies.[2] Since this taxonomic information is available for the entire population of higher educational institutions, the results summarized below should be applicable to the nearly 1,000 four-year institutions not included in our original sample of 246.

Type of Curriculum

Using information provided by the U. S. Office of Education in its 1962-63 *Education Directory: Part III* (*Higher Education*), we separated

[2] A table showing the contingency coefficients associated with each factor and each type category and a table showing the percentages of each type of institution scoring above the median on each factor, are given in Appendix H.

244 of the institutions into four curricular types: universities (N = 48); liberal arts colleges; (N = 170); teachers' colleges (N = 20); technological institutions (N = 6). Two institutions in the sample, classified by the U. S. Office of Education as "professional only," are excluded from this analysis.

Universities. Both the college environment and the college image of the typical university differ in several ways from the environments and images of the other three types of institution. The peer environment of the typical university, for example, tends to be highly competitive (more than nine of every ten universities score above average on this factor). There is also a high frequency of organized dating among the students and a relatively large amount of drinking, but relatively few of them participate in musical and artistic activities. The students in the typical university also lack cohesiveness and use the library infrequently.

The most characteristic feature of the typical university's classroom environment is that the instructor and students tend not to be personally involved in the class (all but two of the 48 universities score below the over-all institutional average on this factor). Similarly, the students are likely to be unfamiliar with their instructors (more than nine out of every ten universities score below average on this factor) and are not inclined to be verbally aggressive in the classroom. Grading practices in most universities tend to be comparatively severe (i.e., a relatively high proportion of failing grades are given).

The disciplinary policies on student drinking are quite lenient in the majority of universities, as are the policies toward heterosexual activity. Policies on aggression and cheating, however, are about average in their severity.

The most striking feature of the image that the student has at the typical university is that there is very little concern with the individual student: Every one of the lowest-scoring 16 institutions on this factor were universities, even though the 48 universities constituted less than 20 percent of the total sample of institutions. Students in the typical university perceive their environment as being relatively permissive, as placing a high degree of emphasis on the student's social life, and as being rather snobbish.

Since about 90 percent of the universities obtained above-average scores on Spread of the Campus, some of the distinguishing characteristics of the university's environment and image (e.g., low scores on Familiarity with the Instructor and on Concern for the Individual Student) are probably attributable in part to its relatively large size.

Liberal Arts Colleges. Because liberal arts colleges form a very heterogeneous category, only a few environmental characteristics can be said to apply to a large percentage of this group of institutions. As might be expected, most of these characteristics reverse the pattern described above for the university: liberal arts colleges are typified by cohesiveness and cooperativeness in the peer environment and by familiarity with the instructor. The only college image factor which seemed to distinguish the liberal arts colleges from the other groups is a high degree of perceived concern for the individual student.

These findings make it clear that, although some characteristics differentiate the average liberal arts college from other types of institutions, the great dissimilarities among institutions in this group suggest that "the liberal arts college" has limited functional significance as a category of institutions.

Teachers Colleges. The peer environment of the typical teachers college is distinguished primarily by femininity, a large amount of leisure time, frequent use of automobiles, and regular sleeping habits. Students at the typical teachers college show less independence and less indecisiveness about their career plans than do students at other types of institutions.

Students and teachers in the typical teachers college seem to be deeply involved in the class, although there is little familiarity with the instructor or verbal aggressiveness. This pattern indicates that, even though the students at the typical teachers college are conscientious about attending classes and taking part in discussions, their participation is relatively passive and their personal interaction with the instructors limited.

The administrative environment of the teachers college is typified by very harsh policies against student aggression, although the policies on student cheating are relatively permissive.

The most striking feature of the environmental image of the teachers college is the very low degree of perceived academic competitiveness: Every one of the 20 teachers colleges scored below average on this factor. Although students at the typical teachers college do not usually view their institution as snobbish, they feel that little concern is shown for the individual student and that school spirit is low.

Since previous research (Astin, 1965d) has revealed that the students entering teachers colleges and public liberal arts colleges are very similar in their abilities and aspirations, it seems likely that the public subgroup within the liberal arts colleges has the features of teachers colleges described above.

Technological Institutions. Previous studies of student inputs to college environments (Astin, 1965d; Astin and Holland, 1961) indicate that, of all the various curricular categories, the technological institutions possess the most unique student bodies and environments. The findings presented here tend to support this notion, but it should be remembered that only six technological institutions were included in this study—a very small sample. For this reason, we shall restrict our description to those factors on which all six of these institutions were either above or below the over-all institutional average.

The peer environment of technological institutions manifests a high degree of independence and competitiveness. On the other hand, it scores low on dating, both organized and informal, on femininity, on leisure time, and on musical and artistic activity.

Its classroom environment is characterized by verbal aggressiveness, and does not tend to be highly organized or formal.

Students at technological institutions see their environment as being exceptionally competitive academically, as having a very inflexible curriculum, and as placing very little emphasis on social activities.

Type of Control

The 246 institutions were divided into four categories on the basis of their source of control: public (N = 56); private nonsectarian (N = 73); Roman Catholic (N = 28); Protestant (N = 89). We considered it particularly important to segregate the privately controlled institutions into nonsectarian, Catholic, and Protestant, because previous research (Astin, 1965d) has shown that using "public versus private control" as a basis for classification has little functional significance; indeed, it obscures many important differences among the private institutions.

Public Institutions. The peer environment of the typical public institution exhibits a relatively large amount of leisure time and competitiveness and relatively little independence, cohesiveness, and musical and artistic activity. In the classroom environment, there is little familiarity with the instructor (about nine out of ten public institutions are below average on this factor) or verbal aggressiveness, and grading practices are rather severe.

More than nine out of ten public institutions obtain below-average scores on the image factor Concern for the Individual Student. Students at the typical public institution also perceive their environment as not being very competitive academically[3] and as emphasizing social activities: public institutions account for ten of the 18 institutions scoring highest on this factor, whereas only two of the lowest-scoring 39 institutions are publicly controlled. Not surprisingly, the typical public institution is usually above average in Spread of the Campus.

Finally, the typical public institution tends to have relatively severe policies against student aggression.

Private Nonsectarian Institutions. Students at private nonsectarian institutions tend to be independent and to engage in a relatively large amount of drinking, whereas their religious activities are limited. Their sleeping habits are somewhat less regular than those of students in the average institution. Although the classroom environment of the private-nonsectarian institution shows a tendency toward frequent verbal aggressiveness, it is in most other respects very similar to the average classroom environment.

Students at private nonsectarian institutions are inclined to have the impression that their environment is relatively snobbish. Whereas 14 of the 16 highest-scoring institutions on snobbishness are private nonsectarian, only two of the 18 least snobbish institutions are of this type. The private-nonsectarian colleges' disciplinary polices about heterosexual activity, aggression, and, in particular, student drinking tend to be relatively permissive.

It is important to stress that the private nonsectarian category comprises a heterogeneous group of institutions. This heterogeneity is created largely by two subgroups: relatively prestigious, selective, and permissive institutions that abandoned their formal religious affiliation many years ago and those institutions that until only recently were formally affiliated with some Protestant denomination. Our inclusion of these two subgroups within this category is probably partially responsible for our failure to find more distinctive features.

Roman Catholic Institutions. The peer environment of the typical Roman Catholic institution has several distinctive features. To begin with, all 28 of these institutions scored above the over-all institutional average on Conflict with Regulations. (The possible significance of this finding was discussed earlier in Chapter 2.) All but one of the Roman Catholic institutions scored below the over-all institutional average on the rate of informal dating. (It seems very likely that this low rate of Informal Dating can be explained by the fact that most of these institutions are not coeducational.)

[3] There were, nevertheless, a few public institutions with very high scores on Academic Competitiveness.

Students at the typical Catholic institution have regular sleeping habits, make frequent use of the library, and have relatively little leisure time.

Although the classroom environments of most Roman Catholic institutions are high in verbal aggressiveness and involvement, there is relatively little familiarity between students and instructors.

Students at most Catholic institutions rate their curricula as being highly inflexible. At the same time, however, they feel that both school spirit and academic competitiveness are high and that there is relatively little snobbishness. Most Catholic institutions are also viewed by their students as placing little emphasis on social activities.

The disciplinary policies of the typical Catholic institution tend to be rather severe in all areas of potential student infractions, particularly heterosexual activity.

Protestant Institutions. Institutions classified as "Protestant" included all those listed by the U. S. Office of Education in 1962 as being affiliated with some Christian religious denomination other than the Roman Catholic or Orthodox Churches. From a denominational point of view, then, this category is extremely heterogeneous.

The peer environments of most Protestant institutions tend to be highly cohesive. The students engage frequently in religious activities and drink relatively infrequently. In the classroom environment, students and instructors tend to be on fairly familiar terms, a finding that may be in part a consequence of the fact that the Protestant institutions are usually physically small.

Students at the typical Protestant institution are inclined to feel that the administrative regulations are somewhat strict. Even though many of such institutions cluster near the over-all institutional mean on Permissiveness, they also account for 30 of the 38 institutions scoring lowest on this factor. At the same time, none of the 16 most permissive institutions is Protestant.

The Protestant institutions' relatively severe policies against student drinking are consistent with the low rate of student drinking mentioned earlier. Nevertheless, their policies against student heterosexual activity are only slightly more severe than those of the typical institution, and their policies toward aggression no different from institutions in general.

Geographic Region

The 246 institutions were divided into four broad geographic regions, as follows: *Northeast* (N = 67). This includes Connecticut, Delaware, District of Columbia, Maine, Maryland, Massachusetts, New Hampshire,

New Jersey, New York, Pennsylvania, Rhode Island, and Vermont; *Southeast* (N = 50). This includes Alabama, Arkansas, Florida, Georgia, Kentucky, Louisiana, Mississippi, North Carolina, South Carolina, Tennessee, Virginia, and West Virginia; *Midwest* (N = 95). This includes Illinois, Indiana, Iowa, Kansas, Michigan, Minnesota, Missouri, Nebraska, North Dakota, Ohio, South Dakota, and Wisconsin; *West and Southwest* (N = 34). This includes Alaska, Arizona, California, Colorado, Hawaii, Idaho, Montana, Nevada, New Mexico, Oklahoma, Oregon, Texas, Utah, Washington, and Wyoming.

For the most part, differences in the environments of institutions in different geographic regions were not as pronounced as were the differences among various types of institutions categorized on the basis of curriculum and control. Furthermore, it appears that those significant regional differences that do occur are partly attributable to the predominance of certain types of institutions in certain regions, rather than to characteristics of the regions per se.

The Northeast. Students in many of the institutions located in the Northeastern states engage in informal dating rather infrequently, probably because most noncoeducational institutions are located in this region of the country (see the section on Sex below). These students are also inclined to drink and to use automobiles relatively frequently and to have little leisure time. Their classroom environments tend to be high in verbal aggressiveness and low in familiarity with the instructor.

Institutions located in the Northeastern states are often perceived by their students as placing little emphasis on athletics and as having relatively inflexible curricula. Most of these institutions have relatively severe policies against student cheating, and many also have severe policies against student heterosexual activities. Their policies concerning student aggression, however, are likely to be permissive.

The Southeast. The peer environment of a typical institution located in the Southeast differs in several ways from the peer environment of institutions located elsewhere. Students at Southeastern institutions tend to have more leisure time, to use automobiles more frequently, and to spend less time working for pay than do students at institutions in other regions of the country. These students are also more likely to be highly cohesive and to engage in religious behavior.

The classroom environment of the typical institution in the Southeast is characterized by relatively severe grading practices (i.e., a high proportion of failing grades) and considerable faculty and student involvement. This latter finding may be explained partly by the fact that institutions located in the Southeast tend to have relatively low scores on Spread of the Campus.

The disciplinary policies of Southeastern institutions tend to be relatively severe with respect to all four categories of student infractions, the most severe being those against heterosexual activity and cheating.

The Midwest. Perhaps because of the fairly large number of Midwestern institutions in the sample (N = 95), the environmental characteristics associated with this geographic category do not deviate much from the average.[4] Consequently, only two environmental characteristics of Midwestern institutions differ sufficiently from those of institutions in general to be worth noting: A relatively high proportion of their students work for pay and their administrative environments have very permissive policies with respect to student cheating. These environmental differences appear to be genuinely geographical in nature, rather than artifacts created by the concentration of particular types of institutions in the Midwest.

The West and The Southwest. The peer environments of institutions located in the Western and Southwestern regions of the country are typified by frequent informal dating, a relatively large amount of leisure time, and a relatively high rate of career indecision. Their classroom environments tend to be informal, but low in faculty and student involvement.

The single most characteristic feature of institutions located in these two areas is their relatively permissive policies toward student cheating. The policies concerning student heterosexual activity are also rather permissive. Finally, students at colleges located in these regions are likely to rate their institutions as having relatively flexible curricula.

Race

Although the sample included only seven colleges which the U. S. Office of Education classified in 1961 as "predominantly Negro," we thought it desirable to analyze this group because of the great interest in the predominantly Negro institution that has been displayed recently by the Federal government, foundations, and others (e.g., see McGrath, 1965). A fuller understanding of some of their distinctive environmental characteristics might be useful in better understanding their unique problems and in guiding future policy. Because of the very small sample size, however, the discussion will be confined to those environmental characteristics upon which

[4] Note that the extent of deviation of any category of institutions from the mean of all institutions is necessarily limited by its size, since all scores were expressed as standard scores.

all seven predominantly Negro institutions scored either above or below the mean score for all 246 institutions.

A relatively high proportion of students at predominantly Negro institutions engage in religious activities (versus drinking). Comparatively few, however, use automobiles or have organized dates. They also tend to be decided in their career plans.

Characteristic features of the classroom environments of predominantly Negro institutions are a high degree of student involvement in the class and relatively severe grading practices.

The administrative environments of these institutions are characterized by relatively severe policies against both drinking and heterosexual activity. Although one institution scored slightly above the over-all institutional average on Severity of Administrative Policy Against Cheating, the six other institutions had very permissive policies on this matter.

Somewhat surprisingly, students at the predominantly Negro institutions are inclined to perceive their institution as showing little concern for the individual student.

Sex

The sample of 246 institutions was sorted into the following three categories: coeducational institutions (N=189), institutions for men (N=31), and institutions for women (N=26). Our analysis of many of the factors discussed earlier makes it clear that we should expect to find certain pronounced differences between institutions for men and institutions for women. It would also be valuable to discover if noncoeducational institutions as a group have certain similarities not generally found in the coeducational institutions.

Coeducational Institutions. Because of the very large size of this category (it made up more than three-fourths of the total sample), one should not expect to find many distinguishing characteristics. Nevertheless, certain features did emerge which, while not applicable to all institutions in the group, were significantly different from the features of the noncoeducational institutions.

The most striking differences between coeducational and noncoeducational institutions involve student dating. Thus, much more informal dating goes on at coeducational institutions, whereas the amount of organized dating is correspondingly greater at the noncoeducational institutions. (The latter difference is much less pronounced than the former.)

The coeducational institutions scored much lower than the noncoeducational institutions on one factor from the classroom environment, Verbal Aggressiveness. This finding is consistent with the fact that the administrative policies concerning student aggression are somewhat more severe in the coeducational institutions, although their policies concerning student cheating are much more lenient.

Students attending coeducational institutions, compared with students at noncoeducational institutions, are more inclined to report that social activities are overemphasized and that the curriculum is flexible. However, the coeducational environments are seen as being less competitive academically and as showing much less concern for the individual student than are the noncoeducational environments.

Institutions for Men. The peer environment of the typical men's college is most distinguished by its competitiveness, lack of informal dating, and masculinity. (On each of these three factors, all 31 institutions for men were on the same side of the over-all institutional mean score.) Other distinguishing features of their peer environments include a high degree of independence and a high rate of drinking (versus religiousness).

The classroom environment of the typical men's college is characterized by verbal aggressiveness and by a lack of involvement in the class. With the exception of the policies against cheating (which are relatively severe), the policies concerning student conduct in the men's colleges are comparatively permissive.

Students at men's colleges typically see their institution as being very competitive academically, as showing a good deal of concern for the individual student, and as being fairly permissive. Men's institutions also tend to have relatively low scores on Spread of the Campus.

Institutions for Women. Since the women's colleges differ from other types of institutions on virtually all measures of the peer environment (with the possible exception of Drinking versus Religiousness), it seems safe to conclude that this category of institution is one of the most unique of all types in its environmental characteristics.

The peer environment of the typical college for women is highly cooperative (rather than competitive) and very feminine. The students often have arranged dates and use the library frequently. (We have already noted from Chapter 2 that the frequency of organized dating is considerably greater in the women's colleges than in the men's colleges, even though both types of noncoeducational institutions have very little informal dating.) Other distinguishing characteristics of the peer environments include a high degree of cohesiveness, much musical and artistic activity, regular sleeping habits, relatively frequent conflict with regulations, and relatively few students who work for pay.

In the classroom environment of the typical women's college, students tend to be verbally aggressive and, along with the faculty, to exhibit a high degree of involvement. The grading practices, furthermore, are relatively permissive (few failing grades are given).

The typical women's college, like the typical men's college, has relatively severe policies against cheating. Somewhat surprisingly, their policies concerning drinking and heterosexual activity are not, on the average, substantially different from policies in coeducational institutions.

Students attending colleges for women are inclined to feel that a good deal of concern is shown for the individual student and that the level of school spirit is high. They are also likely to see their institution as having a rather rigid curriculum and as de-emphasizing both athletics and social activities.

IMPLICATIONS FOR ADMINISTRATION

In the previous section, we touched on some of the implications that these findings have for educational administration. For example, the traditional "public versus private" dichotomy seems to have little significance in measuring either the college environment or the college image. Although geographic region may be somewhat more related to certain environmental factors, it is largely unimportant once other administrative features of the institution, such as the type of curriculum and the sex of the students attending the institution, are taken into account.

Perhaps the most significant finding—as far as its implications for administration are concerned—is the great diversity that was observed in most of the environmental factors. This diversity is important in two ways. First, it affords an opportunity for the administrator to assess critically the relative effectiveness of his own environment and administrative practices. Because each institution can probably locate several other institutions that have contrasting environments, the administrator can examine the effect of his institution's environment by means of collaborative longitudinal studies involving the joint participation of the contrasting institutions. Such studies (which are discussed in more detail in the section on educational research in this chapter) should eventually yield information that will enable the administrator to maximize those educational outcomes which he thinks desirable, either by making appropriate alterations in the institutional environment or by changing his admissions procedures so that those students most likely to benefit from the particular environment are selected.

The second implication of the environmental diversity documented in this study concerns the question of innovation. In recent years, a considerable amount of governmental and foundation money has been used to support projects involving innovations in higher education. One possible effect of such projects is that still more diversity will be introduced into the system, even before the extensive diversity that already exists has been adequately evaluated. A more likely consequence, however, is that the current diversity will lessen as certain attractive new approaches gain widespread acceptance. One possible danger here is that the tendency to accept innovation uncritically may mean that certain practices will be abandoned before their possible value has been adequately appraised.[5] Because of this danger, the administrator should, perhaps, resist the temptation to adopt new practices on any large scale until their superiority over the old practices has been demonstrated.

The administrator who wishes to utilize these results in changing his environment may be hindered by the fact that he does not have complete control over it. For example, he may not be able to alter those environmental factors—such as Competitiveness versus Cooperativeness—that are largely dependent on the characteristics of the entering students, unless he has available a large heterogeneous pool of applicants from which to select his student body. Changing the input of students in certain ways may also be unfeasible because of certain long-standing policies or traditions. Thus, the president of a women's college would probably find it very difficult to change any characteristic that is primarily dependent on the sex of the student body (e.g., Femininity).[6]

One important institutional characteristic that *is* often subject to direct administrative control is the size of the student body. The environmental characteristics most highly related to the number of students enrolled are:

[5] One possible example of this phenomenon is the conversion of teachers colleges into liberal arts colleges or, in some instances, into universities. Although there may be strong a priori arguments in favor of a general liberal arts education for prospective teachers, the fact is that the relative effectiveness of the teachers college in preparing teachers has never been adequately examined empirically. Thus, it is likely that one of the unique types of higher educational institutions will virtually disappear before its efficacy has been tested.

[6] Nevertheless, the obvious environmental differences between men's colleges and women's colleges as described in the previous section might be useful in rendering an administrative judgment concerning the desirability either of making a noncoeducational institution coeducational (as is currently the case with some Roman Catholic institutions) or in coordinating or combining two noncoeducational institutions (e.g., the recent proposal to combine Vassar College and Yale University).

Concern for the Individual Student ($r = -.72$)
Spread of the Campus ($r = .67$)
Involvement in the Class ($r = -.58$)
Familiarity with the Instructor ($r = -.52$)
Competitiveness (vs. Cooperativeness) ($r = .45$)
Cohesiveness ($r = -.42$)

In the environments of large institutions, as compared with those of the smaller ones, there is little concern for the individual student, lack of involvement in the class, little familiarity with the instructor, greater competitiveness, and little cohesiveness. This pattern of variables lends some support to the notion that the larger institutions give the students some feeling of depersonalization. However, the moderate size of the coefficients suggests that some relatively large institutions do not manifest this pattern and some relatively small ones do. It would be useful if future research on these atypical institutions could be undertaken to determine which administrative practices[7] are most successful in avoiding the undesirable consequences of large size.

Thus it seems clear that administrators need to know which environmental features are subject to their manipulation and which are largely a product of the input of students to the institution. Some of the research that could be conducted on these matters is discussed in the section on educational research.

IMPLICATIONS FOR TEACHING

The results of this study have suggested a variety of hypotheses about the effects of certain classroom teaching practices; some of these are discussed in detail in the section on "Implications for Research." Several other findings from the analyses of the classroom environment, however, are worth noting because of their apparent implications for classroom teaching.

The considerable interinstitutional diversity in certain aspects of the classroom environment suggests that teachers might gain some added perspective and insight by examining their own practices in the light of this diversity. Although a particular classroom procedure may be universally practiced in the instructor's own institution, it may be atypical at most other institutions. Examples of such atypical practices are not taking attendance, permitting students to smoke in class, and calling students by their first names.

[7] For example, the fragmentation of large universities into smaller, semi-autonomous "cluster" colleges.

Instructors who want to create a particular type of classroom environment ought to be aware that certain features probably depend more on the type of students making up the class than they do on the deliberate efforts of the instructor. Students majoring in education, for example, are more likely to become involved in what goes on in the class than are students majoring in science. Similarly, instructors who wish to encourage the development of close personal relationships with their students may have to make a special effort in the case of the commuter student.

The existence of a somewhat absolute standard of grading in the higher educational system suggests that instructors in some—but not all—of the more selective institutions recognize that the average level of student performance is likely to be very high in comparison to the typical institution. But the fact that the instructors in a few selective institutions do not give average grades that are higher (or, in a few cases, even as high) as the grades given by instructors in the unselective institutions suggests that grading standards embody serious inequities that could affect the talented student's chances of being admitted to graduate or professional school, winning a fellowship or assistantship, or obtaining a particular job after college. While many employers and graduate schools probably make some effort to compensate for these differences in standards, the obvious inconsistencies among schools at the same level of selectivity suggest that some effort should be made, perhaps at the national level, to develop a more systematic set of procedures for comparing the grade-point averages of students who attend different undergraduate institutions.

IMPLICATIONS FOR GUIDANCE AND COUNSELING

The variety of environmental variables identified in this study and the great institutional diversity would seem to justify the considerable attention that most students give to the problem of college choice. While the long-range impact that each environmental characteristic has on the student can only be discovered through longitudinal studies, these data show clearly that the student's choice of an institution can largely determine the kinds of environmental stimuli to which he will be exposed during his undergraduate years. If administrators could be persuaded to publish data concerning some of these environmental characteristics, the prospective college student would have a much sounder basis for making an appropriate choice among available institutions. This is not to suggest that the student would necessarily want to select an institution where the characteristics of the other students match his own; it means simply that, knowing some of these environmental stimulus variables, he would be better able to judge whether or not he will find a given college generally congenial. Of course, the availability of such information could eventually serve to redistribute students among institutions, thereby changing those environmental characteristics that are dependent on the student input. For this reason, it may be important to monitor institutional environments regularly in order to keep track of any such changes.

One should recognize that many distinct subenvironments exist within a given institution, especially within the complex university,[8] and that the actual patterns of environmental stimuli to which an individual student is exposed may depend as much on his particular subenvironment as on the institution itself. An examination of the correlates of the 27 environmental stimulus factors and the eight college image factors suggests that the student must consider at least three contingencies in estimating what his experiences are likely to be: whether he intends to reside on campus or live at home, what curriculum he intends to pursue, and what his (or her) sex is.

If a student decides to live at home rather than in a dormitory or some other kind of student housing, he should probably attach relatively little weight to the characteristics of the peer environment and perhaps even less weight to the administrative and physical environments of his institution. Except in the classroom, commuter students often spend little time with other students, and they are generally not subject to the same types of rules and regulations as are the resident students.

If the student intends to enroll at a large, complex university, his evaluation of the environmental attributes of that institution should depend in part on the course of study he intends to pursue. In particular, if he intends to pursue a course within a technological school of the university, his environmental experiences are likely to be very different from those he would have were he to enroll in the liberal arts college at the same institution. The nature of some of these differences is suggested by the characteristics of technological institutions discussed earlier. Specifically, we should expect the environment of the technological institute within the university, as

[8] The original plan to compare item results for different schools or colleges within the complex universities was abandoned when it was discovered that, in many universities, the number of students enrolled in colleges other than arts and sciences was too small for us to compute stable estimates of the factor scores. In future studies, it would be advisable to sample disproportionately large numbers of students from those smaller schools, since recent research (Pace, 1963, Table 29) suggests that there may be pronounced differences among the environments of these different schools within the university.

compared with that of the college of arts and sciences, to be competitive (rather than cooperative), independent, verbally aggressive, and academically competitive. On the other hand, it would tend to manifest a lesser degree of the following environmental characteristics: informal dating, musical and artistic activity, femininity, leisure time, use of the library, and organization in the classroom. Those students planning to enroll in the arts and sciences college within a complex university would probably find the opposite pattern of environmental stimuli. In short, a knowledge of the over-all environmental features of a large complex university should be tempered by an awareness of the particular school that the student plans to attend. (Future studies, described in the following section, will be devoted to analyzing some of these differences among the subenvironments of larger institutions.)

The third contingency to be taken into account by the prospective college student, sex, is relevant if he intends to enroll at a coeducational institution. The student's environmental experience at the coeducational college is likely to depend on his sex for two reasons. First, we have already seen that certain environmental characteristics are highly dependent on the sex ratio of the student body. Second, since the sexes in most coeducational institutions are partially segregated, the student is much more likely to be exposed to the environmental stimuli supplied by students of like sex. Fortunately, however, only two of the environmental stimulus factors showed substantial correlations with the percentage of men in the student body: Competitiveness (versus Cooperativeness) ($r = .80$) and Femininity ($r = -.77$). Thus, the male student would normally encounter a pattern of environmental stimuli that is more competitive and less cooperative and feminine than is indicated by the over-all environmental measure for his institution. He would also be more likely than a female student at the same institution to encounter high degrees of independence ($r = .41$) and drinking versus religiousness ($r = .43$). The woman student, on the other hand, could normally expect to encounter a pattern of stimuli characterized by more than the over-all amount of musical and artistic activity ($r = -.48$).

IMPLICATIONS FOR EDUCATIONAL RESEARCH

As is true of most research studies, this project has raised as many questions as it has answered. In this section, we shall describe some of the avenues for further research that are suggested by the findings.

Environmental Effects on Student Development

In Chapter 1, it was proposed that measures developed through research of this type are valuable chiefly because they provide a basis for interpreting the differential impact of colleges in environmental terms. Definitive studies of college effects will, of course, require longitudinal data in order to rule out many of the plausible rival interpretations of the relationships observed in this study. Several provocative hypotheses, however, are suggested by the correlations obtained between certain environmental factors and certain aspects of students' behavior.

1. One of the most intriguing findings from the analyses of stimuli in the peer environment is that the factor Drinking versus Religiousness has a close negative relationship to Severity of Administrative Policies Against Drinking. From an administrator's point of view, one might argue that the amount of student drinking that goes on can be lessened by making the policies against it more strict. This interpretation, though plausible at first glance, makes less sense when one examines the other pole of the Drinking versus Religiousness factor: Is it likely that stiffening policies against drinking will lead to increased religious activity among the students? The improbability of this hypothesis suggests an alternative interpretation: namely, that the severity of the administrative policy represents in part an accommodation to the amount of drinking that the students are likely to engage in, because of the kind of people they are. The bipolar factor would thus be a reflection of the fact that drinking is most likely to occur among students who are relatively nonreligious. These rival hypotheses could be examined in longitudinal studies which would attempt to determine if the actual amount of drinking as opposed to religiousness can be predicted solely from the characteristics of the students entering the institution, or if administrative policies are also a factor in shaping these behaviors.

2. Another interesting hypothesis suggested by the analyses of stimuli from the peer environment concerns the positive relationship between the prevalence of career indecision and the proportion of students who receive vocational counseling. Once again, at least two alternative interpretations of this finding are possible. The proportion of students who receive counseling may be merely a function of the amount of career indecision in the student body. Or, alternatively, the counseling process itself may contribute to this indecision. A more important question is, how may career indecision affect the student's later vocational development? While it can be argued that his being undecided or changing career plans impedes his vocational development, a case can also be made for flexibility and tentativeness dur-

ing the college years (Baird, in press; Holland & Nichols, 1964). Students whose choices are fixed and not subjected to scrutiny through vocational counseling may end up in the long run dissatisfied with their careers. Answers to questions such as these must, of course, await further longitudinal studies which follow the students beyond their undergraduate years.

3. A third suggestive relationship observed in the analyses of the stimuli from the peer environment is the positive correlation between the regularity of the students' sleeping habits and the percentage of students who live at home during their freshman year. This relationship suggests that when the student is away from home for the first time, his former sleeping habits may be disrupted. An alternative hypothesis is that this relationship is mediated by personal differences between commuters and noncommuters (e.g., being Catholic) that are also related to regularity of sleeping habits. That is, Catholic students may be more likely than non-Catholic students both to commute and to have regular sleeping habits.

4. Another provocative finding from the analysis of the peer environment is the complex relationship between the student's being employed, his cheating on examinations, and his spending relatively little time studying. The most obvious interpretation is that the student who has to work in order to stay in school has less time for studying and therefore finds it more necessary to cheat on examinations in order to pass. Of course, it may also be that those students who have a paying job are less committed to academic work and also less concerned about the practical or moral consequences of cheating. Obviously, these and other alternative interpretations of these relationships need to be tested in future longitudinal research.

5. One of the most interesting patterns of relationships observed in the analyses of the classroom environment is the positive association between Involvement in the Class and the teacher's knowing the student's names, encouraging class discussion, giving pop quizzes, and taking roll. This type of behavior was also associated with the student's coming to class on time. These relationships suggest several hypotheses that could be tested at individual campuses. Specifically, experiments could be designed to determine which, if any, of these techniques actually increases the student's degree of involvement in classroom activities. At the same time, it would be valuable to determine whether the instructor's personal involvement in his classroom responsibilities could be increased if he were encouraged to perform regularly one or more of these simple activities.

6. The finding from the analyses of the classroom environment that the student's familiarity with the instructor tends to be associated with a small

student body, a low proportion of instructors who are engaged in research, and a low proportion of commuter students also provokes speculation. A variety of alternative hypotheses to account for these relationships could be tested experimentally. Is the degree of familiarity with the instructor necessarily limited by the size of the class? Does the instructor's being deeply committed to research interfere with his getting to know his undergraduate students personally? Are commuting students less likely to be concerned about developing a personal relationship with their instructors, or are instructors relatively indifferent to the commuter? Are all three relationships mediated by one common factor, such as the over-all size of the institution or its emphasis on research over teaching?

7. Still another implicative finding from the analyses of stimuli from the classroom environment was that, in highly organized classes, the proportion of students who report that they come late to class is small. It would be useful to determine through experimental studies whether the practices that define this factor (assigning seats, taking attendance, holding the class at a regularly scheduled time and place) do indeed increase the likelihood that the student will be prompt.

8. Several hypotheses concerning the possible effects of administrative practices on student behavior are suggested in the analyses of stimuli from the administrative environment. We have already discussed (in No. 1, above) the possible effects of policies on student drinking. A similar causal hypothesis is suggested by the negative correlation between the amount of independence shown by the students and the severity of administrative policies against student aggression. The interpretation of this finding is clouded by the fact that the ability level of the student body is positively correlated with Independence and negatively correlated with Severity of Administrative Policy Against Aggression. Does this mean that the policies concerning student aggression are, once again, merely an accommodation to the demands of the students and that highly able students are more likely to make demands on the administration? Or is it possible that the amount of independence shown by the students is at least partially controlled by the administrative policies and that harsh policies lead to passivity and dependence?

Development and Change in College Environments

Although this study does not provide any definitive answers to the question of environmental effects on student development, it does demonstrate certain important facts about college environments. First, it is now clear that colleges do not differ along just one or even a few measurable dimensions. Thus, any attempt to describe colleges in terms of only one or two factors, such as size or prestige, represents a drastic and perhaps destructive oversimplification. Furthermore, the absolute differences among institutions in the frequency with which the stimuli that make up each environmental dimension occur are considerable. Many stimuli are reported by virtually all of the student observers at some institutions and by virtually none of the students at others. In short, this study clearly demonstrates that institutional environments in American higher education are extraordinarily diverse, both quantitatively and qualitatively.

A very practical problem, from the point of view of academic administration and educational planning is to discover what factors determine the particular character of any given college environment. This study, and several earlier ones (Astin, 1961; 1963b; 1965d), suggest strongly that college environments depend, to a considerable extent, on the kinds of students who are recruited into the institution. However, the correlations between student input characteristics and college environments are less than perfect and, in some cases, very low, which suggests that certain aspects of the college environment are largely determined by factors other than the student input. Presumably, these aspects are more subject to direct administrative control through rules and regulations, living arrangements, physical facilities, teaching practices, and other institutional characteristics. Because these characteristics are directly under the control of the institution, and because many institutions would find it extremely difficult to change their student inputs, it seems desirable that future research be designed (a) to identify aspects of the college environment that are independent of student input; and (b) to determine what administrative techniques can be used to augment or diminish the usual effects of the student input characteristics on other environmental characteristics. Answers to questions such as these would be of immediate value to administrators who want to change specific aspects of their institutional environments.

It is probable that research on the genesis of the college environment will also necessitate longitudinal studies in which the relevant contributions of student inputs and of administrative practices to the college environment can be assessed. Such studies would require an adequate appraisal of the entering students' potential for the behaviors that define the environmental stimulus factors, as well as an assessment of current administrative practices. The results of these studies would be useful in future studies of institutional impact, since they would identify environmental characteristics that are unrelated to or independent of the student input. The effects of such characteristics on student development could then be assessed directly; it would no longer be necessary to apply statistical controls first in order to allow for differences in student inputs.

Studies of Other Environmental Characteristics

In spite of the diversity of the environmental and image factors identified in this study, it is likely that they represent only some of the important differences among colleges and universities. Research could probably be done on other institutional characteristics; some possibilities are given below.

1. It was suggested in Chapter 5 that the measures of the physical environment used in this study were probably insufficient to account for many of the important institutional differences in this area. It would seem desirable to obtain more detailed information about the physical characteristics of the students' living quarters, the demographic and geographic features of the college town, the location of the campus with respect to various cultural and recreational facilities in the town, and the weather. In particular, an attempt to assess those environmental characteristics that are associated with the differences between the rural and the urban community environments seems called for.

2. This study utilized almost no information about the environmental stimuli that impinge upon the faculty and administration. These stimuli would include the quality and quantity of interactions among the faculty members within a department, between departments, and between faculty and administrative personnel. They would also include characteristics of the faculty members' office, laboratory or work space, recreational or club facilities, and so forth. Knowledge of such environmental differences could be used in future studies concerned with such outcomes as faculty productivity and faculty mobility. Such environmental characteristics may not affect students directly, but perhaps they serve as indirect influences on many students because they affect the manner in which the typical faculty member conducts his classes, deals with his academic advising, and otherwise interacts with students in and out of the classroom. Also, of course, students will be affected by, for instance, rapid turnover of faculty in their major field (especially if this is caused by faculty dissatisfaction within the department).

3. One possible weakness with the approach taken in this study is that we have treated each institution as if it were a single environmental entity. While this approach is relevant in the sense that decisions about college

choice and administrative policy are often made with the total institution in mind, there is no doubt that many important environmental differences *within* institutions have been confounded. These differences may not be especially great in the relatively small, homogeneous colleges, but they are probably extensive within the large, complex universities. In fact, it is likely that the environmental differences between colleges within the complex university are just as great, if not greater, than the differences between the total environments of different institutions of this type.

One problem in attempting to study institutional subenvironments is that of defining the relevant environmental units. In some universities, the technological school, the liberal arts college, the business school, and the school of nursing may be geographically segregated and, in most other respects, completely separate units. On the other hand, freshmen in different units of other large universities may share common dormitories and otherwise interact with professors and students in all colleges, even though they are technically enrolled in separate colleges within the university. In any event, it would seem desirable in future research to identify the functional administrative units within large institutions and to attempt to measure environmental differences among them.

4. A fourth area for possible future research on environmental characteristics is that of the relationship between the environmental stimuli and the college image. This study has shown that although there are consistencies between the students' perceptions of their college environments and the observable stimuli at the college, these relationships are far from perfect. Apparently, many observable stimulus properties of the environment are not assessed by the college image factors that we have identified, and, by implication, some aspects of the students' perceptions of their institutions cannot be accounted for in terms of observable stimuli. In future research, it would be useful to determine if these discrepancies between the college image and the observable stimuli are attributable simply to our not having adequately covered the actual stimuli in the initial pool of items, or if factors other than the observable environmental stimuli determine the students' perceptions. At the same time, it would be interesting to discover whether there are environmental stimuli of which the student is not aware, but which nevertheless affect his behavior.

CONCLUSION

In this study we have described and measured some of the important differences among the educational and social environments of American undergraduate institutions. Although we have not documented all of the relevant environmental differences, those that we have been able to identify emphasize the great quantitative and qualitative diversity of environmental stimuli that can confront the entering college student. This diversity makes reasonable the anxiety that many students express in choosing an appropriate college and underscores the need for providing more and better information about differences in the environments of specific institutions. At the same time, these results demonstrate dramatically that we must come to a better understanding of how environmental differences actually affect the students' educational and personal development.

It is hoped that the findings of this study will stimulate administrators and faculty members to greater efforts to understand how their institutional environments may be improved and that the measurement techniques used here will prove helpful to other researchers who may be concerned with measuring institutional differences and assessing their impact on student development.

A

The Inventory of College Activities (ICA)

NATIONAL MERIT SCHOLARSHIP CORPORATION

1580 Sherman Avenue, Evanston, Illinois GReenleaf 5-2552

August, 1962

Dear Student:

When you registered for college last Fall you filled out a form in which you indicated some of your high school activities and future college plans. This form was administered by your college as a part of a survey of entering freshmen conducted by the National Merit Scholarship Corporation.

We are now attempting to follow-up a selected group of students to determine their recent activities and current plans, and also to obtain their impressions of the freshman year in college. This study is one of a series which we are conducting to learn more about how different colleges affect the development of the student.

We would greatly appreciate your completing this booklet and returning it to us in the enclosed envelope. All of the information is to be coded and used in group comparisons for research purposes only, so your responses will be kept entirely confidential.

Since we are following up only a limited sample of students, it is important to secure as complete a response as possible. We hope you will be able to participate.

Thank you for your consideration.

Sincerely,

John M. Stalnaker
President

The Inventory of College Activities—*Continued*

ID______________ (5-8)

Your Name____
Last First Middle
(Maiden name, if married)

Home Address____
Number and Street City State

1 (9)

Your sex (Circle one)
Male. 1 (10)
Female. . . . . 2 m

INSTRUCTIONS: You can answer most of the questions by circling a number or letter, as follows:
I am now (Circle one):
A high school graduate 7
A college graduate 8
A graduate student 9

If you make an error, mark out the incorrect response like this:

Yes No
I am over 25 years of age . . . . y n

---

1. In what college did you enroll in Fall, 1961?

____
Name of College City State

2. (Circle one):
I completed my freshman year at this college. 3
I left this college before completing my freshman year, and did not enter another college 4
I changed colleges during my freshman year. 5

3. Do you plan to return to college this Fall? (Circle one)
Yes, in the same college (#1, above) 6
Yes, but in a different college. 7
Name of College______________________
Not sure 8
No 9

4. Did you take the National Merit Scholarship Qualifying Test when you were in high school?
(Circle one) Yes. 0
Not sure x
No . . . . y

5. At what high school did you take the test? (If you are not sure whether, or where, you took the test, name the high school you were attending in your <u>junior</u> year).

____
High School City State

6. What is the highest level of education you expect to complete? (Circle one)
Less than bachelor's degree. 1 (11)
B.A. or B.S. 2
M.A. or M.S. 3
Ph.D. or Ed.D. 4
M.D. or DD.S.. 5
LL.B.. 6
B.D. 7
Other (Circle and specify)______________ . . 8

The Inventory of College Activities—*Continued*

7. What is your present (or probable) major field of study?______________________

8. What occupation will you pursue after you complete your education?______________
____

9. The following activities cut across a number of specific jobs. How desirable would each of these activities be in your future job? (Circle one number for each job activity)

Activity:	Desirable		Neutral		Undesirable	(12-14)
Teaching	1	2	3	4	5	m
Research	6	7	8	9	0	
Administration	1	2	3	4	5	
Service to patients or clients	6	7	8	9	0	
Working mainly with people	1	2	3	4	5	
Working mainly with things	6	7	8	9	0	

10. Were you regularly employed during your freshman year? (Circle one)
    No 1 (15)
    Yes--
    Full-time job which was relevant to my anticipated career field 2
    Full-time job which had nothing to do with my anticipated career field. . . . 3
    Part-time job which was relevant to my anticipated career field 4
    Part-time job which had nothing to do with my anticipated career field. . . . 5

YOUR ACTIVITIES AT COLLEGE

11. Did you do any of the following things during your freshman year? (Circle either yes or no for each item) ←

	Yes	No
Gained more than ten pounds in weight	1	n
Lost more than ten pounds in weight	2	n
Flunked a course	3	n
Took a course over and above requirements	4	n
Became pinned or engaged	5	n
Broke-up with girlfriend or boyfriend	6	n
Got married	7	n
Participated in a student demonstration against some administrative policy	8	n
Won an award in an art competition (painting, ceramics, etc.)	9	n

	Yes	No	(16-17)
Was elected to a student office	1	n	m
Participated in the Undergraduate Research Program (URP) sponsored by the National Science Foundation	2	n	
Fell in love	3	n	
Changed your major field	4	n	
Dropped a course	5	n	
Wanted to take a course but couldn't because of other requirements	6	n	
Changed your long-term career plans	7	n	
Wrote an article for the school paper or magazine	8	n	
Had a lead in a college play	9	n	

12. What is your average grade so far in college? (Circle one)
    A . . . . 1 (18) m
    A- or B+. 2
    B 3
    B- or C+. 4
    C 5
    C- or D+. 6
    D or less 7

13. Is your average grade as reported above a fair indication of your ability? (Circle one)
    It grossly under-represents my ability 8
    It slightly under-represents my ability. 9
    It is a fair representation of my ability. 0
    It slightly over-represents my ability x
    It grossly over-represents my ability. . . . . y

The Inventory of College Activities—*Continued*

14. In an average week during your freshman year, how much time did you spend in each of the following activities?

IMPORTANT: Fill in the boxes with two digits indicating the average number of hours spent in each activity during a typical seven-day period. Indicate time to the nearest hour. Do not write in fractional hours.

FOR EXAMPLE: If you spent about 8 hours a night sleeping, you slept 7 x 8 or 56 hours a week, which you would indicate thus: [5|6]

If you attended movies or plays about twice a week for about 2 hours each time, you would indicate your 4 hours of movie attendence thus: [0|4]

NOTE: If less than 10 hours were spent in an activity, write in the preceding zero. Five hours is indicated as "05", 1 hour as "01". If you did not engage in an activity, write in "00".

Activity	No. of Hrs. (19-38)
Attending class	[ ][ ]
Attending lab	[ ][ ]
Studying for school assignments	[ ][ ]
Reading for pleasure.	[ ][ ]
Talking informally with others.	[ ][ ]
Watching TV	[ ][ ]
Attending movies and plays	[ ][ ]
Watching athletic events (inter-collegiate or intramural)	[ ][ ]
Working on other projects or hobbies not directly related to course work or a job . . .	[ ][ ]
Personal care (bathing, fixing hair, shaving, putting on make-up, etc.)	[ ][ ]

Activity	No. of Hrs. (39-56)
Sleeping.	[ ][ ]
Working for a salary or hourly wage.	[ ][ ]
Daydreaming	[ ][ ]
Working on your own private business enterprise.	[ ][ ]
Participating in sports and practice sessions.	[ ][ ]
Attending club or organizational activities (meetings, pledge-duties, etc.)	[ ][ ]
Participating in musical, dramatic or artistic activities.	[ ][ ]
Playing games (cards, chess, etc.).	[ ][ ]
Traveling (include commuting or other regular trips away from campus; exclude vacations). . . .	[ ][ ]

15. Of which of the following organizations were you a member?

Organization	Active member	Inactive member	Not a member
Social Fraternity or Sorority . .	1	2	n
Intramural athletic team.	3	4	n
College athletic team	5	6	n
Student government.	7	8	n
Choir or glee club.	9	0	n
Concert band or orchestra	x	y	n
Marching band	1	2	n
Religious club.	3	4	n

Organization	Active member	Inactive member	Not a member (57-59) m
Subject matter club.	1	2	n
Hobby club	3	4	n
Drama club	5	6	n
Service organization	7	8	n
Campus ratio or TV station	9	0	n
Athletic booster club (pep club, card section, etc.). . . .	x	y	n

The Inventory of College Activities—*Continued*

16. Below is a list of things that college students sometimes do. Indicate which of these things you did during your freshman year in college. (Exclude things which you did only while on vacations.) If you engaged in an activity regularly with a frequency appropriate for that activity, circle the number under "frequently". If you engaged in an activity one or more times, but not frequently, circle the number under "occasionally". Circle "Not at all" ("n"), if you never performed the activity.
(Circle one for each item)

	Frequently	Occasionally	Not at all
Played chess	1	2	n
Picked-up a date in a bar, restaurant or similar place	3	4	n
Donated money to charity	5	6	n
Prayed (not including grace before meals)	7	8	n
Said grace before meals	9	0	n
Discussed how to make money with other students	x	y	n
Listened to modern (progressive) jazz	1	2	n
Listened to New Orlean's (Dixieland) jazz	3	4	n
Listened to folk music	5	6	n
Went to a party	7	8	n
Gambled with cards or dice	9	0	n
Attended a campus political rally or meeting	x	y	n
Drove a car over 80 M.P.H.	1	2	n
Played a practical joke or prank on another student	3	4	n
Stayed up all night	5	6	n
Attended a public lecture (not for a course)	7	8	n
Drank wine	9	0	n
Attended a public recital or concert	x	y	n
Lost privileges for infraction of college rules	1	2	n
Gave a prepared talk to a class	3	4	n
Listened to the radio	5	6	n
Listened to a friend discuss a personal problem	7	8	n
Made wisecracks in class	9	0	n
Played a musical instrument	x	y	n
Loaned money to a friend	1	2	n
Drank whisky, gin or other hard liquor	3	4	n
Hazed freshmen	5	6	n
Went to sleep in class	7	8	n
Came late to class	9	0	n
Studied with another person or persons	x	y	n
Took No-Doz or other stay-awake pills	1	2	n
Changed clothes during the day (exclude gym or athletics)	3	4	n
Donated blood	5	6	n
Performed pledge duties	7	8	n
Said "hello" to students you didn't know	9	0	n
Took a sleeping pill	x	y	n
Cooked a complete meal	1	2	n
Daydreamed in class	3	4	n

	Frequently	Occasionally	Not at all
Did voluntary work for a hospital or service organization (Red Cross, Heart Fund, etc.)	5	6	n (60-72) m
Arranged a date for another student	7	8	n
Loaned money to another student	9	0	n
Went social (ballroom) dancing	x	y	n
Went square dancing	1	2	n
Argued with a teacher in class	3	4	n
Bought a paper-back book (not for a class)	5	6	n
Listened to classical or semi-classical music	7	8	n
Bit your fingernails	9	0	n
Rode in a sports car	x	y	n
Borrowed money from another student	1	2	n
Took a nap or rest during the day	3	4	n
Talked to another student in a language other than English	5	6	n
Picked-up a hitch-hiker	7	8	n
Tutored someone for money	9	0	n
Tutored someone for free	x	y	n
Went to a night club with a floor show	1	2	n
Had psychotherapy or personal counseling (with a psychologist or psychiatrist)	3	4	n
Made bets on a game or other event (not cards or dice)	5	6	n
Attended a burlesque show	7	8	n
Went to an overnight or week-end party	9	0	n
Went to the movies	x	y	n
Attended a professional stage play	1	2	n
Went swimming	3	4	n
Saw a foreign movie	5	6	n
Rode a bicycle	7	8	n
Took tranquilizing pills	9	0	n
Attended a student stage play	x	y	n
Drove a car	1	2	n
Took Metrecal or similar dietary formula	3	4	n
Attended an orchestral concert	5	6	n
Attended a formal dance	7	8	n
Discussed sex with friends	9	0	n
Took vitamins	x	y	n
Drank beer	1	2	n
Participated in a drag race	3	4	n
Attended a fashion show	5	6	n
Visited a museum	7	8	n
Argued with other students	9	0	n

The Inventory of College Activities—*Continued*

	Frequently	Occasionally	Not at all
Voted in a student election	1	2	n
Discussed religion with other students	3	4	n
Took a laxative	5	6	n
Been interviewed as a client in the college counseling center	7	8	n
Studied in the library	9	0	n
Ate lunch or dinner alone	x	y	n
Called a teacher by his first name	1	2	n
Felt homesick	3	4	n
Put up decorations for a party	5	6	n
Attended a ballet performance	7	8	n
Overslept and missed a class or appointment	9	0	n
Checked out a book or journal from the college library	x	y	n
Violated college rules or regulations without getting caught	1	2	n
Visited a person in a hospital	3	4	n
Painted (oil, watercolor, pastel, etc.)	5	6	n
Played table tennis or ping-pong	7	8	n
Read the Bible	9	0	n
Had a blind date	x	y	n

	Frequently	Occasionally	Not at all	(73-79) m
Danced the twist	1	2	n	
Tried on clothes in a store without buying anything	3	4	n	
Pushed a stalled car (other than your own)	5	6	n	
Drew pictures or doodles in a notebook during class	7	8	n	
Attended an art exhibition	9	0	n	
Served as a subject in a psychological experiment or demonstration	x	y	n	
Cut class	1	2	n	
Wrote letters home	3	4	n	
Drank in a bar or club	5	6	n	
Told jokes	7	8	n	
Lost your temper	9	0	n	
Cheated on examinations	x	y	n	
Attended Sunday School	1	2	n	
Attended church	3	4	n	
Cried	5	6	n	
Discussed sports with other students	7	8	n	
Asked questions in class	9	0	n	
Participated in informal group singing	x	y	n	
Became intoxicated	1	2	n	

17. What is your current marital or dating status? (Circle one) **(80)**

- Married (children or expecting) 1
- Married (no children) 2
- Engaged 3
- Pinned or going steady. 4
- Usually date same person. 5
- Usually date different person 6
- Do not date at all. 7

2 (9)

18. What was the frequency of your dates while at college? Indicate the average number of dates of each type that you had per month. If less than one every two months, write in "00". (If married, indicate the number of times you and your spouse went out together to these events.) (10-15)

Casual coke, coffee or study dates (No. per month) → [|]

Informal dates to movies, student gatherings, etc. (No. per month) → [|]

Formal dates to dances and big parties (No. per month) → [|]

19. Below is a brief list of personal traits or characteristics. Circle all which are accurate descriptions of yourself. (16-17) m

Intelligent	1	Argumentative	1
Lazy	2	Take my studies seriously	2
Impulsive	3	Popular with the opposite sex	3
Considerate	4	Ambitious	4
Immature	5	Religious	5
Like to talk	6	Good sense of humor	6
Social climber	7	Talented	7
Politically conservative	8	Messy	8

The Inventory of College Activities—*Continued*

FOR MEN:

20\. When attending class, I wore:

	Usually	Occasionally	Seldom or Never
Suit	1	2	n
Sport jacket and tie	3	4	n
Sport jacket (no tie)	5	6	n
Sport shirt and slacks	7	8	n
Sweat shirt or tee shirt and slacks	9	0	n
Blue jeans (levis, dungarees)	x	y	n

At dinner, I wore:

	Usually	Occasionally	Seldom or Never
Suit	1	2	n
Sport jacket and tie	3	4	n
Sport jacket (no tie)	5	6	n
Sport shirt and slacks	7	8	n
Sweat shirt or tee shirt and slacks	9	0	n
Blue jeans (levis, dungarees)	x	y	n

FOR WOMEN:

When attending class, I wore: (18-19) m

	Usually	Occasionally	Seldom or Never
Suit or dress	1	2	n
Skirt with sweater or blouse	3	4	n
Slacks	5	6	n
Blue jeans (levis, dungarees)	7	8	n
Bermudas	9	0	n
Shorts	x	y	n

At dinner, I wore:

	Usually	Occasionally	Seldom or Never
Suit or dress	1	2	n
Skirt with sweater or blouse	3	4	n
Slacks	5	6	n
Blue jeans (levis, dungarees)	7	8	n
Bermudas	9	0	n
Shorts	x	y	n

DESCRIPTION OF ONE OF YOUR CLASSES

21\. Name below the course you took this past year which was most closely related to your primary field of interest:

Name of Course	Department	Time at which class met

← (20-24)

22\. Approximate number of students in class (lecture only): [ ][ ][ ]   What was the approximate age of the instructor: [ ][ ] years

23\. Please circle "yes" for all of the following statements which apply to this course. Circle "no" if the statement does not apply. (If the course had a lab portion, check only those items which apply to the lecture portion.)

	Yes	No
The class met only at a regularly scheduled time and place	1	n
Students had assigned seating	2	n
Attendance was usually taken every day	3	n
Students were permitted to smoke in class	4	n
The class was taught by a graduate student	5	n
The lectures followed the text book closely	6	n
The instructor was a woman	7	n
The instructor called students by their first names	8	n
The instructor encouraged a lot of class discussion	9	n
The instructor was exceptionally well-grounded in the course subject matter	0	n
The instructor outlined the day's lecture or discussion at the beginning of each class	x	n

← (25-26) m

	Yes	No
The instructor was enthusiastic	1	n
The instructor had a good sense of humor	2	n
The instructor was often sarcastic in class	3	n
The instructor spoke in a monotone	4	n
The instructor usually wore a coat and tie to class	5	n
The instructor was often dull and uninteresting	6	n
The instructor knew me by name	7	n
The instructor was engaged in research of some kind	8	n
We sometimes had unannounced or "pop" quizzes	9	n
The examinations were usually of the "objective" type (multiple choice, matching, etc.), rather than the "essay" type	0	n
I almost never spoke in class unless I was called on	x	n

The Inventory of College Activities—*Continued*

	Yes	No
If he had wanted, a student could probably have passed this course mainly on "bluff". . .	1	n
I knew the instructor's first name	2	n
I knew which institution awarded the instructor his degree.	3	n
I usually did all of the assigned reading in this course	4	n
I took notes regularly in class. . .	5	n →

	Yes	No	
I sometimes argued openly with the instructor	6	n	(27) m
I sometimes argued openly with other students in the class. . . .	7	n	
I usually typed my written assignments.	8	n	
I was in the instructor's office one or more times.	9	n	
I was a guest in the instructor's home one or more times	0	n	

YOUR LIVING QUARTERS

24. Where did you live during your freshman year at college (Circle any which apply)

Dormitory	1	(28) m
Fraternity or Sorority House.	2	
Other student housing	3	
Private room or apartment (on campus)	4	
Private room or apartment (off campus).	5	
At home (exclude vacations)	6	

NOTE: If you lived only at home, skip to question #33, page 10.

25. About how many other students lived in the same residence where you lived? (29-31)

26. How many roommates did you have?

None (Circle and skip to question #28).	1	(32)
One	2	
Two	3	
Three or more	4	

27. The following items apply to your roommate. (If you had more than one roommate, describe the one whom you knew best.) Circle all of the following which accurately describe your roommate.

Intelligent	1	Argumentative	1	(33-34) m
Noisy	2	Drank a lot	2	
Minded his own business	3	Popular with the opposite sex	3	
Went out on a lot of dates.	4	Ambitious	4	
Took his studies seriously.	5	Dressed very well	5	
Considerate	6	Good sense of humor	6	
Immature.	7	Talented.	7	
Liked to talk	8	A close friend of mine.	8	
Social climber.	9	Had a lot of money.	9	
Politically conservative.	0	Messy	0	

28. Which of the following did you have displayed in your room at college? (Circle all that apply)

Pennants.	1	Abstract painting	7	(35) m
Souvenirs from dates (programs, flowers, favors, etc.).	2	Other painting or drawing	8	
Cartoons or jokes	3	Sports trophies	9	
Scientific models	4	Photographs of friends.	0	
Pin-ups	5 →	Religious articles.	x	
Schedule.	6	None of these	y	

29. In your living quarters did you have a: (circle only one)

Housemother	1	(36)
Dorm counselor.	2	
Head resident	3	
None of these (Circle and skip to question #31) . . .	4	

The Inventory of College Activities—*Continued*

30. How would you describe this person? (Circle all which apply)

Friendly	1	(37)
Strict, but fair	2	
Strict, but showed favoritism.	3	
Strict almost to the point of being ruthless	4	
Listened to your problems.	5	
Generally permissive, but had limits	6	
Permissive, let you get away with almost anything.	7	

31. What action (if any) would be taken by the administration at your college if a student in <u>your</u> living quarters were known to have done the following:

	No policy against this	Reprimand or minor disciplinary action	Major disciplinary action (possible expulsion from college)	Sure expulsion from college	
Coming in from date 10-15 minutes late	1	2	3	4	(38-42) m
Coming in from date 2 hours late	5	6	7	8	
Cheating on examinations	9	0	x	y	
Drinking in student union. . . .	1	2	3	4	
Drinking in living quarters. . .	5	6	7	8	
Drinking somewhere off campus. .	9	0	x	y	
Being drunk.	1	2	3	4	
Being alone with a date in your room during the daytime.	5	6	7	8	
Being alone with a date in your room at night	9	0	x	y	
Having a date with a faculty member	1	2	3	4	
Staying off campus overnight without permission	5	6	7	8	
Organizing a student demonstration against some administrative policy.	9	0	x	y	
Writing off-color stories in a student publication . . .	1	2	3	4	
Participating in a water fight or dormitory raid. . . .	5	6	7	8	

32. How long did it take you to get from your living quarters to the following places (indicate traveling time in minutes by the means you usually used; e.g., if you walked, give walking time; if you usually drove, give driving and parking time, etc.). For example, if it took 5 minutes to get to the library from your living quarters, you would write in the first pair of boxes: [0|5] mins. Please fill in all items.

← (43-56)

Library . . . . [|] mins.

Student Union . . . . [|] mins.

Your most distant classroom . . . . [|] mins.

Nearest restaurant or snack bar . . . . [|] mins. →

Closest place where you could visit and talk with people your own age of the opposite sex . . . . . [|] mins.

Nearest bar that served alcoholic beverages to students . . . . [|] mins.

Nearest movie theater. . . [|] mins.

The Inventory of College Activities—*Continued*

33. How far was the campus from your hometown? (Circle one)

0 - 9 miles	1	(57)
10 - 19 miles	2	
20 - 49 miles	3	
50 - 99 miles	4	
100 - 199 miles	5	
200 - 499 miles	6	
500 - 999 miles	7	
1,000 or more miles	8	

34. My hometown is located (Circle one):

in the same state as the college.	1	(58) m
in a different state.	2	
in a foreign country.	3	

35. Compared with my hometown, the weather at my college was (Circle one):

the same.	4
much warmer	5
somewhat warmer	6
somewhat colder	7
much colder	8

IMPRESSIONS OF YOUR COLLEGE

36. Answer each of the following as it applies to your college:

	Yes	No
It is a friendly campus.	1	n
The students are under a great deal of pressure to get high grades	2	n
The student body is apathetic and has little "school spirit"	3	n
Most of the students are of a very high calibre academically	4	n
The students here are not particularly concerned about their personal appearance.	5	n
The students have a sense of superiority with regard to most other colleges.	6	n
There is a keen competition among most of the students for high grades	7	n
The students are not well-rounded.	8	n
Upperclassmen go out of their way to help new students	9	n
It's important socially to be in the right group or club	0	n
Freshmen have to take orders from upperclassmen for a period of time.	x	n
There isn't much to do except go to class and study.	y	n
I felt "lost" when I first came to the campus	1	n
The campus paper and humor magazine are carefully censored by the administration.	2	n
There is a narrow political point of view on campus.	3	n

	Yes	No (59-61) m
The administration is not really very concerned about the individual student	4	n
Athletes are given special privileges	5	n
A great deal of independence is granted the student.	6	n
The library here is well run and convenient to use.	7	n
Being in this college builds poise and maturity	8	n
This college has an outstanding reputation nationally.	9	n
There are too many required courses here	0	n
Athletics are overemphasized here	x	n
There is a large group of "avant-guarde" students on campus	y	n
The social activities are overemphasized	1	n
The intellectual atmosphere is definitely on the theoretical, rather than the practical side	2	n
There is a great deal of conformity among the students	3	n
The classes are usually run in a very informal manner	4	n
The students are often noisy and inattentive at concerts and lectures	5	n
There is too much emphasis on fraternities and sororities.	6	n
The campus is too big.	7	n
The library is too noisy	8	n

The Inventory of College Activities—*Continued*

Answer each of the following as it applies to your college:

	Yes	No		Yes	No	(62) m
The student publications often openly ridicule administrative policies	1	n	The faculty seem to be interested more in research than in teaching students	4	n	
The faculty go out of their way to help the student.	2	n	The faculty is usually liberal in interpreting regulations and treat violations with understanding and tolerance. . . .	5	n	
Most students are more like "numbers in a book".	3	n				

37. How many students did you call by their first names or by nickname? (Estimate this as best as you can) [ ][ ][ ]

How many of these students did you consider close friends? [ ][ ][ ] (63-68)

38. Where did the majority of your friends at college live?

Dormitory 1 (69)
Fraternity or sorority house. 2
Off campus room or apartment. 3
With parents. 4
Other________________________________ . . 5

39. To what extent does each of the following describe the psychological climate or atmosphere at your college? (Circle one number for each)

	Very Descriptive	In Between	Not at all Descriptive	(70-74) m
Intellectual	1	2	3	
Snobbish	4	5	6	
Competitive.	7	8	9	
High Morale.	0	x	y	
Impersonal	1	2	3	
Conventional	4	5	6	
Arty	7	8	9	
Social	0	x	y	
Victorian.	1	2	3	
Practical-minded	4	5	6	
Warm	7	8	9	
Enterprising	0	x	y	
Realistic.	1	2	3	
Tense.	4	5	6	
Liberal.	7	8	9	
Carefree	0	x	y	
Sophisticated.	1	2	3	

40. Have you ever felt "out of place" at this college? (Circle one)

Yes, all of the time. . . . . 1 (75) m
Yes, frequently 2
Yes, but only occasionally. 3
No, never 4

41. What is your over-all evaluation of your college so far? (Circle one)

Very satisfied with my college. 5
Satisfied with my college 6
On the fence. 7
Dissatisfied with my college. 8
Very dissatisfied with my college 9

The Inventory of College Activities—*Continued*

42. All in all, in terms of your own needs and desires, how much of the following did you receive during your freshman year? (Circle the appropriate number after each item)

	Too much or too many	Just about the right amount	Not enough	(76-80) m
Personal direction in studies and in course selection	1	2	3	
Freedom in course selection.	4	5	6	
Opportunity for classroom discussion	7	8	9	
Social life.	0	x	y	
Extracurricular activity	1	2	3	
Intellectual activity.	4	5	6	
Personal contacts with classmates.	7	8	9	
Personal contacts with faculty	0	x	y	
Time for social activity	1	2	3	
Time for extracurricular activity.	4	5	6	
Time for intellectual activity	7	8	9	
Work required of you in courses.	0	x	y	
Outlets for creative activities.	1	2	3	
Occupational or professional preparation . . .	4	5	6	
Liberal studies not closely related to any occupation.	7	8	9	
Examinations on course material.	0	x	y	
Dates.	1	2	3	
Friends.	4	5	6	
Sleep.	7	8	9	
Exercise	0	x	y	

THIS IS THE END OF THE BOOKLET

THANK YOU VERY MUCH.

B

Analyses to Determine the Probable Effects of Bias in the Sample of Student Respondents to the Questionnaire

SURVEY RESEARCH has firmly established that persons who respond to mailed questionnaires differ in certain respects from nonrespondents. For this reason, we considered it important to determine the extent to which the results of this study may have been affected by biases in the sample of students who completed and returned the Inventory of College Activities.

The present study afforded an unusual opportunity to estimate these effects since some data were available on all subjects (respondents and nonrespondents alike) from the questionnaire they completed when they first entered college in the fall of 1961. Table B1 compares the freshman input data of a random sample of 1,069 students who completed and returned the ICA in 1962 with input data from a random sample of 1,028 students who did not return the ICA. The rate of response is significantly ($p < .01$) higher among female than among male students. In addition, the respondents had higher grades in high school than did the nonrespondents and were generally more likely to have achieved in extracurricular areas. The differences in extracurricular achievements, however, appear to be trivial, with the possible exceptions of "Had leads in high school or church-sponsored plays" and "Edited the school paper or literary magazine."

The findings in Table B1 do indeed reveal certain biases in the responding sample. But the primary methodological question in the current study is how these biases may have affected the *relationships* among the environmental variables studied. If there is reason to believe that they have altered the *relative* ordering of institutions on certain variables, then the generalizability of the results of this study is open to serious question. In order to explore these possibilities more directly, freshman input measures were computed for each of the 246 colleges, using only the 1961 freshman data originally provided by those students who later completed and returned the ICA in 1962. Correlations among the input characteristics scored in this manner were then compared with the correlations based on data provided by all entering students, as reported in the earlier study of student inputs (Astin, 1965d, Table E1). Table B2 compares these two sets of intercorrelations using the 18 extracurricular achievements and two of the variables which showed the largest differences between respondents and nonrespondents: percentage of males in the student body and percentage of students who edited their high school paper. The first column of coefficients in Table B2 shows the correlations between the percentage of males in the student body and each of the 18 extracurricular achievements, using only the data from those students who later responded to the follow-up questionnaire. The

Table B1

Freshman Input Characteristics of Random Samples of Respondents and Nonrespondents to the ICA

Characteristic	Respondents (N=1,069)		Nonrespondents (N=1,028)	
	Mean	S.D.	Mean	S.D.
Sex (% male)	47.5		38.3	
High school class size	4.0	2.14	4.1	2.17
Average high school grade	5.4	1.75	4.9	1.79
Highest degree sought	2.7	0.84	2.6	0.82
Father's educational level	3.7	1.54	3.5	1.44
Percentage who:				
Placed in school science contest	9.5		8.2	
Placed in state science contest	3.8		2.4	
Placed in national science contest	0.3		0.1	
Leads in H. S. or church-sponsored plays	28.5		22.8	
Placed in state speech or debate contest	5.1		6.1	
Placed in national speech or debate contest	0.1		0.4	
Elected to student offices	45.3		41.5	
Elected president of H. S. class	9.5		10.1	
Won awards for leadership	34.3		31.2	
Participated in national music contest	2.5		1.8	
Received high rating in state music contest	12.4		10.0	
Received high rating in national music contest	1.3		0.7	
Won awards in art competition	3.8		5.1	
Exhibited works of art at H. S.	7.1		6.8	
Exhibited works of art other than at H. S.	5.5		4.1	
Edited school paper or magazine	14.3		10.7	
Had poems, short stories, etc. published	10.2		8.3	
Won awards for creative writing	6.2		3.5	

second column in Table B2 shows the same correlations based on data provided by all entering freshmen in 1961 (both respondents and nonrespondents to the 1962 follow-up, as well as students who were not randomly sampled for the follow-up). The last two columns in Table B2 show the correlations, again computed two different ways, between the percentage of students who edited the school paper or literary magazine and the other 17 nonacademic achievements. Note that in addition to the differences in the samples of students used to compute the input scores, correlations in the second and fourth columns differ from correlations in the first and third columns in the number of institutions used (248 rather than the 246 selected for the follow-up study).

A comparison of the coefficients in Table B2 shows clearly that the two sets of correlations correspond very closely. The tendency for correlations based on all students to be slightly higher than the correlations based only on respondents to the follow-up may be attributable to the somewhat reduced variance among institutions that occurs as a result of the response bias. Nevertheless, the relative size of the coefficients is almost identical: the rank-difference correlation

Table B2

The Effects of Respondent Bias on Correlations Among Selected Student Input Characteristics

1961 Student Input Characteristics	Correlation with Percent Males in Student Body		Correlation with Percent Who Edited School Paper	
	Respondents to 1962 Follow-up (246 colleges)	All Students* (248 colleges)	Respondents to 1962 Follow-up (246 colleges)	All Students* (248 colleges)
Percentage who:				
Placed in school science contest	.10	.11	.30	.30
Placed in state science contest	.16	.15	.18	.26
Placed in national science contest	.11	.08	.21	.27
Leads in H. S. or church-sponsored plays	−.22	−.25	.18	.25
Placed in state speech or debate contest	.01	−.02	.20	.19
Placed in national speech or debate contest	−.11	−.11	.06	.14
Elected to student offices	−.36	−.38	.60	.64
Elected president of H. S. class	.24	.31	.07	.06
Won awards for leadership	−.18	−.18	.55	.58
Participated in national music contest	−.31	−.33	−.02	.05
Received high rating in state music contest	−.06	−.08	−.06	−.06
Received high rating in national music contest	−.26	−.31	.08	.18
Won awards in art competition	−.43	−.44	.37	.40
Exhibited works of art at H. S.	−.49	−.50	.52	.52
Exhibited works of art other than at H. S.	−.42	−.45	.42	.49
Edited school paper or literary magazine	−.32	−.37	—	—
Had poems, short stories, etc. published	−.31	−.36	.65	.71
Won awards for creative writing	−.39	−.36	.74	.79

* From A. W. Astin, *Who goes where to college?* (Chicago, Ill.: Science Research Associates, 1965), 116–117.

between the coefficients in the first two columns of Table B2 is .984; the rank-difference correlation between the last two columns of coefficients in Table B2 is .983.

In short, these findings show that the bias in the sample of respondents has little effect on the relative ordering of institutions in terms of their 1961 student input characteristics. Although these findings cannot be taken as proof that the relative ordering of institutions on the *environmental* data collected in 1962 was not affected by the response biases, they do suggest that the magnitude of such effects is likely to be small.

C

Range and Median Institutional Mean Scores[1] for All Items in the ICA

Item	Range of Scores		
	Lowest Institution	Median Institution	Highest Institution
I completed my freshman year at this college. (Percentage answering "yes")	80.4	96.0	100.0
Do you plan to return to college this fall? (Percentage answering "yes")	54.3	83.6	98.1
Did you take the National Merit Scholarship Qualifying Test when you were in high school? (Percentage answering "yes")	21.3	67.0	96.3
What is the highest level of education you expect to complete?			
Expect to complete Ph.D. or Ed. D.	.0	10.9	80.9
Expect to complete M.D. or D.D.S.	.0	5.7	30.4
Expect to complete LL.B.	.0	1.9	23.3
Expect to complete graduate degree	23.6	58.1	99.1
The following activities cut across a number of specific jobs. How desirable would each of these activities be in your future job?[2]			
Teaching	5.5	23.9	37.4
Research	56.5	78.4	86.5
Administration	21.6	30.0	36.8
Service to patients or clients	58.1	75.5	88.7
Working with people	11.8	70.6	88.0
Working with things	59.3	84.5	93.3
Were you regularly employed during your freshman year? (Percentage answering "no")	9.2	72.7	98.8
Activities in college:			
Did you do any of the following things during your freshman year? (Percentage answering "yes")			
Gained more than ten pounds in weight	10.1	22.8	42.1
Lost more than ten pounds in weight	5.0	12.6	27.8
Flunked a course	2.3	19.0	56.5
Took a course over and above requirements	4.3	35.1	67.2
Became pinned or engaged	.0	7.4	21.1
Broke up with girlfriend or boyfriend	17.6	31.5	47.8
Got married	.0	.7	7.0
Participated in a student demonstration against some administrative policy	.0	11.4	80.6

[1] Unless otherwise indicated, all scores are percentages.
[2] All except "working with people" are scored in reverse (i.e., the percentage checking the two categories at the "undesirable" end).

Range and Median Institutional Mean Scores for All Items in the ICA—*Continued*

Item	Range of Scores		
	Lowest Institution	Median Institution	Highest Institution
Won an award in an art competition (painting, ceramics, etc.)	.0	1.3	8.0
Was elected to a student office	2.6	16.4	40.4
Participated in the Undergraduate Research Program (URP) sponsored by the National Science Foundation	.0	.6	7.3
Fell in love	8.6	23.6	37.4
Changed your major field	4.3	26.3	43.4
Dropped a course	.6	18.4	55.5
Wanted to take a course but couldn't because of other requirements	11.0	46.4	81.3
Changed your long-term career plans	6.5	25.9	39.1
Wrote an article for the school paper or magazine	1.0	10.8	40.6
Had a lead in a college play	.0	2.6	16.7
What is your average grade so far in college? (7=A; 1=D or less)	3.16	3.97	4.90
Is your average grade as reported above a fair indication of your ability? (Scored on a scale of 1–5, where 5="grossly under-represents my ability." See Appendix A, item 13)	3.50	3.85	4.20
Median hours per week spent in the following activities:			
Attending class	12.2	18.0	22.9
Attending lab	.5	3.5	9.6
Studying for school assignments	15.8	28.0	38.6
Reading for pleasure	2.3	3.4	5.9
Talking informally with others	7.7	12.6	17.1
Watching TV[3]	3.5	52.6	96.9
Attending movies and plays	.6	2.4	4.1
Watching athletic events (intercollegiate or intramural	.6	2.6	4.2
Working on other projects not directly related to course work or job	.7	2.1	4.0
Personal care (bathing, fixing hair, shaving, etc.)	4.5	7.8	10.7
Sleeping	39.0	49.0	54.0
Working for a salary or hourly wage[3]	6.7	71.2	100.0
Daydreaming	1.5	3.0	5.0
Working on your own private business enterprise[3]	76.4	93.0	99.0
Participating in sports and practice sessions	.8	2.6	9.4
Attending club or organizational activities (meetings, pledge duties, etc.[3])	7.4	23.7	100.0
Participating in musical, dramatic, or artistic activities[3]	28.6	66.1	88.5
Playing games (cards, chess, etc.)	.7	2.0	4.5
Traveling (include commuting or other regular trips away from the campus; exclude vacations)	.6	2.4	12.2

[3] Percentage of students reporting no hours per week spent in the activity. Scoring of these items was reversed for the factor analyses.

Range and Median Institutional Mean Scores for All Items in the ICA—*Continued*

Item	Range of Scores		
	Lowest Institution	Median Institution	Highest Institution
Of which of the following organizations were you a member?			
Social fraternity or sorority	.0	25.4	97.8
Intramural athletic team	6.0	37.6	84.5
College athletic team	1.4	15.8	75.5
Student government	1.2	15.2	63.4
Choir or glee club	.0	15.2	42.8
Concert band or orchestra	.0	6.1	30.9
Marching band	.0	3.2	26.0
Religious club	4.6	33.8	98.2
Subject-matter club	4.0	19.0	88.0
Hobby club	.0	5.3	22.6
Drama club	.0	6.0	52.6
Service organization	2.4	21.7	67.0
Campus radio or TV station	.0	1.8	26.6
Athletic booster club (pep club, card section, etc.)	.0	13.9	71.0
Activities: (Percentage checking either "frequently" or "occasionally")			
Played chess	5.3	25.0	67.6
Picked up a date in a bar, restaurant, or similar place	1.2	14.6	43.2
Donated money to charity	46.5	77.4	98.2
Prayed (not including grace before meals)[4]	7.1	48.3	100.0
Said grace before meals[4]	.0	45.9	99.2
Discussed how to make money with other students[4]	4.6	19.1	39.6
Listened to modern (progressive) jazz	43.8	76.0	96.5
Listened to New Orleans (Dixieland) jazz	26.1	62.0	94.2
Listened to folk music[4]	4.5	21.9	74.7
Went to a party[4]	.9	28.4	74.1
Gambled with cards or dice	.0	20.0	54.0
Attended a campus political rally or meeting	18.3	56.8	94.1
Drove a car over 80 mph	.8	18.8	48.2
Played a practical joke or prank on another student	55.6	85.2	97.7
Stayed up all night	8.7	57.3	89.9
Attended a public lecture (not for a course)	35.3	75.4	98.0
Drank wine	.8	23.6	82.8
Attended a public recital or concert	33.0	77.2	98.9
Lost privileges for infraction of college rules	.0	7.4	61.7
Gave a prepared talk to a class	8.9	57.4	100.0
Listened to the radio[4]	7.0	60.5	86.8
Listened to a friend discuss a personal problem	27.3	59.2	88.2
Made wisecracks in class	8.4	30.8	67.3
Played a musical instrument	10.7	37.6	68.3
Loaned money to a friend[4]	4.5	14.3	34.0

[4] Percentage checking "frequently" only.

Range and Median Institutional Mean Scores for All Items in the ICA—*Continued*

Item	Range of Scores		
	Lowest Institution	Median Institution	Highest Institution
Drank whiskey, gin, or other hard liquor	1.3	45.6	87.5
Went to sleep in class	14.0	30.2	67.1
Came late to class	20.9	62.6	89.3
Studied with another person or persons[5]	9.7	31.0	53.3
Took No-Doz or other stay-awake pills	4.5	28.6	65.1
Changed clothes during the day[5]	4.0	27.1	82.6
Donated blood	.0	4.1	59.5
Performed pledge duties	.0	30.8	97.7
Said "hello" to students you didn't know[5]	5.9	57.2	94.0
Took a sleeping pill	.9	5.9	35.0
Cooked a complete meal	.9	27.9	77.2
Daydreamed in class	66.7	89.3	98.3
Did voluntary work for a hospital or service organization (Red Cross, etc.)	1.3	14.5	55.1
Arranged a date for another student	13.8	54.5	95.3
Loaned money to another student	70.3	86.8	97.4
Went social (ballroom) dancing	.8	69.1	89.9
Went square dancing	.0	10.8	92.2
Argued with a teacher in class	10.5	36.3	72.3
Bought a paperback book (not for class)	28.0	71.2	97.0
Listened to classical or semiclassical music	9.3	29.0	80.0
Bit your fingernails	21.6	43.0	61.8
Rode in a sports car	3.0	47.8	87.0
Borrowed money from another student	44.5	70.8	91.0
Took a nap or rest during the day[5]	6.5	23.7	45.5
Talked to another student in a language other than English	6.2	45.8	90.7
Picked up a hitchhiker	.0	12.5	55.6
Tutored someone for money	.0	1.9	10.8
Tutored someone for free	25.0	44.0	69.7
Went to a night club with a floor show	.0	13.9	74.1
Had psychotherapy or personal counseling (with a psychologist or psychiatrist)	.0	3.8	43.3
Made bets on a game or other event (not cards or dice)	.0	21.2	56.8
Attended a burlesque show	.0	5.7	60.8
Went to an overnight or week-end party	5.3	25.0	80.9
Went to the movies[5]	.0	31.1	61.1
Attended a professional stage play	4.5	31.6	86.6
Went swimming	11.3	70.1	99.1
Saw a foreign movie	10.1	49.6	97.9
Rode a bicycle	2.6	34.5	98.7
Took tranquilizing pills	.0	6.0	24.6
Attended a student stage play	10.3	80.4	99.0
Drove a car	6.9	66.3	92.8
Took Metrecal or similar dietary formula	.0	6.5	29.4
Attended an orchestral concert	17.4	55.5	96.3
Attended a formal dance	.0	65.8	93.1

[5] Percentage checking "frequently" only.

Range and Median Institutional Mean Scores for All Items in the ICA—*Continued*

Item	Range of Scores		
	Lowest Institution	Median Institution	Highest Institution
Discussed sex with friends[6]	4.0	28.1	51.0
Took vitamins	15.6	43.4	67.0
Drank beer	1.8	50.6	93.4
Participated in a drag race	.0	5.3	23.8
Attended a fashion show	.0	19.5	90.8
Visited a museum	6.0	32.8	99.1
Argued with other students[6]	1.8	20.6	61.1
Voted in a student election[6]	9.0	59.3	91.8
Discussed religion with other students[6]	17.4	42.6	85.7
Took a laxative	.9	10.6	53.9
Been interviewed as a client in the college counseling center	.0	10.2	56.4
Studied in the library[6]	4.4	50.7	87.5
Ate lunch or dinner alone	15.7	60.2	90.4
Called a teacher by his first name	.6	14.4	66.1
Felt homesick	1.8	50.0	86.8
Put up decorations for a party	9.7	52.5	92.2
Attended a ballet performance	.0	6.5	79.9
Overslept and missed a class or appointment[6]	8.7	47.3	87.2
Checked out a book or journal from the college library[6]	15.4	56.4	88.8
Violated college rules or regulations without getting caught	22.2	56.6	91.3
Visited a person in a hospital	10.4	44.3	88.2
Painted (oil, watercolor, pastel, etc.)	2.7	15.8	71.1
Played table tennis or ping-pong	17.5	62.9	93.3
Read the Bible	23.5	66.7	100.0
Had a blind date	7.1	53.0	95.5
Danced the twist[6]	.0	38.7	82.4
Tried on clothes in a store without buying anything	13.1	53.6	91.7
Pushed a stalled car (other than your own)	1.3	40.8	81.0
Drew pictures or doodles in a notebook during class[6]	7.9	23.2	41.9
Attended an art exhibition	10.2	56.2	96.4
Served as a subject in a psychological experiment or demonstration	.0	14.7	86.8
Cut class	1.7	85.0	100.0
Wrote letters home[6]	.0	47.6	79.5
Drank in a bar or club	.9	30.5	88.4
Told jokes[6]	8.8	22.8	41.5
Lost your temper	53.6	77.2	90.0
Cheated on examinations	.0	10.8	38.4
Attended Sunday School	1.0	17.7	96.4
Attended church[6]	6.9	53.7	98.9
Cried	8.3	50.0	93.0

[6] Percentage checking "frequently" only.

Range and Median Institutional Mean Scores for All Items in the ICA—*Continued*

Item	Range of Scores		
	Lowest Institution	Median Institution	Highest Institution
Discussed sports with other students[7]	5.4	29.4	65.5
Asked questions in class[7]	17.7	36.7	64.1
Participated in informal group singing	35.0	74.5	96.4
Became intoxicated	.0	24.8	71.5
What is your current marital status?			
Married	.0	1.5	12.9
Median number of dates per month:			
Casual coke, coffee, or study dates	1.90	2.89	9.24
Informal dates to movies, student gatherings, etc.	.47	1.80	7.36
Formal dates to dances and big parties	.11	.41	.77
Below is a list of personal traits or characteristics. How would you best describe yourself, choosing any or several of these?			
Intelligent	52.4	77.5	98.4
Lazy	10.1	34.8	55.8
Impulsive	22.9	40.5	55.5
Considerate	69.0	83.2	93.9
Immature	3.6	16.7	33.3
Like to talk	50.0	71.6	87.5
Social climber	1.8	11.1	27.0
Politically conservative	13.3	38.3	62.7
Argumentative	21.5	40.0	65.5
Take my studies seriously	52.1	71.4	88.7
Popular with the opposite sex	20.0	44.4	68.1
Ambitious	43.3	62.7	84.1
Religious	19.8	55.6	94.8
Good sense of humor	69.0	85.2	94.9
Talented	14.6	33.6	56.3
Messy	1.6	21.8	43.9
Description of one of your classes:			
Approximate number of students in class (lecture only)[8]	20.0	35.0	168.0
What was the approximate age of the instructor[8]	30.0	43.0	55.0
(Percentage answering "yes"):			
The class met only at a regularly scheduled time and place	82.5	95.3	100.0
Students had assigned seating	.0	47.9	90.1
Attendance was usually taken every day	.8	79.5	100.0
Students were permitted to smoke in class	.0	5.1	94.7
The class was taught by a graduate student	.0	15.8	47.6
The lectures followed the textbook closely	6.0	50.5	76.1
The instructor was a woman	.0	18.0	97.3
The instructor called students by their first names	1.6	34.9	97.4
The instructor encouraged a lot of class discussion	25.7	64.4	88.1
The instructor was exceptionally well-grounded in the course subject matter	76.0	90.4	97.8

[7] Percentage checking "frequently" only.
[8] Median.

Range and Median Institutional Mean Scores for All Items in the ICA—*Continued*

Item	Range of Scores		
	Lowest Institution	Median Institution	Highest Institution
The instructor outlined the day's lecture or discussion at the beginning of each class	22.1	41.9	65.5
The instructor was enthusiastic	61.9	85.5	98.2
The instructor had a good sense of humor	66.4	85.7	97.4
The instructor was often sarcastic in class	4.9	24.0	53.9
The instructor spoke in a monotone	3.9	18.5	42.5
The instructor usually wore a coat and tie to class	1.8	72.3	99.0
The instructor was often dull and uninteresting	3.9	18.9	43.3
The instructor knew me by name	21.5	89.0	100.0
The instructor was engaged in research of some kind	18.0	45.0	89.9
We sometimes had unannounced or "pop" quizzes	6.3	41.7	85.7
The examinations were usually of the "objective" type (multiple choice, matching, etc.), rather than the "essay" type	3.1	42.1	89.5
I almost never spoke in class unless I was called on	14.6	40.5	65.7
If he had wanted, a student could probably have passed this course mainly on "bluff"	1.1	10.7	26.4
I knew the instructor's first name	33.0	71.6	97.1
I knew which institution awarded the instructor his degree	24.2	51.4	86.7
I usually did all of the assigned reading in this course	67.3	86.5	99.3
I took notes regularly in class	55.4	79.1	96.4
I sometimes argued openly with the instructor	4.7	21.5	51.1
I sometimes argued openly with other students in the class	7.9	28.4	67.4
I usually typed my written assignments	2.1	28.3	72.5
I was in the instructor's office one or more times	28.9	67.2	98.7
I was a guest in the instructor's home one or more times	.0	7.0	39.0
Your Living Quarters:			
Where did you live during your freshman year at college?			
Dormitory	.0	82.7	100.0
Fraternity or sorority house	.0	.0	62.8
Private room or apartment (on or off campus)	.0	2.6	49.2
Lived at home	.0	10.8	100.0
About how many other students lived in the same residence where you lived?[9]	7.0	239.0	396.0
How many roommates did you have?[9]	.0	2.4	5.7
The following items apply to your roommate. (If you had more than one roommate, describe the one whom you knew best.)			
Intelligent	52.3	80.1	98.3
Noisy	8.3	20.6	43.3

[9] Median.

Range and Median Institutional Mean Scores for All Items in the ICA—*Continued*

Item	Range of Scores		
	Lowest Institution	Median Institution	Highest Institution
Minded his own business	38.4	55.5	75.3
Went out on a lot of dates	9.1	34.5	58.8
Took his studies seriously	40.9	61.9	83.1
Considerate	46.1	68.6	82.5
Immature	10.4	26.3	44.4
Liked to talk	37.0	69.3	82.8
Social climber	3.9	18.2	40.0
Politically conservative	10.0	28.2	50.6
Argumentative	13.3	33.9	60.8
Drank a lot	.0	12.8	36.3
Popular with the opposite sex	20.9	44.6	63.1
Ambitious	33.3	52.4	76.6
Dressed very well	21.6	57.8	80.5
Good sense of humor	52.4	75.7	90.5
Talented	10.0	41.7	63.5
A close friend of mine	36.5	66.6	85.3
Had a lot of money	3.4	16.6	37.7
Messy	10.3	28.0	55.4
Which of the following did you have displayed in your room at college?			
Pennants	.0	28.6	76.0
Souvenirs from dates (programs, flowers, favors, etc.)	6.1	61.3	95.6
Cartoons or jokes	16.1	57.8	79.7
Scientific models	.0	3.6	17.8
Pin-ups	.0	16.0	54.0
Schedule	35.7	81.0	100.0
Abstract painting	.9	18.4	60.2
Other painting or drawing	.0	44.8	91.4
Sports trophies	.0	9.2	30.4
Photographs of friends	24.6	65.2	91.5
Religious articles	4.0	24.3	95.7
None of these	.0	2.6	18.2
In your living quarters did you have a housemother, dorm-counselor, or head resident? (Percentage answering "yes.")	7.2	96.4	100.0
How would you describe this person?			
Friendly	7.7	76.7	97.1
Strict, but fair	7.7	45.3	78.9
Strict, almost to the point of being ruthless	.0	3.8	76.9
Listened to your problems	7.7	53.2	83.6
Permissive	.0	5.4	45.3
Travel time from your living quarters to: (Median time in minutes)			
Library	2.1	5.1	15.1
Student Union	1.0	4.5	15.8
Most distant classroom	4.2	6.7	16.0
Nearest restaurant or snack bar	2.2	5.5	15.5

Range and Median Institutional Mean Scores for All Items in the ICA—*Continued*

Item	Range of Scores		
	Lowest Institution	Median Institution	Highest Institution
Closest place to visit with the opposite sex	1.6	3.8	40.8
Nearest bar serving students	5.2	15.2	51.2
Nearest movie theater	4.6	15.5	35.8
How far was the campus from your hometown? Median miles: 1=0–9; 8=1000 or more miles	.8	5.2	8.1
My hometown is located in the same state	2.0	69.2	100.0
My hometown is located in a foreign country	.0	.7	2.2
Compared with my hometown, the weather at college was the same.	10.5	56.3	100.0
Impressions of your college (Percentage answering "yes")			
It is a friendly campus	50.6	96.9	100.0
The students are under a great deal of pressure to get high grades	.0	37.8	89.1
The student body is apathetic and has little "school spirit"	.0	35.9	86.3
Most of the students are of a very high calibre academically	10.9	65.0	100.0
The students here are not particularly concerned about their personal appearance	3.7	20.2	93.9
The students have a sense of superiority with regard to most other colleges	5.1	36.8	96.4
There is a keen competition among most of the students for high grades	10.0	51.0	93.3
The students are not well-rounded	5.4	18.8	58.1
Upperclassmen go out of their way to help new students	23.5	67.6	98.7
It's important socially to be in the right group or club	.0	29.5	90.0
Freshmen have to take orders from upperclassmen for a period of time	.0	45.0	100.0
There isn't much to do except go to class and study	4.6	29.0	70.0
I felt "lost" when I first came to the campus	14.7	29.4	64.3
The campus paper and humor magazine are carefully censored by the administration	.8	41.7	90.7
There is a narrow political point of view on campus	2.7	14.8	54.7
The administration is not really very concerned about the individual student	3.0	15.6	55.5
Athletes are given special privileges	.0	25.6	86.2
A great deal of independence is granted the student	3.5	79.7	100.0
The library here is well run and convenient to use	45.2	91.9	100.0
Being in this college builds poise and maturity	47.1	84.8	100.0
This college has an outstanding reputation nationally	11.2	62.9	100.0

Range and Median Institutional Mean Scores for All Items in the ICA—*Continued*

Item	Range of Scores		
	Lowest Institution	Median Institution	Highest Institution
There are too many required courses here	3.9	30.8	73.1
Athletics are overemphasized here	.0	3.2	56.0
There is a large group of "avant-garde" students on campus	1.6	12.4	67.7
The social activities are overemphasized	.0	8.6	55.6
The intellectual atmosphere is definitely on the theoretical, rather than the practical side	6.0	25.2	82.4
There is a great deal of conformity among the students	3.1	59.5	92.9
The classes are usually run in a very informal manner	22.6	65.8	99.2
The students are often noisy and inattentive at concerts and lectures	.0	8.6	41.6
There is too much emphasis on fraternities and sororities	.0	20.8	86.6
The campus is too big	.0	8.0	39.5
The library is too noisy	.0	9.6	71.7
The student publications often openly ridicule administrative policies	.0	34.8	96.0
The faculty go out of their way to help the student	35.4	81.1	100.0
Most students are more like "numbers in a book"	.0	6.7	79.5
The faculty seem to be interested more in research than in teaching students	.0	3.6	53.2
The faculty is usually liberal in interpreting regulations and treat violations with understanding and tolerance.	28.7	79.0	96.0
Where did the majority of your friends at college live?			
Dormitory	.0	89.1	100.0
Fraternity or sorority house	.0	6.0	63.4
With parents	.0	2.7	100.0
To what extent does each of the following describe the psychological *climate* or *atmosphere* at your college?			
(Mean score: 1 = very descriptive; 2 = in-between; 3 = not at all descriptive)			
Intellectual	1.00	1.76	2.31
Snobbish	1.63	2.66	2.96
Competitive	1.11	1.71	2.30
High Morale	1.10	1.68	2.35
Impersonal	1.70	2.45	2.90
Conventional	1.54	1.89	2.92
Arty	1.37	2.33	2.79
Social	1.14	1.83	2.63
Victorian	2.12	2.59	2.98
Practical-minded	1.25	1.64	2.35
Warm	1.03	1.40	2.30
Enterprising	1.30	1.72	2.05
Realistic	1.23	1.53	1.85
Tense	1.49	2.46	2.84

Range and Median Institutional Mean Scores for All Items in the ICA—*Continued*

Item	Range of Scores		
	Lowest Institution	Median Institution	Highest Institution
Liberal	1.05	1.77	2.69
Carefree	1.55	2.22	2.80
Sophisticated	1.37	1.78	2.69
All in all, in terms of your own needs and desires, how much of the following did you receive during your freshman year?			
(Mean scores: 1 = too much; 3 = not enough)			
Personal direction in studies and in course selection	2.03	2.22	2.53
Freedom in course selection	1.68	2.15	2.72
Opportunity for classroom discussion	1.99	2.16	2.41
Social life	1.89	2.24	2.84
Extracurricular activity	1.64	2.23	2.50
Intellectual activity	1.95	2.23	2.46
Personal contacts with classmates	1.86	2.07	2.29
Personal contacts with faculty	2.11	2.37	2.83
Time for social activity	1.95	2.24	2.89
Time for extracurricular activity	1.95	2.30	2.66
Time for intellectual activity	1.95	2.25	2.54
Work required of you in courses	1.65	2.00	2.50
Outlets for creative activities	2.09	2.41	2.65
Occupational or professional preparation	2.04	2.36	2.59
Liberal studies not closely related to any occupation	1.77	2.02	2.56
Examinations on course material	1.89	2.06	2.59
Dates	2.06	2.28	2.89
Friends	1.96	2.10	2.22
Sleep	2.17	2.50	2.76
Exercise	1.68	2.38	2.76

D

Weights Used to Score the Environmental Factors

Factors and Items	Multiple R Between Factor and Three Items	Standard Partial Regression Coefficient
Competitiveness vs. Cooperativeness:	.922	
Gambled with cards or dice		.4862
Participated in informal group singing		−.4215
Voted in a student election		−.2138
Organized Dating:		
Arranged a date for another student	.907	.5182
Had a blind date		.2613
Went to an overnight or week-end party		.2579
Independence:	.801	
Argued with other students		.4339
Member of college athletic team		.3539
Participated in a student demonstration against some administrative policy		.2951
Cohesiveness:	.873	
Number of close friends among fellow students		.5233
Discussed how to make money with friends		.3427
Freshmen have to take orders from the upperclassmen		.2798
Informal Dating:	.854	
Number of casual coke, coffee, or study dates		.6096
Fell in love		.3405
Discussed sex with other students		.1542
Femininity:	.878	
Tried on clothes in a store without buying anything		.4455
Took Metrecal or similar dietary formula		.4243
Attended a ballet performance		.1789
Drinking vs. Religiousness:	.951	
Drank beer		.5249
Drank wine		.3835
Prayed (not including grace before meals)		−.1648
Musical and Artistic Activity:	.847	
Attended a public recital		.5707
Played a musical instrument		.3225
Listened to folk music		.2151
Leisure Time:	.867	
Time spent attending movies and plays		.5074

Weights Used to Score the Environmental Factors—*Continued*

Factors and Items	Multiple R Between Factor and Three Items	Standard Partial Regression Coefficient
Went to the movies		.2607
Time spent playing games (cards, chess, etc.)		.2674
Career Indecision:	.778	
Changed your major field		.4457
Changed your long-term career plans		.2675
Been interviewed as a client in the college counseling center		.3067
Regularity of Sleeping Habits:	.786	
Time spent sleeping		.3252
Stayed up all night		−.4621
Took No-Doz or other stay-awake pills		−.2239
Use of the Library:	.668	
Checked out a book or journal from the college library		.4285
Studied in the library		.2805
Time spent reading for pleasure		.2492
Conflict with Regulations:	.734	
Lost privileges for infraction of college rules		.4292
Attended church		.4457
Drank in a bar or club		.3473
Student Employment:	.883	
Regularly employed during the school year		.7921
Cheated on examinations		.2519
Drank in a bar or club		.2436
Use of Automobiles:	.798	
Drove a car		.6241
Listened to New Orleans (Dixieland) jazz		.3773
Cheated on examinations		−.3478
Involvement in the Class:	.890	
Instructor encouraged a lot of class discussion		.4714
Instructor knew me by name		.2697
Overslept and missed a class or appointment		−.3750
Verbal Aggressiveness:	.905	
I sometimes argued openly with the instructor		.5646
Asked questions in class		.3226
Made wisecracks in class		.2286
Extraversion of the Instructor	.907	
Instructor was enthusiastic		.3582
Instructor had a good sense of humor		.1177
Instructor was often dull and uninteresting		−.5446

Weights Used to Score the Environmental Factors—*Continued*

Factors and Items	Multiple R Between Factor and Three Items	Standard Partial Regression Coefficient
Familiarity with the Instructor:	.859	
I knew the instructor's first name		.3618
I was a guest in the instructor's home one or more times		.3545
I was in the instructor's office one or more times		.3169
Organization in the Classroom:	.737	
Students had assigned seating		.5053
Class met only at a regularly scheduled time and place		.1868
Came late to class		−.2972
Severity of Grading:	.875	
Flunked a course		.6074
Lectures followed the textbook closely		.1715
I usually typed my written assignments		−.2719
*Administrative Factors**		
Spread of the Campus:	.919	
Travel time to most distant classroom		.4877
Travel time to the library		.2612
Travel time to the student union		.2780
Friendliness of the Dorm Counselor or House-mother:	.883	
Friendly		.4343
Listened to your problems		.3375
Strict, almost to the point of being ruthless		−.2740
Academic Competitiveness:	.936	
Students are under a great deal of pressure to get high grades		.3997
There is keen competition among most of the students for high grades		.3918
Most of the students are of a very high calibre academically		.2430
Conern for the Individual Student:	.929	
Warm		.3430
Most students are more like "numbers in a book"		−.5236
I felt "lost" when I first came to the campus		−.2225

* The four Administrative Factors were not scored by regression procedures (see Chapter 4).

Weights Used to Score the Environmental Factors—*Continued*

Factors and Items	Multiple R Between Factor and Three Items	Standard Partial Regression Coefficient
School Spirit:	.841	
Being in this college builds poise and maturity		.3823
Student body is apathetic and has little "school spirit"		−.4603
There isn't much to do except go to class and study		−.3132
Permissiveness:	.922	
Liberal		.5501
Classes are usually run in a very informal manner		.2292
Victorian		−.3082
Snobbishness:	.882	
Snobbish		.3702
Practical-minded		−.3572
Realistic		−.3785
Emphasis on Athletics:	.757	
Athletics are overemphasized here		.4794
Athletes are given special privileges		.4329
Not enough exercise		−.2955
Flexibility of the Curriculum:	.783	
Not enough outlets for creative activities		−.4276
Not enough freedom in course selection		−.4014
Too much work required in courses		−.3153
Emphasis on Social Life:	.896	
Social		.5390
Not enough social life		−.3985
Not enough personal contacts with classmates		−.1901

E

Administrator's Questionnaire

NATIONAL MERIT SCHOLARSHIP CORPORATION

1580 Sherman Avenue, Evanston, Illinois GReenleaf 5-2552

August, 1962

Since sending you the summary of the data from our survey of entering freshmen, we have computed norms for the 18 high school achievements of the students. Enclosed you will find copies of these norms for the total sample of institutions and for your institutional subgroup.

We are now attempting to relate certain characteristics of the 248 colleges to the characteristics of the students admitted. We have already obtained some data about each institution from various sources such as American Universities and Colleges, college catalogues, etc., but there are still certain items of information which we need. We would, therefore, be grateful if you would complete this booklet and return it to us at your earliest convenience. We have enclosed a return envelope for this purpose.

In the future we plan to mail a brief follow-up questionnaire to a random subsample of the 1961 entering freshmen. Through this follow-up we hope to be able to relate different college experiences to changes in the students' career plans and educational aspirations.

We will continue to keep you informed of the progress of these studies and will send you results as they become available.

Thank you once again for your interest and help.

Sincerely yours,

Alexander W. Astin

Alexander W. Astin,
Project Director

Administrator's Questionnaire—*Continued*

Name of Institution________________________________

Name of College Official Providing Data________________________

Position________________________

IMPORTANT: We are now preparing certain reports of our freshmen survey data for publication in monograph form. This monograph will be intended primarily for the use of professionals (high school counselors, college administrators, etc.). In order to protect the anonymity of each institution, we are at this time planning only to list all the participating institutions at the end of the monograph. However, we now believe that certain of our analyses of institutional subgroups will be much more meaningful to the reader if we can identify the specific institutions involved. We would, therefore, appreciate your indicating below whether or not it would be permissible to identify your institution by name in some of the subgroup analyses. (We will, of course, abide by whatever decision you make.)

It is permissible to identify our institution in the subgroup analyses____

We would prefer not to be identified in the subgroup analyses____

Most of the following questions can be answered by circling a number after the appropriate alternative (e.g., 1 ② 3). Additional space is provided for any items which ask for narrative information.

1. The institution operates on the
   - semester system. 1
   - quarter system 2
   - Other (circle and specify)________________ . . 3

2. Are male students required to live on campus?
   - Yes. 1
   - Only under certain conditions* 2
   - No 3
   - No male students 4

   *These conditions are ________________________

3. Are female students required to live on campus?
   - Yes. 1
   - Only under certain conditions* 2
   - No 3
   - No female students 4

   *These conditions are ________________________

4. Are students permitted to keep their own automobiles on campus?
   - Yes. 1
   - Yes, but only under certain conditions*. . . 2
   - No 3

   *These conditions are ________________________

5. Are instructors required to report class attendence?
   - Yes. 1
   - No 2

6. What are the regulations (if any) governing class cuts?________________________

Administrator's Questionnaire—*Continued*

7. Are students' grades routinely reported to parents?
   - Yes, both mid-term and final 1
   - Yes, final grades only 2
   - No 3

8. Are warnings of unsatisfactory work <u>routinely</u> reported to: (Circle one alternative for each item)

	Yes	No
students?	1	2
parents?	1	2
advisors?	1	2

9. Which one(s) of the following do you have? (Circle one alternative for each item)

	Yes	No
National social fraternities or sororities	1	2
Local social fraternities or sororities	1	2
Eating clubs or other formal social organizations	1	2

10. Do you have a student counseling bureau or guidance center which is staffed by professional counselors or psychologists?
    - Yes. 1
    - No 2

    If yes, approximately how many full-time counselors work in the center?__________

11. Are examinations proctored?
    - Routinely. 1
    - Varies with the instructor . . . 2
    - No ("honor system"). 3

12. Does the administration hire staff with atheistic or agnostic beliefs?
    - This would not be a consideration in hiring staff 1
    - An individual might not be hired because of such beliefs. . . . 2
    - Such individuals would never be hired with the knowledge of the administration 3

13. What are the regulations (if any) governing attendance at chapel or religious services?

    ____

    ____

14. Do student assemblies usually open or close with prayer?
    - Yes. 1
    - No 2

15. Is "hazing" of freshmen traditional?
    - Yes, generally 1
    - Yes, but on a small scale. . . . 2
    - No 3

16. Are special student holidays ever declared because of some outstanding success in intercollegiate athletics?
    - No 1
    - Rarely (less than once a year) 2
    - About once a year. 3
    - More than once a year. 4

Administrator's Questionnaire—*Continued*

17. How are major student disciplinary problems usually handled? (Circle only one)
    - By a governing body composed exclusively of representatives from the faculty and/or administration. 1
    - By a governing body composed exclusively of students 2
    - By a governing body composed of both students and administration officials, with final authority for disposition resting primarily with:
      - faculty or administration. 3
      - students 4
      - students and faculty or administration equally 5

18. What action (if any) would be taken by the administration if a student were known to have done the following: (Circle one alternative for each item)

	No policy against this	Reprimand or minor disciplinary action	Major disciplinary action (possible expulsion from college	Sure expulsion from college
Organizing a student demonstration against some administrative policy	1	2	3	4
Writing off-color stories in a student publication	1	2	3	4
Participating in a water fight or dormitory raid	1	2	3	4
Cheating on examinations	1	2	3	4
Drinking in student union	1	2	3	4
Drinking in living quarters	1	2	3	4
Drinking somewhere off campus	1	2	3	4
Being drunk	1	2	3	4
For Female Students only: (skip to question #19 if you have only male students)				
Coming in from date 2 hours late	1	2	3	4
Staying off campus overnight without permission	1	2	3	4
Wearing shorts to class	1	2	3	4
Wearing slacks to class	1	2	3	4

19. Could you estimate the number of each of the following types of social events which are held annually at your institution? (Circle one alternative for each item)

House party weekends	0	1	2	3	4	5 or more
Formal or semi-formal dances or proms.	0	1	2	3	4	5 or more
Parents' weekends, e.g., mother's day, father's day, etc	0	1	2	3	4	5 or more
Teas or receptions	0	1	2	3	4	5 or more
Homecoming	0	1	2	3	4	5 or more
Interfraternity Council weekend.	0	1	2	3	4	5 or more
Other (cirle and specify)________________ . .	0	1	2	3	4	5 or more

20. The space below is provided in case you wish to qualify or elaborate any of your answers to the above questions.

THANK YOU VERY MUCH.

F

Reliabilities of the 35 Environmental Factors

THE STATISTICAL RELIABILITY of the measures of each of the 35 environmental factors was estimated by separating the student observers at each college into two groups: "Odds" and "Evens" as determined by the units position of the eight-digit identification number that was originally printed on the information forms that they completed when they first entered college in the fall of 1961. Scores on each factor were computed separately for the Odds and Evens subjects at each institution. The Pearson product-moment correlations between these two sets of scores are shown in the first column of data in Table F1; the second column shows the same coefficients corrected by means of the Spearman-Brown formula. The purpose of this formula is to estimate the reliability of the scores based on all of the subjects: that is, the reliability coefficient that would be obtained if the scores based on all subjects were correlated with scores obtained from another, independent sample of the same size.

These coefficients show clearly that the split-half reliabilities of the ICA factors are very high: the median corrected reliability coefficient is .931. Eight of the factors produced reliabilities exceeding .950. Only three of the ICA factors (Career Indecision, Verbal Aggressiveness and Extraversion of the Instructor) yielded reliabilities of less than .850. It seems likely that the relatively low reliability of these three factors is a consequence of the low variability among institutions on the items making up these factors (see Appendix C).

One intriguing technical problem concerns the actual number of student observers at each institution. While conventional reliability theory (which provides the major justification for the use of the Spearman-Brown formula) assumes that reliability would increase montonically as the number of student observers is increased, it is of interest to determine *empirically* whether these very high coefficients would be still higher if the number of student observers at the smaller institutions were increased. Thus, two additional analyses were performed to determine the possible effects on the reliability coefficients of the number of observers at the various institutions. In the first analysis, the 13 institutions where the number of student observers was fewer than 60 were excluded and the reliability coefficients recomputed using the remaining 233 institutions. In the second analysis, a more stringent criterion was used: the 32 institutions with fewer than 75 observers were excluded and the coefficients recomputed on the remaining 214 institutions. The results of these analyses are shown in Table F2. With the exception of only one factor—Severity of Administrative Policy Against Cheating—excluding institutions with fewer than 60 student observers raises the reliability coefficients, and excluding those that enroll fewer than 75 students raises them even higher. These findings indicate that the reliability of the ICA factor scores can be improved by increasing the number of student observers beyond 75.

Table F1

Split-half Reliabilities of the 35 ICA Factors

ICA Factor	Correlation Between Scores Based on Odd-numbered and Even-numbered Subjects: Uncorrected (r_{12})	Corrected $\left[r_{tt} = \frac{2r_{12}}{1+r_{12}}\right]$
Competitiveness vs. Cooperativeness	.875	.933
Organized Dating	.866	.928
Independence	.871	.931
Cohesiveness	.907	.951
Informal Dating	.891	.942
Femininity	.874	.933
Drinking vs. Religiousness	.936	.967
Musical & Artistic Activity	.833	.909
Leisure Time	.832	.908
Career Indecision	.608	.756
Regularity of Sleeping Habits	.740	.850
Use of the Library	.805	.892
Conflict with Regulations	.930	.964
Student Employment	.816	.899
Use of Automobiles	.870	.930
Involvement in the Class	.873	.932
Verbal Aggressiveness	.664	.798
Extraversion of the Instructor	.484	.652
Familiarity with the Instructor	.862	.926
Organization in the Classroom	.872	.932
Severity of Grading	.888	.941
Severity of Administrative Policy Against Drinking	.976	.988
Severity of Administrative Policy Against Aggression	.933	.965
Severity of Administrative Policy Against Heterosexual Activity	.953	.976
Severity of Administrative Policy Against Cheating	.890	.942
Spread of the Campus	.884	.938
Friendliness of the Dorm Counselor or Housemother	.807	.893
Academic Competitiveness	.930	.964
Concern for the Individual Student	.889	.941
School Spirit	.868	.929
Permissiveness	.850	.919
Snobbishness	.820	.901
Emphasis on Athletics	.822	.902
Flexibility of the Curriculum	.765	.867
Emphasis on Social Life	.918	.957

Table F2

Corrected Split-half Reliabilities of the ICA Factors Using Various Samples of Institutions

ICA Factor	Corrected Odd-Even Reliability Based on		
	All Institutions (N = 246)	All Institutions with 60 or more student observers (N = 233)	All Institutions with 75 or more student observers (N = 214)
Competitiveness vs. Cooperativeness	.933	.942	.950
Organized Dating	.928	.932	.940
Independence	.931	.933	.943
Cohesiveness	.951	.955	.955
Informal Dating	.942	.946	.951
Femininity	.933	.938	.941
Drinking vs. Religiousness	.967	.967	.971
Musical & Artistic Activity	.909	.920	.924
Leisure Time	.908	.919	.920
Career Indecision	.756	.781	.783
Regularity of Sleeping Habits	.850	.859	.867
Use of the Library	.892	.896	.900
Conflict with Regulations	.964	.966	.966
Student Employment	.899	.908	.921
Use of Automobiles	.930	.935	.942
Involvement in the Class	.932	.938	.941
Verbal Aggressiveness	.798	.811	.821
Extraversion of the Instructor	.652	.666	.694
Familiarity with the Instructor	.926	.930	.937
Organization in the Classroom	.932	.936	.942
Severity of Grading	.941	.943	.951
Severity of Administrative Policy Against Drinking	.988	.989	.991
Severity of Administrative Policy Against Aggression	.965	.966	.972
Severity of Administrative Policy Against Heterosexual Activity	.976	.980	.981
Severity of Administrative Policy Against Cheating	.942	.943	.938
Spread of the Campus	.938	.941	.943
Friendliness of the Dorm Counselor or Housemother	.893	.899	.911
Academic Competitiveness	.964	.966	.967
Concern for the Individual Student	.941	.948	.952
School Spirit	.929	.940	.943
Permissiveness	.919	.924	.930
Snobbishness	.901	.914	.926
Emphasis on Athletics	.902	.914	.928
Flexibility of the Curriculum	.867	.868	.874
Emphasis on Social Life	.957	.960	.966

In summary, these analyses indicate that nearly all of the ICA factor scores can be measured with a relatively high degree of precision. Those few factors with relatively low reliabilities tend to be based on items that show relatively small variation in frequency of occurrence among the different institutions.

G

Lists of Items, Correlation Matrices and Unrotated Factor Matrices:

G1. Interpersonal Peer Environment
G2. Noninterpersonal Peer Environment
G3. Mode of Dress
G4. Classroom Environment
G5. Administrative Environment
G6. Physical Environment
G7. The College Image

Because of their very large size, the tables listed above have been deposited as Document number 9665 with the ADI Auxiliary Publications Project, Photoduplication Service, Library of Congress, Washington, D.C. 20504. A copy may be secured by citing the Document number and by remitting $21.25 for photoprints, or $6.25 for 35 mm microfilm. Advance payment is required. Make checks or money orders payable to: Chief, Photoduplication Service, Library of Congress. Prices of separate tables available on request to Chief, Photoduplication Service.

H

Distribution of ICA Environmental Factor Scores by Type of Institution

Table H1. ICA Factor Scores by Type of Curriculum

ICA Factor	Percentage of Institutions with Scores Above Median Among				Contingency Coefficient*
	Universities (N=48)	Liberal Arts (N=170)	Teachers Colleges (N=20)	Technological (N=6)	
Competitiveness vs. Cooperativeness	91.7	34.7	65.0	100.0	0.58
Organized Dating	79.2	46.5	25.0	0.0	0.44
Independence	37.5	51.8	20.0	100.0	0.49
Cohesiveness	6.3	62.4	55.0	33.3	0.54
Informal Dating	56.3	49.4	55.0	0.0	0.42
Femininity	52.1	47.1	85.0	0.0	0.54
Drinking vs. Religiousness	85.4	38.8	35.0	83.3	0.47
Musical & Artistic Activity	20.8	61.8	40.0	0.0	0.66
Leisure Time	52.1	47.1	85.0	0.0	0.46
Career Indecision	70.8	52.9	15.0	16.7	0.49
Regularity of Sleeping Habits	31.3	55.9	90.0	50.0	0.50
Use of the Library	22.9	59.4	60.0	16.7	0.61
Conflict with Regulations	31.3	56.5	60.0	16.7	0.47
Student Employment	41.7	48.8	65.0	33.3	0.45
Use of Automobiles	58.3	42.4	85.0	50.0	0.44
Involvement in the Class	4.2	56.5	85.0	50.0	0.67
Verbal Aggressiveness	31.3	53.5	20.0	100.0	0.48
Extraversion of the Instructor	41.7	48.8	55.0	66.7	0.53
Familiarity with the Instructor	8.3	66.5	20.0	16.7	0.58
Organization in the Classroom	39.6	51.8	65.0	0.0	0.53
Severity of Grading	68.8	42.9	55.0	66.7	0.43
Severity of Administrative Policy Against Drinking	18.8	58.2	55.0	16.7	0.47
Severity of Administrative Policy Against Aggression	56.3	45.3	90.0	33.3	0.64
Severity of Administrative Policy Against Heterosexual Activity	31.3	56.5	75.0	33.3	0.50
Severity of Administrative Policy Against Cheating	54.2	49.4	15.0	66.7	0.57
Spread of the Campus	89.6	22.9	45.0	33.3	0.61
Friendliness of the Dorm Counselor or Housemother	52.1	53.5	35.0	83.3	0.49
Academic Competitiveness	45.8	54.7	0.0	100.0	0.58
Concern for the Individual Student	6.3	69.4	15.0	66.7	0.65
School Spirit	64.6	51.8	20.0	16.7	0.61
Permissiveness	72.9	42.9	40.0	33.3	0.44
Snobbishness	68.8	52.4	15.0	50.0	0.53
Emphasis on Athletics	41.7	48.2	70.0	66.7	0.45
Flexibility of the Curriculum	62.5	45.3	55.0	0.0	0.48
Emphasis on Social Life	75.0	40.6	75.0	0.0	0.63

* For purposes of the cross-tabulation, ICA factor scores were grouped into 12 intervals of .5 standard deviations each.

Table H2

ICA Factor Scores by Type of Control

ICA Factor	Percentage of Institutions with Scores Above Median Among				Contingency Coefficient*
	Public (N=56)	Private Non-Sectarian (N=73)	Roman Catholic (N=28)	Protestant (N=89)	
Competitiveness vs. Cooperativeness	80.4	52.1	50.0	30.3	0.60
Organized Dating	55.4	60.3	53.6	36.0	0.63
Independence	23.2	80.8	35.7	40.4	0.61
Cohesiveness	26.8	35.6	35.7	80.9	0.57
Informal Dating	55.4	52.1	3.6	59.6	0.61
Femininity	69.6	39.7	46.4	46.1	0.54
Drinking vs. Religiousness	57.1	78.1	60.7	16.9	0.67
Musical & Artistic Activity	28.6	60.3	39.3	58.4	0.48
Leisure Time	73.2	38.4	28.6	51.7	0.61
Career Indecision	50.0	57.5	64.3	46.1	0.43
Regularity of Sleeping Habits	60.7	28.8	85.7	58.4	0.58
Use of the Library	35.7	53.4	78.6	49.4	0.48
Conflict with Regulations	41.1	41.1	100.0	50.6	0.67
Student Employment	46.4	39.7	64.3	52.8	0.51
Use of Automobiles	64.3	34.2	35.7	56.2	0.45
Involvement in the Class	39.3	30.1	75.0	59.6	0.57
Verbal Aggressiveness	17.9	67.1	89.3	37.1	0.55
Extraversion of the Instructor	44.6	56.2	60.7	40.4	0.39
Familiarity with the Instructor	10.7	61.6	14.3	75.3	0.60
Organization in the Classroom	51.8	41.1	67.9	49.4	0.47
Severity of Grading	76.8	35.6	42.9	47.2	0.46
Severity of Administrative Policy Against Drinking	39.3	20.5	64.3	74.2	0.66
Severity of Administrative Policy Against Aggression	78.6	24.7	64.3	51.7	0.61
Severity of Administrative Policy Against Heterosexual Activity	51.8	34.2	82.1	59.6	0.57
Severity of Administrative Policy Against Cheating	37.5	61.6	57.1	41.6	0.40
Spread of the Campus	76.8	31.5	35.7	21.3	0.52
Friendliness of the Dorm Counselor or Housemother	37.5	64.4	64.3	48.3	0.43
Academic Competitiveness	16.1	69.9	78.6	43.8	0.53
Concern for the Individual Student	7.1	64.4	71.4	64.0	0.65
School Spirit	60.7	32.9	85.7	48.3	0.47
Permissiveness	53.6	63.0	57.1	30.3	0.59
Snobbishness	46.4	75.3	25.0	46.1	0.52
Emphasis on Athletics	62.5	35.6	28.6	59.6	0.44
Flexibility of the Curriculum	60.7	53.4	7.1	48.3	0.46
Emphasis on Social Life	80.4	46.6	21.4	40.4	0.51

* For purposes of the cross-tabulation, ICA factor scores were grouped into 12 intervals of .5 standard deviations each.

Table H3

ICA Factor Scores by Geographic Region

ICA Factor	Percentage of Institutions with Scores Above Median in the				Contingency Coefficient*
	North-east (N = 67)	South-east (N = 50)	Mid-west (N = 95)	West & South-west (N = 34)	
Competitiveness vs. Cooperativeness	58.2	48.0	49.5	41.2	0.41
Organized Dating	53.7	60.0	38.9	55.9	0.41
Independence	62.7	36.0	44.2	47.1	0.38
Cohesiveness	37.3	68.0	49.5	50.0	0.44
Informal Dating	28.4	52.0	52.6	82.4	0.46
Femininity	38.8	50.0	52.6	61.8	0.45
Drinking vs. Religiousness	68.7	28.0	43.2	58.8	0.45
Musical & Artistic Activity	50.7	36.0	52.6	61.8	0.41
Leisure Time	32.8	76.0	54.7	32.4	0.45
Career Indecision	50.7	40.0	53.7	70.6	0.45
Regularity of Sleeping Habits	53.7	56.0	55.8	41.2	0.33
Use of the Library	55.2	56.0	44.2	52.9	0.36
Conflict with Regulations	58.2	50.0	52.6	35.3	0.46
Student Employment	43.3	24.0	66.3	47.1	0.46
Use of Automobiles	31.3	68.0	46.3	64.7	0.48
Involvement in the Class	44.8	68.0	45.3	32.4	0.41
Verbal Aggressiveness	64.2	40.0	42.1	41.2	0.38
Extraversion of the Instructor	50.7	48.0	43.2	58.8	0.35
Familiarity with the Instructor	37.3	54.0	56.8	47.1	0.33
Organization in the Classroom	61.2	36.0	56.8	26.5	0.41
Severity of Grading	47.8	82.0	40.0	35.3	0.52
Severity of Administrative Policy Against Drinking	43.3	58.0	50.5	44.1	0.35
Severity of Administrative Policy Against Aggression	38.8	66.0	52.6	50.0	0.42
Severity of Administrative Policy Against Heterosexual Activity	61.2	72.0	45.3	29.4	0.47
Severity of Administrative Policy Against Cheating	82.1	68.0	25.3	17.6	0.57
Spread of the Campus	41.8	34.0	36.8	44.1	0.29
Friendliness of the Dorm Counselor or Housemother	52.2	38.0	58.9	55.9	0.41
Academic Competitiveness	56.7	38.0	49.5	50.0	0.38
Concern for the Individual Student	59.7	36.0	54.7	52.9	0.39
School Spirit	46.3	58.0	46.3	61.8	0.33
Permissiveness	55.2	44.0	43.2	55.9	0.35
Snobbishness	61.2	54.0	46.3	50.0	0.31
Emphasis on Athletics	35.8	60.0	55.8	44.1	0.42
Flexibility of the Curriculum	26.9	46.0	56.8	67.6	0.54
Emphasis on Social Life	38.8	58.0	46.3	64.7	0.35

* For purposes of the cross-tabulation, ICA factor scores were grouped into 12 intervals of .5 standard deviations each.

Table H4

ICA Factor Scores by Type of Student Body

ICA Factor	Percentage with Scores Above Median Among			Contingency Coefficient*
	Coed. Instit. (N = 189)	Men's Instit. (N = 31)	Women's Instit. (N = 26)	
Competitiveness vs. Cooperativeness	49.2	100.0	0.0	0.68
Organized Dating	42.3	54.8	96.2	0.52
Independence	43.4	87.1	34.6	0.51
Cohesiveness	52.4	64.5	15.4	0.35
Informal Dating	64.0	0.0	7.7	0.73
Femininity	51.3	0.0	96.2	0.73
Drinking vs. Religiousness	42.9	93.5	42.3	0.48
Musical & Artistic Activity	48.7	35.5	76.9	0.46
Leisure Time	54.5	38.7	30.8	0.32
Career Indecision	51.9	45.2	65.4	0.31
Regularity of Sleeping Habits	52.9	38.7	73.1	0.40
Use of the Library	46.0	48.4	88.5	0.44
Conflict with Regulations	46.6	58.1	76.9	0.49
Student Employment	51.3	54.8	23.1	0.35
Use of Automobiles	55.0	45.2	11.5	0.38
Involvement in the Class	47.1	22.6	84.6	0.43
Verbal Aggressiveness	35.4	93.5	80.8	0.52
Extraversion of the Instructor	43.9	61.3	65.4	0.39
Familiarity with the Instructor	48.1	64.5	42.3	0.37
Organization in the Classroom	49.2	54.8	46.2	0.28
Severity of Grading	51.3	64.5	23.1	0.49
Severity of Administrative Policy Against Drinking	52.9	22.6	53.8	0.39
Severity of Administrative Policy Against Aggression	56.1	32.3	38.5	0.42
Severity of Administrative Policy Against Heterosexual Activity	55.0	35.5	57.7	0.52
Severity of Administrative Policy Against Cheating	39.7	77.4	76.9	0.44
Spread of the Campus	42.9	19.4	30.8	0.32
Friendliness of the Dorm Counselor or Housemother	49.7	64.5	57.7	0.32
Academic Competitiveness	41.3	87.1	61.5	0.40
Concern for the Individual Student	42.9	80.6	84.6	0.44
School Spirit	46.6	51.6	80.8	0.38
Permissiveness	45.0	80.6	34.6	0.40
Snobbishness	51.3	51.6	61.5	0.31
Emphasis on Athletics	54.0	41.9	26.9	0.29
Flexibility of the Curriculum	55.0	29.0	19.2	0.39
Emphasis on Social Life	54.5	35.5	26.9	0.42

* For purposes of the cross-tabulation, ICA factor scores were grouped into 12 intervals of .5 standard deviations each.

Table H5

ICA Factor Scores for Predominantly Negro Institutions (N=7)

	Percentage Above the Median	Contingency Coefficient*
Competitiveness vs. Cooperativeness	42.9	0.13
Organized Dating	0.0	0.41
Independence	28.6	0.12
Cohesiveness	71.4	0.24
Informal Dating	57.1	0.22
Femininity	57.1	0.21
Drinking vs. Religiousness	0.0	0.23
Musical & Artistic Activity	71.4	0.14
Liesure Time	71.4	0.40
Career Indecision	0.0	0.23
Regularity of Sleeping Habits	57.1	0.30
Use of the Library	85.7	0.39
Conflict with Regulations	85.7	0.19
Student Employment	14.3	0.23
Use of Automobiles	0.0	0.50
Involvement in the Class	100.0	0.33
Verbal Aggressiveness	57.1	0.11
Extraversion of the Instructor	57.1	0.14
Familiarity with the Instructor	28.6	0.16
Organization in the Classroom	28.6	0.19
Severity of Grading	100.0	0.31
Severity of Administrative Policy Against Drinking	100.0	0.28
Severity of Administrative Policy Against Aggression	85.7	0.20
Severity of Administrative Policy Against Heterosexual Activity	100.0	0.33
Severity of Administrative Policy Against Cheating	14.3	0.34
Spread of the Campus	42.9	0.13
Friendliness of the Dorm Counselor or Housemother	14.3	0.17
Academic Competitiveness	57.1	0.19
Concern for the Individual Student	0.0	0.23
School Spirit	71.4	0.13
Permissiveness	42.9	0.12
Snobbishness	57.1	0.12
Emphasis on Athletics	71.4	0.29
Flexibility of the Curriculum	42.9	0.16
Emphasis on Social Life	85.7	0.24

* For purposes of the cross-tabulation, ICA factor scores were grouped into 12 intervals of .5 standard deviations each.

Bibliography

Astin, A. W. A re-examination of college productivity. *Journal of Educational Psychology,* 1961, *52,* 173-178.

Astin, A. W. An empirical characterization of higher educational institutions. *Journal of Educational Psychology,* 1962, *53,* 224-235. (a)

Astin, A. W. Productivity of undergraduate institutions. *Science,* 1962, *136,* 129-135. (b)

Astin, A. W. Differential college effects on the motivation of talented students to obtain the Ph.D. degree. *Journal of Educational Psychology,* 1963, *54,* 63-71. (a)

Astin, A. W. Further validation of the Environmental Assessment Technique. *Journal of Educational Psychology,* 1963, *54,* 217-226. (b)

Astin, A. W. The classroom environment in different fields of study. *Journal of Educational Psychology,* 1965, *56,* 275-282. (a)

Astin, A. W. Effects of different college environments on the vocational choices of high aptitude students. *Journal of Counseling Psychology,* 1965, *12,* 28-34. (b)

Astin, A. W. The introductory college course in psychology: An empirical analysis. *Psychology in the Schools,* 1965, *2,* 309-317. (c)

Astin, A. W. *Who goes where to college?* Chicago, Ill.: Science Research Associates, 1965. (d)

Astin, A. W. Environmental correlates of student protests. Washington, D.C.: American Council on Education, 1967. (mimeo)

Astin, A. W., & Holland, J. L. The Environmental Assessment Technique: A way to measure college environments. *Journal of Educational Psychology,* 1961, *52,* 308-316.

Astin, A. W., & Holland, J. L. The distribution of "wealth" in higher education. *College and University,* 1962, *37,* 113-125.

Astin, A. W., Panos, R. J., & Creager, J. A. A program of longitudinal research on the higher educational system. *ACE Research Reports,* 1966, *1*(1).

Astin, A. W., Panos, R. J., & Creager, J. A. National norms for entering college freshmen, Fall 1966. *ACE Research Reports,* 1967, *2*(1). (a)

Astin, A. W., Panos, R. J., & Creager, J. A. Supplementary national norms for freshmen entering college in 1966. *ACE Research Reports,* 1967, *2*(3). (b)

Baird, L. L. The indecision scale: A reinterpretation. *Journal of Counseling Psychology,* in press.

Davis, J. A. *Undergraduate career decisions.* Chicago, Ill.: Aldine Publishing Co., 1965.

Gibb, C. A. Teacher behavior—Here and there. *Australian Journal of Psychology,* 1957, *9,* 135-140.

Holland, J. L. Determinants of college choice. *College and University,* 1959, *35,* 11-28. (a)

Holland, J. L. A theory of vocational choice. *Journal of Counseling Psychology,* 1959, *6,* 35-45. (b)

Holland, J. L. *The psychology of vocational choice.* Waltham, Mass.: Blaisdell Publishing Co., 1966.

Holland, J. L., & Nichols, R. C. The development and validation of an indecision scale: The natural history of a problem in basic research. *Journal of Counseling Psychology,* 1964, *11,* 27-34.

Lindquist, E. F. An evaluation of a technique for scaling high school grades to improve prediction of college grades. *Educational and Psychological Measurement,* 1963, *23,* 623-646.

McConnell, T. R., & Heist, P. The diverse college student population. Chapter 5 in N. Sanford (ed.), *The American college.* New York: Wiley, 1962.

McGrath, E. J. *The predominantly negro colleges and universities in transition.* New York: Bureau of Publications, Teachers College, Columbia University, 1965.

Murray, H. M. *Explorations in personality.* New York: Oxford University Press, 1938.

Pace, C. R. Five college environments. *College Board Review,* 1960, *41,* 24-28.

Pace, C. R. *College and university environmental scales.* Princeton, N.J.: Educational Testing Service, 1963.

Pace, C. R., & Stern, G. G. An approach to the measurement of psychological characteristics of college environments. *Journal of Educational Psychology,* 1958, *49,* 269-277.

Panos, R. J., & Astin, A. W. Attrition among college students. *American Educational Research Journal,* in press.

Peterson, R. E. Organized student protests in 1964-65. *Journal of the National Association of Woman Deans and Counselors,* 1966-67, *30,* 50-56.

Ryans, D. G. *Characteristics of teachers: Their description, comparison, and appraisal.* Washington, D.C.: American Council on Education, 1960.

Sasajima, D. M., Davis, J. A., & Peterson, R. E. Organized student protest and institutional climate. Educational Testing Service *Research Bulletin,* 1967, *15.*

Stern, G. G. *Scoring instructions and college norms for the activities index and the college characteristics index.* Syracuse, N.Y.: Psychological Research Center, 1963.

Stern, G. G., Stein, M. I., & Bloom, B. S. *Methods in personality assessment.* Glencoe, Ill.: Free Press, 1956.

Thistlethwaite, D. L. College press and changes in study plans of talented students. *Journal of Educational Psychology,* 1960, *51,* 222-234.